Russia
Soviet Union
1917-1945

FROM TSAR TO STALIN

Russia
Soviet Union
1917-1945

FROM TSAR TO STALIN

DAVID THOMAS AND MARK MCANDREW

HODDER EDUCATION
A division of Hodder Headline Australia

ACKNOWLEDGEMENTS

To
Pebbles, Gump, Jonesy
and ACA-the maddest chauffeur of them all.

The authors and the publisher would like to thank the following sources for assistance with respect to copyright material:

R.K.Massie, *Nicholas and Alexandra,* Victor Gollancz Ltd, London 1992 (pp 27); Alan Bullock, *Hitler and Stalin: Parallel Lives,* Harper Collins, London 1991 (pp 200, 850–2); P. Baker and J. Bassett, *Stalin's Revolution: The USSR 1924–57,* Heinemann, Auckland 1988 (pp 52, 64)

Every effort has been made to trace and acknowledge copyright. The publishers apologise for any accidental infringement and welcome information that would rectify any error or omission in subsequent editions.

Hodder Education
A Division of Hodder Headline Australia
(a member of the Hodder Headline Group)
10-16 South St
Rydalmere NSW 2116

First published by
Hodder Education in 1995
© Thomas, McAndrew 1995

National Library of Australia
Cataloguing-in-publication data

Thomas, David.
Russia, Soviet Union 1917 - 1945 From Tsar to Stalin

ISBN 0 7336 0682 2

1. Soviet Union - History - 1917 -1936. 2. Soviet Union -
History - 1925 - 1953. 3. Soviet Union - History - 1917 - 1936
Sources. 4. Soviet Union - History - 1925 - 1953 - Sources.
5. Soviet Union - History - 1925 -1953 - Problems, exercises, etc.
I. McAndrew, Mark.
II. Title

947.084

Text and cover design by R. T. J. Klinkhamer
Edited by Robert Coupe
Typeset in 9/10 pt Franklin Gothic Book by Midland Typesetters, Victoria
Printed in Australia by Ligare Pty. Ltd. Riverwood, NSW

Contents

THERE IS a traditional Russian parable which speaks of the Russian nation as a car being driven around the countryside by a chauffeur. The Russian people are all sitting in the back of the car while the leader of the country drives them in whichever direction he sees fit. The safety and survival of the entire nation is in the hands of one man. Should he choose to take a wrong turning, or ignore the warning signs which are given by his vehicle, disaster could strike.

What would happen if the chauffeur was totally mad or misguided or paranoid or obsessed with the idea that he was heading in the right direction, oblivious to what was going on and heedless of the consequences of his actions? What would happen if Tsar Nicholas II was a mad chauffeur? What would happen if Alexander Kerensky was a mad chauffeur? What would happen if Vladimir Lenin was a mad chauffeur? What would happen if Josef Stalin was a mad chauffeur?

This is their story.

The Demise of Tsarism

At the end of this topic you should attempt to answer the following question:
After 1905, was revolution against the Tsarist regime In Russia Inevitable?

THE PROBLEMS AND ISSUES

In this topic the relevant Problem and Issue for analysis in the HSC is:
Revolution and Counter-Revolution
Revolution may be seen as the replacement of an established system of government by an alternative system.
Counter-revolution may be viewed as the attempts of the established system of government to either retain its power or return to power.

Background Events

1905–1914

FOCUS QUESTIONS In what ways did the reforms of 1905 and 1906 help avert Tsardom's collapse before the First World War?
Why was there no revolution until 1917?

TIME LINE

1905	'Bloody Sunday Massacre'—revolutionary turmoil in Russia
	Tsar Nicholas II promises constitution
	Formation of St Petersburg Soviet
	Tsar issues October Manifesto authorising elections to the State Duma
1906	Tsar issues 'Fundamental Law'
	First Duma meets—Pyotr Stolypin, Prime Minister, commences agrarian reforms
1907	Second Duma—Stolypin alters electoral laws and begins process of additional social and political reforms
1907–12	Third Duma

1911	Assassination of Stolypin
1912	Massacre on Lena goldfield—renewal of industrial unrest
1912–17	Fourth Duma
1914	Germany declares war on Russia
1915	Tsar assumes direct control of Russian war effort—civilian government left in hands of Tsarina and Rasputin—deterioration of relations between government and Duma
1916	Assassination of Rasputin
1917	Strikes and civil unrest in Petrograd—troops join the revolutionary movement
	Formation of Petrograd Soviet of Workers' Deputies—issues Order No. 1
	Abdication of Tsar and formation of Provisional Government
	Overthrow of Provisional Government by Bolsheviks

THE CHARACTER OF TSAR NICHOLAS II

Tsar Nicholas II and his wife, Alexandra. The young boy being carried is the heir to the throne, Alexei.

AT THE BEGINNING of the twentieth century the Russian empire was on the verge of momentous political and social change. Despite the pressures exerted by war, famine, industrialisation, increased contact with the West, the failure of agricultural reform and the growing political demands of revolutionary groups, Nicholas II, Tsar of Russia, managed to hold onto his supreme power. Although he had been reluctant to take up the reins of autocratic government in 1894, once he ascended the throne Nicholas II was determined to rule as his forebears had done. He maintained this attitude until his abdication in 1917. A family-oriented man, he was out of touch with the people he ruled. He visited neither the poor villages nor the new, overcrowded factories of the growing industrial cities. He appointed all his ministers and based his decisions upon the censored reports which they sent him. He was also ruled by his wife, Alexandra, and preoccupied with the problem of his son's haemophilia. Control at a local level was enforced through the local councils (*zemstvas*), the local landlords and the Tsar's troops. Yet the personal devotion of the ordinary people to their Tsar remained strong. Power was dispensed from above, and at the lowest levels of society it was ruthlessly imposed.

The autocratic nature of the Tsarist state at the beginning of the twentieth century was also reflected in the continuing inequalities in society. The majority of the population continued to belong to the peasant class: they were extremely poor, and their hopes of ever rising above their station in life was limited. The reforms and 'emancipations' of Alexander II in the 1860s had done very little to overcome the problems in agriculture. Plots of land were small, machinery was very primitive and agricultural methods were uneconomic and inefficient. The spread of industrialisation at the end of the nineteenth century had brought many peasants to the growing urban areas, but rather than alleviating the problems this only served to create a mass of disgruntled workers, many of whom lived in appalling conditions. The inability of this urban working class to influence change through peaceful means led to outbreaks of strikes and industrial unrest in the period 1899–1904.

At the top of society, and forming a very small percentage of the entire population, were the landlords, the church and the armed forces. They made up the military, religious and administrative basis and support structures for the Tsarist regime. This privileged elite gave little thought to the remainder of the population and contributed little to its development. At the very top the Tsar and his advisers were completely out of touch with the people they governed.

This lack of empathy by the Tsar's government contributed further to the discontent at a time when there was already general social and economic instability. The historian Bernard Pares has pointed out the role played by the university disturbances of 1899. He argues that the autocracy's unwillingness to believe that the students' protests were a genuine desire for reform, and its determination to see them simply as 'seditious elements', marked the beginning of the revolution. Pares therefore recognises one of Tsardom's most telling blind spots: its inability to seek the centre ground between 'reform' and 'reaction'. Alan Wood uses the analogy of the 'inflexible vessel' to describe the situation. In this all-or-nothing social and political system there was no safety valve of moderation and compromise: extreme solutions were the only ones possible. The situation which developed is clearly shown by the fact that some members of the police force even worked as 'double agents' as they strove to protect and undermine the regime at one and the same time.

The economic hardship that faced the majority of the people also made their lives miserable, and again there was little chance of improvement. Wages for the industrial workers fell, yet the cost of living rose. This created conditions for an outbreak of strikes, acts of violence and assassinations. The railways and the engineering workshops were the hardest hit by these waves of discontent. The Tsar's government, in reaction, sent more troops than ever before to restore order. In the countryside poor conditions and a series of harsh seasons led to outbreaks of violence against the local landlords and, more significantly, against the central government. While not all of these disturbances were economic in nature, they were now being directed at the autocracy itself.

THE NATURE OF THE TSARIST STATE, c. 1900

THE EMERGENCE OF DISCONTENT

WAR WITH JAPAN

In the midst of these deteriorating economic conditions, Russia embarked upon a war against Japan, and was decisively defeated. The humiliating losses and the growing discontent at home led to the greatest threat that had confronted the Tsarist state to date.

From 1903 there was an increase in the number of strikes in St Petersburg and other industrial centres protesting at the declining working conditions in the factories. Out of this situation emerged a number of reformers and agitators, one of whom was Father Georgi Gapon, a priest-police informer-humanitarian-socialist sympathiser. In January 1905 he decided that the best way to alert the Tsar to the conditions being suffered by the people was by personal confrontation. He organised a march to the Winter Palace so the Tsar could witness the distress of his subjects and then receive a petition outlining the steps necessary to create improved conditions.

'BLOODY SUNDAY', 1905

The opposite eventuated. Innocent demonstrators lost their lives when the troops opened fire. Although not in the Palace at the time, the Tsar was held responsible for the massacre. Workers went on strike in many cities and towns throughout Russia. 'Bloody Sunday' was the spark that set the masses alight. To a large extent these uprisings were spontaneous outpourings of the people's frustration and anger, and the government of the Tsar was quickly brought to a standstill. Councils (known as *soviets*) formed throughout the country to represent the workers and urged them to remain on strike until their demands were met. In 1905, however, these councils were slow to pick up the mood and attitude of the people and so lost this initial opportunity to topple the Tsar's regime. For example, the St Petersburg Soviet (Council) of Workers' Deputies, which represented all workers in the city, was not formed until October, well after the initial disturbances and too late for it to be able to take any effective action. More important was the complete breakdown of law and order in the provinces. Many of the peasants took this opportunity to exact their vengeance upon the local landlords and officials with assassination becoming a popular form of retribution.

THE OCTOBER MANIFESTO, 1905

To meet this crisis Nicholas II appointed Count Sergei Witte to the position of Prime Minister. Witte advised the Tsar that some reforms were required in order to stem the revolutionary tide. Other liberal-minded people, under the influence and direction of Pavel Miliukov, established an organisation called the Union of Unions which pressed the Tsar to introduce political changes. Finally, and only after many deaths and significant damage to his regime, Nicholas II reluctantly

Count Sergei Witte,
Prime Minister of Russia, 1905–06

issued the 'October Manifesto'. This granted some concessions and fore-shadowed a new political relationship between the Tsar and his subjects. In particular, the Manifesto allowed for the election of a representative political body known as the State Duma (or Constituent Assembly). While the newly elected members of this Duma could discuss matters and have minor legislative powers, the Tsar retained ultimate control. Ministers were still appointed by, and remained responsible only to, the Tsar. It was the upper/middle classes who benefited most from these changes.

Nicholas II imposed further restrictions upon these elected representatives when he issued the 'Fundamental Laws' in 1906. This reaffirmed his supremacy within the State by restating his power to veto any legislation passed by the Duma. As well, the Tsar limited the franchise for the Duma to men of property and made the selection process so complicated that very few urban workers actually had the right to vote. Nicholas II consistently refused all calls for the introduction of universal suffrage: at no time in the Duma's history (1906–17) was it accepted by the Tsar as being a legitimate political institution. By his actions in 1905–06, Nicholas II may have saved his regime, but his spineless introduction and subsequent emasculation of limited reforms ensured that the real crisis was still to come.

THE FUNDAMENTAL LAWS, 1906

The Tsar's opponents were quick to see these actions as those of a frightened and weak leader. The revolutionary movement, slow to get organised in 1905, and seemingly crushed by the Tsar's internal security forces, may have been silenced, but it was only the lull before the storm. New political parties (Octobrists and Kadets) were formed, while others, such as the Socialist Revolutionary Party and the Social Democratic Workers' Party returned from their pre-1905 hiding and/or exile. However, the issuing of the Fundamental Law, the conflict between the various groups within the Duma, the political chasm that continued to exist between the workers and their elected representatives and the unwillingness of the Tsar to countenance any transfer of real power meant that there were very few formal political changes between 1905 and 1914.

THE POLITICS OF THE DUMAS

The more revolutionary parties continued to strive for mass proletarian support, but their isolation from the Duma, and the effective surveillance by the internal police, kept them underground for most of the period to 1914. The real winners in 1905 were the middle-ground politicians, the Octobrists, the Kadets and other liberal-minded people. Even among these people, the Tsar's unwillingness to grant true reforms led to flirtation with revolutionary solutions. The sticking point remained 'the urban masses'. What was the power of these people? How controllable or reliable would they prove?

The leaders of the revolutionary movement did not help the cause for change. Lenin's public criticism of the Duma allowed the Tsar to treat it with further disdain. At the same time, the moderates in the Duma turned a blind eye to terrorism as a political tactic—not because they favoured it, but because the Tsar was not willing to make genuine reform.

Thus the focus after 1905 turned to re-establishing order and stability based on support for the Tsar. Support was sought from the traditional

THE REFORMS OF PYOTR STOLYPIN

working classes of the countryside, the peasants. To create a class of peasants who would become independent and prosperous supporters of the regime, Pyotr Stolypin, Prime Minister from 1906, introduced a number of agricultural reforms. The most important of these was the cancellation of all redemption payments, which had kept many peasants in servitude for more than forty years. This, the granting of the right of each peasant to sell his plot and leave his village, and the removal of the *mir* (the local rural governing body) from a position of authority over the peasant were designed to bolster Tsarist control. In practice they did little more than reduce the number of rural disturbances. Also Stolypin's ruthless repression of political dissidents—the hangman's noose was nicknamed the 'Stolypin necktie'—showed again it was a case of reform without change.

THE RE-EMERGENCE OF DISCONTENT

In the years immediately before the outbreak of the First World War industrial production in Russia increased, but the real impact of this improvement was muted. The conditions of the industrial workers actually worsened, and after 1910 there was a rise in the number of strikes and civil disturbances in all major centres. These years also saw a minor thaw in relations between the government and the revolutionary movement, allowing the latter to once again produce their newspapers and broadsheets criticising the government's actions. Widespread discontent was re-emerging.

Thus by 1914 the political fabric of the Russian state was again precariously balanced. The use of repression and the granting of limited reforms gave the Tsar's government some stability, but there were signs of future trouble. Industrial discontent, the need for continued repression, the narrow reform base and the growing instability of the proletariat were signs that the State was not in complete control.

Perhaps the strongest alarm bells should have sounded for the Tsarist regime with the gradual, but growing, notion of a collective mentality among the working class. Seemingly abandoned by both the Tsarist regime and the middle-class moderates in the Duma, the workers began to act on their own. The upper classes in the Duma feared the collective power of the working class and sought to influence it, while not letting it get the upper hand. The educated classes were keen to gain power for themselves. However, the working-class trend towards independent action was an ominous sign for the future.

Pyotr Stolypin,
Prime Minister of Russia, 1906–11

SUMMARY

- Russia continued to be an autocratic state governed by a leader who had little interest in the plight of his people.
- The autocracy was unwilling to face the political demands of the people.
- The reforms of 1905 did little to overcome the demands of those who sought political change.
- The reforms of Stolypin failed to provide the regime with the support it required to survive.
- Criticism of the Duma by the Tsar meant that this institution found it difficult to combat the attacks made by the more radical political factions within Russia.
- The working class became the key factor in the developments in Russia.

Nicholas II: Tsar of Russia, 1894–1917; born 1868, died 1918; early training was rigidly militaristic; disliked formal, public occasions and seemed ill at ease with his subjects; many believe he was completely dominated by his wife, Alexandra—it was her influence that led to the rise of characters such as Rasputin; was more comfortable receiving censored positive reports about his realm than reading the more accurate official dispatches; belief in maintaining autocratic rule led him to distrust any minister who suggested political reform; 1905, disregarded the advice of Sergei Witte about constitutional reform; dismissed Witte and the first two Dumas because they placed pressure upon him to grant more reforms; 1906, reiterated his power through the Fundamental Laws; proved incapable of running foreign affairs, e.g. the war with Japan in 1904–05 and Russia's involvement in the First World War; 1915, assumed direct control over Russia's military forces, leaving Alexandra and Rasputin to run the country; 1917, his attempts to stop the riots and disturbances by using troops failed; abdicated in 1917; he and his family were assassinated by Communists at Ekaterinburg in 1918.

Father Georgi Gapon: Orthodox priest, police informer, trade union organiser, strike leader and humanitarian; born 1870, died 1906; led a march on the Winter Palace in St Petersburg, 22 January 1905—the protest failed; fled to Finland; hanged by the Socialist Revolutionaries who maintained he was acting as a spy.

Count Sergei Yulievich Witte: Minister and adviser to Tsar Alexander III and Tsar Nicholas II; born 1849, died 1915 Minister for Commerce 1892, Minister for Finance 1893–1903, Prime Minister 1905–06; used high tariffs to protect Russian industry and boost Russia's balance of pay-

KEY PERSONALITIES, GROUPS, TERMS

A Russian cartoon from 1900. Above the workers are the capitalists: 'We do the eating'; then the army: 'We shoot you'; the clergy: 'We mislead you'; and the royal family: 'We rule you'.

ments position; improved economic position; helped attract foreign investment, particularly from France; helped begin the Trans-Siberian Railway after the signing of a treaty with China in 1896; 1905, represented Russia at the Treaty of Portsmouth to end the war with Japan; 1905, urged Tsar Nicholas II to issue the October Manifesto to end the civil disturbances; appointed Prime Minister but resigned soon after when he failed to gain the support of the Duma.

Pyotr Arkadevich Stolypin: Minister and adviser to Tsar Nicholas II; born 1862, died 1911; Minister of Internal Affairs 1906, Prime Minister 1906–11; believed that the hereditary autocracy must change itself to a limited monarchy but with the executive remaining strong; sought to avoid conflict with the Duma; hoped that by providing State loans to the peasants and releasing them from the redemption payments (set up in 1861 under the reforms of Tsar Alexander II) a better relationship would be established between the executive and the people; began migration of large groups of people to the east to encourage agriculture; severely repressed the revolutionary movements using the 'Stolypin necktie' (hangman's noose); assassinated in 1911.

Socialist Revolutionaries: Political party; political agitators who grew out of the reforms of Alexander II in the 1860s; their different approaches to reform limited their overall effectiveness; believed in a combination of socialism and the nationalisation of the land; attempted to form a new organisation in the 1890s and finally became organised in 1902; most support was found in the intelligentsia and amongst rural workers; main tactics were assassination and generating support in rural areas; some members believed that Russia would never be fully industrialised and that revolution had to come from the rural masses; the movement lacked the gifted leaders it needed to be an effective voice for change; sometimes referred to as the Essars (SRs).

Social Democratic Workers' Party: Political party; formed in Minsk in 1898 by splinter Marxist groups; stressed the importance of the industrial workers in the fight against the autocracy; Central Committee was immediately arrested and sent into exile; on their return, Lenin and others went abroad to establish the movement away from the surveillance of the security police; party newspaper was *Iskra* (the Spark); 1902, Lenin published *What is to be done?* setting out his views of the future role of the Russian socialist movement and arguing that the party must be centralised and consist of professional revolutionaries who were initially from the intelligentsia but would later come from the working class—Lenin believed it was mandatory for the revolutionaries to educate the working class and that only by confronting the ruling class would the condition of the working class improve; 1903, London Party Conference saw a split over the future direction of the Party—Lenin became leader of the 'majority' faction (Bolsheviks), the 'minority' became known as the Mensheviks.

Duma: Parliamentary body also known as the State Deliberative Assembly; along with the State Council it made up the government of Russian between 1906 and 1917; established by Nicholas II in the October Manifesto (1905) and designed to have power to discuss all legislation; 1906, Fundamental Laws deprived the Duma of control over ministers and over aspects of the budget and limited its power to initiate legislation; there were four Dumas— from May to July 1906, from March to June 1907, from November 1907 to June 1912, and from November 1912 to March 1917— and the Tsar retained absolute power when it was not in session; the First Duma demanded radical reforms in the redistribution of landed estates, the granting of amnesties for political prisoners, religious autonomy and freedom for Poland—it was dissolved by the Tsar; the Second Duma was more conservative in nature but still too radical for the Tsar, who dissolved it; the franchise was restricted to the more prosperous people and so the Third and Fourth dumas supported the Tsar's agricultural policy and plans for the reorganisation of the military; the more conservative nature of the last two dumas allowed them to conduct freer meetings with more open debate; 1912, introduced legislation on health insurance for industrial workers; during the First World War the Fourth Duma grew increasingly critical of the government's conduct of the war effort and it demanded the creation of a government which held the confidence of the nation; by 1917 the Fourth Duma was the focal point for formal opposition to the Tsarist regime; 1917, a committee of the Duma established itself as the Provisional Government to oversee the transfer of power to a representative Constituent Assembly.

Kadets: Political party; also known as the Constitutional Democrats; the first liberal party formed in Russia to implement the reforms outlined by the Tsar in 1905; believed in the movement towards a constitutional monarchy.

Octobrists: Political party; group of liberal-minded politicians formed to implement the reforms of the Tsar in 1905; more conservative than the Kadets, and took their name from the October Manifesto.

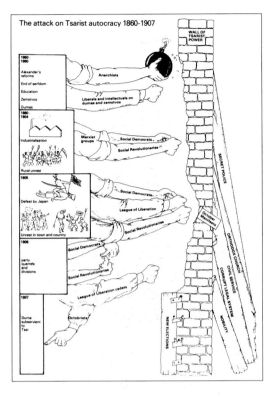

Diagram from Peter Moss, Modern World History, *showing the forces opposing and supporting the Tsarist regime between 1860 and 1907*

A British cartoon from the satiric magazine, Punch, *1905*

The Czar of all the Russias.

EXERCISES

1. a Examine the three cartoons on pages 8, 9 and 10.
From these cartoons draw up a list of the forces which were supporting the existing regime in Russia, and a list of forces which could be considered revolutionary or opposed to the Tsarist regime.
  b What comment is each of these cartoons making about the Tsar's position in Russia at the start of this century?
  c What is each of these cartoons suggesting about the conditions of the Russian people at the start of the century?
2. Industrialisation began on a large scale from the late 1880s.
  a What were the major factors that stimulated this industrial growth in the years to 1914?
  b What were the major industries affected by this growth? How were they affected?

   c What effect did industrialisation have upon the living conditions and political beliefs of the people of Russia?

   d What was the role of Count Sergei Witte in the industrialisation of Russia at the end of the nineteenth century?

3. What was the purpose behind the Tsar's government going to war with Japan in 1904?

4. It has been suggested that the outbreak of revolution in 1905 was to a great extent 'spontaneous'.

   a What evidence would you produce to support or refute this claim?

   b What were the main aims of the major groups involved in the 1905 Revolution?

   c What preparations had the revolutionary leaders made to cope with an event of this nature?

   d What groups stayed loyal to the government in 1905? How did their loyalty help to keep the Tsar in power?

   e What factors determined the outcome of the events of 1905?

   f In what ways would you consider that the revolution of 1905 was successful?

   g What were the major legacies of 1905–06 that augured poorly for the future of the Tsarist regime?

5. a What were the major reforms of Pyotr Stolypin?

   b What were the main aims of these reforms?

   c What were their major effects upon Russian society in the years preceding the First World War?

6. a Describe the nature of the Duma.

   b In what ways did the aims of the Duma change in the period 1906–14?

7. When the first Duma met in 1906, Lenin's position was significant. He advised his followers to have nothing to do with it at all. He believed that this constitutional experiment 'debauched the consciousness of the people'.

   a What did he mean by this statement?

   b Do you believe he was justified in describing the Duma in this way?

   c How important was the attitude of Lenin and the Bolsheviks to the failure of the Duma?

DOCUMENT STUDY No. 1

Read the following historical sources and answer the questions which follow.

A message from Count Sergei Witte, October 1905   **SOURCE 1.A**
quoted in D. Shub, *Lenin*, Penguin, 1971, p. 96
The present movement for freedom is not of new birth. Its roots are imbedded in centuries of Russian history . . . 'Freedom' must become the slogan of the government. No other possibility for the salvation of the state exists. The march of historical progress cannot be halted. The idea of civil liberty will triumph if not through reform then by the path of revolution. In the latter eventuality, the idea of freedom will rise again only from the ashes of the destroyed thousand-year-old Russian past . . . The horrors of this Russian insurrection may surpass all records in the history of mankind. A possible foreign intervention may dismember the country . . . The government must be ready to proceed along constitutional lines . . .

Extract from The Workers' Petition, 22 January 1905, quoted in D. Christian,   **SOURCE 1.B**
Power and Privilege, pp. 137–8
Every worker and peasant is at the mercy of your officials, who accept bribes, rob

the Treasury and do not care at all for the people's interests. The bureaucracy of the government has ruined the country, involved it in a shameful war and is leading Russia nearer and nearer to utter ruin. We, the Russian workers and people have no voice at all in the great expenditure of the huge sums collected in taxes from the impoverished population. We do not even know how our money is spent. The people are deprived of any right to discuss taxes and their expenditure. The workers have no right to organise their own labour unions for the defence of their own interests.

Is this, O Sovereign, in accordance with the laws of God, by whose grace you reign? And how can we live under such laws? Break down the wall between yourself and the people . . . let the election of members of the Constituent Assembly take place in conditions of universal, secret and equal suffrage.

This is our chief request; upon it all else depends . . .

An account of the events of 1905

SOURCE 1.C

From Williams C. Askew, 'An American View of Bloody Sunday', *Russian Review*, 1952

It is now clear to every impartial observer that the credulity of the workingmen had been worked upon by a group of socialists with Father Gapon, raised by this press to the position of a demi-god—a sort of Second Saviour—at its head, although he has to his record the violation of a young girl of twelve years of age. My authority for this, and he told me that he spoke with knowledge, is the Austro-Hungarian Ambassador Baron d'Aehrenthal.

The correspondent of the *Standard* . . . who had an interview with this renegade priest, has told me that the latter was a thorough-placed revolutionist, and that he had utterly deceived the workingmen into the belief that his sole purpose was to aid them to better their condition, and secure from their employers concessions on the lines indicated in the appeal to the Emperor, which was drawn up by him . . . there seems little doubt that his real intention was to get possession of the person of the Emperor and hold him as a hostage.

SOURCE 1.D

Extract from The October Manifesto, 30 October 1905

We, Nicholas the Second, by the grace of God, Emperor and Autocrat of All Russia, etc, etc, declare to all our loyal subjects:

The rioting and agitation in the capitals and in many localities of our Empire fills our heart with great and deep grief. The welfare of the Russian Emperor is bound up with the welfare of the people, and its sorrows are his sorrows. The turbulence which has broken out may confound the people and threaten the integrity and unity of our Empire.

The great vow of service by the Tsar obligates us to endeavour, with all our strength, wisdom and power, to put an end as quickly as possible to the disorders, lawlessness and violence, and to protect peaceful citizens in the quiet performance of their duties. We have found it necessary to unite the activities of the Supreme Government, so as to ensure the successful carrying out of the general measures laid down by us for the peaceful life of the state.

We lay upon the government the execution of our unchangeable will:

1. To grant to the population the inviolable right of free citizenship, based on the principles of the freedom of the person, conscience, speech, assembly, and union.

2. Without postponing the intended elections for the State Duma and in so far as possible, in view of the short time that remains before the assembling of that body, to include

in the participation of the work of the Duma those classes of the population that have been until now entirely deprived of the right to vote, and to extend in the future, by the newly created legislative way, the principles of the general right of election.

3. To establish as an unbreakable rule that no law should go into force without its con-firmation by the State Duma and that persons elected by the people shall have the opportunity for actual participation in supervising the legality of the acts of authorities appointed by us.

We call on all the true sons of Russia to remember their duties toward their country, to assist in combating these unheard-of disturbances, and to join us with all their might in re-establishing quiet and peace in the country . . .

Nicholas

Questions

a i) What advice is Count Witte offering the Tsar in Source 1.A?

ii) What were the major demands contained in The Workers' Petition of 1905 (Source 1.B)?

b From your own knowledge, describe what happened on 'Bloody Sunday', 1905.

c In what ways are Sources 1.A and 1.C useful to an historian who is seeking to understand the events of January 1905? (Consider the nature, origins, reliability and motive of each source as well as its content.)

d Using all four sources and your own knowledge, explain why there was an attempted revolution in Russia in 1905 and explain why the Tsarist regime survived.

DOCUMENT STUDY No. 2

Read the following historical sources and answer the questions which follow.

Leon Trotsky on The October Manifesto, published 1905   SOURCE 1.E

So a constitution is granted. Freedom of assembly is granted . . . but the assemblies are surrounded by the military. Freedom of speech is granted: but censorship exists exactly as before. Freedom of knowledge is granted, but the universities are occupied by troops. Inviolability of person is granted, but the prisons are overflowing with the incarcerated . . . A constitution is given, but the autocracy remains. Everything is given—and nothing is given.

SOURCE 1.F

Photograph of Tsar Nicholas II addressing a joint meeting of the State Duma and the State Council, 1906

SOURCE 1. G

**Extract from *Russia and the Soviet Union*
by American historian W.B. Walsh, published in 1958**
Elections to the Duma were arranged, the government often interfering to exclude individuals . . . The people watched with interest which was buoyed by hope but tempered with great doubts. Despite the boycotts against the election announced by the Essars and Social Democrats, the majority of the people exercised their new rights of suffrage to choose the best men. The general participation of the peasants in the elections to the first two Dumas is contrary proof to the often-heard claim that the Russian people never had any interest in governing themselves. When they had any chance at self-govern-ment—as in the Zemstva and these two Dumas and, again in the Constituent Assembly of 1917–18—they showed a lively and intelligent interest . . . just four days before it [the First Duma] was scheduled to open the Imperial government announced not the con-stitution which had been expected but a revision of the Fundamental Laws of the Empire, which contained in its first section the two following sentences: 'The supreme autocratic power belongs to the Emperor of All the Russias. Acceptance of his authority is dictated not alone by fear and conscience, but also by God Himself.'

SOURCE 1. H

**Extract from *Russia: Why Revolution?*
by British historians M. Bucklow and G. Russell, published in 1981**
The Tsar never accepted the Duma. It was a concession granted reluctantly in a moment of panic; when the crisis subsided it was a concession he was only too happy to retract . . .
The Duma was also to share power with an upper house, the Imperial Council. This consisted half of members appointed by the Tsar and half of elected members, the rep-resentatives in both cases belonging to the wealthier commercial and professional classes. As such it tended to be very conservative . . .
The Duma had very little control over government finances, and in the event of a dispute between the two houses over budgetary matters the government could accept the decision of either house. Each house was elected for a five-year period, but

the Tsar could dissolve them at any time provided he set the date for a new election. When the Duma was not in session, and in 'exceptional circumstances', the emperor could legislate on his own account.

Questions

a i) From Source 1.E, what were two criticisms Trotsky made of the October Manifesto?

ii) According to the Fundamental Laws (Source 1.G), where did supreme power reside?

b Using Source 1.F, Source 1.G and your own knowledge, describe the nature of the Dumas.

c In what ways would an historian find Source 1.E, Source 1.F and Source 1.H of use when trying to understand the political changes introduced in Russia after 1905? (Consider the nature, origins, reliability and motive of each source as well as its content.)

d Using all four sources and your own knowledge, explain the extent to which Russia was changed by the 1905 Revolution.

Structured Essay

EXTRA WRITING

a What measures were promised in the October Manifesto in 1905?

b How did the Tsarist regime attempt to reassert its authority between 1905 and 1914?

c To what extent was the Tsarist regime still in control of events in Russia by 1914?

Essay

Why did the Tsarist regime survive the 1905 Revolution?

THE PROBLEMS AND ISSUES

At this point recall the Problem and Issue:
Revolution and Counter-Revolution
in relation to the period 1905–14.
The **revolutionary** forces were:
• some of the workers   • some of the peasants   • the rank-and-file soldiers
• the SRs   • the SDs
The **counter-revolutionary** forces included:
• the Tsar   • the bureaucracy   • the upper class   • the officer corps
Ask yourself, why did the **counter-revolutionary** forces prevail?
• bullets   • the loyalty of sections of the army   • the offers of reform
• the lack of preparedness among the revolutionaries
• the nature of the demands
• the lack of cooperation among the revolutionaries
• the lack of a 'revolutionary consciousness' among the people

---

A. Wood, *The Origins of the Russian Revolution*   EXTRA READING
B. Pares, *The Russian Revolution*
J.N. Westwood, *Endurance and Endeavour*
M. Bucklow and G. Russell, *Russia: Why Revolution?*
L. Kochan and A. Abraham, *The Making of Modern Russia*
D. Christian, *Power and Privilege*
Robert K. Massie, *Nicholas and Alexandra*

M. McAndrew and D. Thomas, *Century of Change: Nineteenth Century Europe*
Richard Pipes, *The Russian Revolution*
E. Radzinsky, *The Last Tsar*
D. Lieven, *Nicholas II*

Russia and the First World War

FOCUS QUESTIONS What was the impact of the First World War upon events in Russia?

TIME LINE

1914
July	Mobilisation of Russian army
	Germany declares war on Russia
August	Russian armies invade East Prussia and Austrian Galicia
	Russian forces defeated in East Prussia (Battles of Tannenberg and Masurian Lakes)
September	Russian forces capture Lemberg

1915
June	Sukhomlinov replaced as Minister of War
July	Russian forces begin to withdraw from Poland
August	Nicholas II assumes personal command of Russian armed forces—moves to army headquarters at Mogilev

1916
June	Brusilov Offensive commences
December	Murder of Rasputin

1917
March	Outbreak of protest and strikes in Petrograd
	Formation of Provisional Government and abdication of Nicholas II
June	Russian offensive against Austria commences
September	Russia abandons Riga to the Germans
October	German forces threaten Petrograd
November	Bolsheviks seize power and declare peace with Germany

1918
March	Russia signs Treaty of Brest-Litovsk

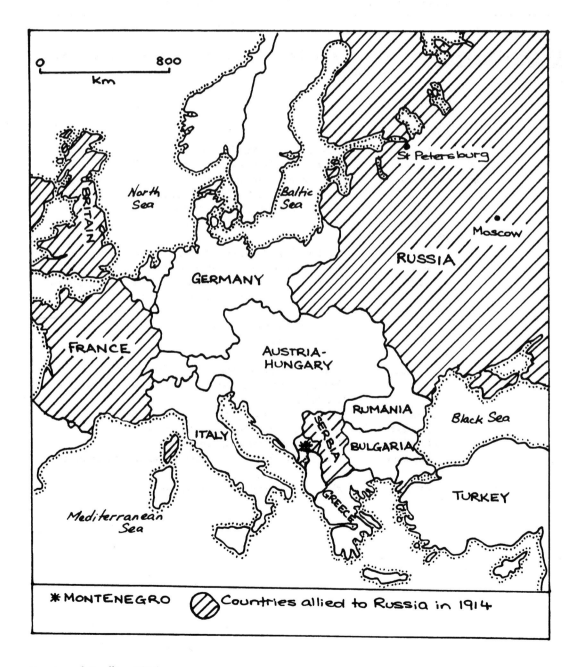

Russia and its allies, 1914

Reasons for Russia's Involvement

FOCUS QUESTION Why did Tsarist Russia become involved in the First World War?

RUSSIAN FOREIGN POLICY IN
THE NINETEENTH CENTURY

AN EXAMINATION of Russian foreign policy over much of the nineteenth century makes it difficult to immediately comprehend how the Russian Empire became involved in a war against Germany in 1914. In post-Napoleonic Europe, Russia had stood as one of the victors, and during the following decades it forged friendships with its natural allies, Prussia and Austria. These three states were keen to maintain the form of government that had drawn them together in the wars against revolutionary France, and Russia, Austria and Prussia remained allies for most of the century. This unity was eventually broken by the desires and dreams of Wilhelm II, Kaiser of Germany from 1888.

In other aspects of its nineteenth-century foreign policy, the Tsarist state had been keen to expand and secure its southern and eastern borders. This was largely a reflection of the Tsar's quest for power, the desire for a specific barrier in the east, and the need for a warm-water seaport in the south. Expansion to the south therefore drew Russia into conflict with the Ottoman Turks. At first Russia sought friendly relations with the Turks, but in the second half of the nineteenth century this turned to a desire for outright control over access to the Black Sea. Some Russians also felt an obligation to free Constantinople (a traditionally Christian city) from 'the infidel'. Consequently, Russia became heavily involved in the Balkans.

The steady collapse of the Turkish Empire in Europe and the growing ambitions of the Austro-Hungarian leaders brought the Balkan crisis to a head in the first decade of the twentieth century. There had been earlier crises in the Balkan area during the second half of the nineteenth century, but Great Power diplomacy had maintained a semblance of order. This situation became more complicated as the Austro-Hungarian Empire was itself unstable. This encouraged the Balkan states to push harder for their independence.

Yet behind the Austro-Hungarians stood the most ambitious nation in Europe: Germany. Its meddling in Balkan affairs and its desire for economic expansion from 'Berlin to Baghdad' created even greater instability in an unstable region. These actions by Germany and Austria-Hungary therefore drew Russia further into the problems of the Balkans as it sought to protect its 'Slavic cousins' in the region. Between 1900 and 1914 war was close on two occasions, but both sides backed down. It was Serbia's desire for independence which kept the issue alive.

Russia therefore had a number of reasons for going to war in 1914: defeat by Japan in 1905 caused the focus of foreign policy to be upon

Europe rather than Asia; the protection of the Slavs against the Austro-Hungarian menace; its ambitions in the Black Sea region; and a desire to divert people's attention away from domestic problems. In each of these reasons the Tsar, Nicholas II, as ruler and autocrat of 'all the Russias' played a crucial role. His decision to order the general mobilisation of Russia's armed forces created the conditions for the war plans of the other Great Powers to come into operation: Russia's mobilisation ensured Germany's invasion of France via Belgium.

SUMMARY

- For much of the nineteenth century Russia was friendlier with Austria-Hungary and Germany than it was with France and Britain.
- Russia moved closer to France and Britain during the 1890s due to:
  —concerns about the Black Sea region
  —the Pan-Slavic movement
  —the need for financial assistance for industrialisation
  —the increasing belligerence of Kaiser Wilhelm II of Germany.
- Russia's actions in 1914 brought the war plans of the other Great Powers into operation.

Sergei Sazonov: Minister of Tsar Nicholas II; born 1861, died 1927; Russian Foreign Minister 1910–16; determined to protect Russian interests; his diplomatic methods gave way to the military demands of the Russian General Staff.

KEY PERSONALITIES, GROUPS, TERMS

Vladimir Sukhomlinov: Minister of Tsar Nicholas II; born 1848, died 1926; Russian Minister for War 1909–15; reorganised the Russian army after 1905; believed he was the right general to lead the army during the war; one of the leading pro-German members of the government, he was dismissed on unspecified charges of 'treasonable negligence'—saved by the Empress and Rasputin; later the Provisional Government reopened his case and sentenced him to hard labour for life; released by the Bolsheviks in 1918 and found refuge in Germany.

Serbia: Country in south-eastern Europe that had been part of the Turkish Empire in Europe; slowly acquired its own semi-independence from the Turks, and then set about uniting all the Slavic peoples of the area under its control; desire to unite all Serbs and Croats together brought them into conflict with the Austro-Hungarians; drew Russia into the dispute through its perception of itself as the protector of the Slavic people.

'Berlin to Baghdad': Ambitious scheme to extend Germany's influence from Berlin (Germany) to Baghdad (Persia) via the construction of a railway—had the effect of bringing Russia and Britain into friendship against Germany.

EXERCISES

1. a What was the Dreikaiserbund?
 b When was it formed?
 c Why was it formed?
 d What does this alliance tell you about the nature of the nations that formed it, and the foreign ambitions of each?

2. What caused the outbreak of the Balkan Wars at the start of the twentieth century? Using maps, and any other material available, explain how the territorial boundaries changed as a result of these wars. What role did Russia play in these conflicts? What did Russia hope to gain from its involvement?

3. Why did the Tsar's government become involved in the First World War?

4. What groups supported the Tsar's government at the outbreak of war in 1914? Why?

5. What were the major aims of the opposition groups in the Duma in August 1914?

6. What were the major problems facing the Tsar's government at the outbreak of war in August 1914?

7. a What role did the Tsar play in the immediate crisis leading up to the outbreak of war in 1914?
 b How important was the Russian decision for partial/full mobilisation in bringing about the beginning of hostilities?

8. It is important to understand how Russian foreign policy worked. Examine the role of the Tsar, the civil service and the generals in the formulation of foreign policy over the years 1815–1914. What conclusions can you draw about Russian foreign policy from this study?

9. Examine Mikhail Lermontov's novel *A Hero of Our Time*. How did the Russian advance into the southern regions of the Caucasus bring it into conflict with the Turks? What effect did this advance have upon the internal government? What light does this novel shed on the role of the military at this time and how the Tsar governed his empire?

STUDYING AN HISTORICAL SOURCE   No. 1

Read the following historical source and then answer the questions which follow.

SOURCE 1.1

from J.N. Westwood, *Endurance and Endeavour. Russian History 1812–1986*, published in 1991

Fundamentally, it was not the Russo-Turkish War but the emergence of a united Germany that was the main event in Russia's foreign relations during Alexander III's reign. Bismarck's work was to have as damaging an effect on Russia's position as it would have on France. Whereas Russia's relations with the German states had been successfully managed in the post-Napoleonic period . . . there was now a completely new situation. For a time, cordiality between the Romanovs and the Hohenzollerns persuaded the former that the old relationships might continue. But the underlying reality, which emerged plainly in 1914, was quite different. With a new and militant power established in central Europe and determined to make its mark, an additional and usually unhelpful voice was heard as the great powers strove to accommodate peacefully the political and social upheavals of the time.

Bismarck was familiar with Russia, having been the Prussian minister in St Petersburg. He had no great regard for the Russians and, like several of his successors, tried to encourage them to turn their attention towards expansion in the east; if kept busy in Asia, Russians would be less concerned with the Balkans, where Austrian ambition,

British anxieties, Ottoman decline, and local nationalisms promised perilous changes. In fact, Russia no more needed encouragement in her military excursions in Central Asia than she did in her continuing pacification of the Caucasus. But despite these preoccupations she was unwilling to turn her back on the Balkans. Alexander was anxious to avoid trouble, yet even the Tsar-Autocrat had to heed the outcry from those of his subjects for whom the tribulations of the Orthodox Christians under the Turks was a burning wrong. Among these subjects of the Tsar it was the Panslavists who were the most vocal, and they were influential not only in Russia but also in the Slavic lands of the Ottoman Empire . . .

Questions
a Is this a primary source or a secondary source?
b Describe the nature of this source.
c Summarise the content of this source.
d What is the purpose of this source?
e How does the author of this source justify the opinions which are expressed?
f What problems or weaknesses are present in this source?
g In what ways would an historian find this source useful for uncovering the details of Russian foreign policy before 1914? (In your answer consider the nature, origin, motive, audience and reliability of the source as well as its content.)

War

FOCUS QUESTION In what ways did Russia's involvement in the First World War contribute to the downfall of the Tsarist government?

Within Russia there was enthusiasm at the outbreak of hostilities as thousands went off in defence of 'Mother Russia'. Even the liberals in the Duma supported military involvement in the hope that an

INITIAL REACTIONS TO THE WAR

Tsar Nicholas II visiting the troops in 1915

Supply wagons making a delivery to Russian troops

alliance with France and Britain would facilitate change in the political situation in Russia. The most vocal opponents were Lenin and his Bolshevik Party who maintained that the war was being fought for imperialist reasons. This stance isolated the Bolsheviks from the other revolutionary groups, many of whom supported the war. Consequently, they were easy prey for the internal security forces. Many of the Bolshevik leaders were arrested, some fled abroad and others went into hiding. However, this public rejection of the Bolshevik Party was not to last.

Throughout Russia the people rallied behind the war effort. Local organisations helped to staff hospitals and relief agencies, there was local input into the War Industries Committee and the Duma (for a short time) adopted a more accommodating role towards the bureaucracy. Soon, however, a 'Progressive Bloc' formed within the Duma. This group, led by Pavel Miliukov, demanded a greater say in the running of the war and believed that Russia's war effort could only be completed successfully with their help. They demanded a 'government of confidence' based on the attitudes of the emerging bourgeoisie.

CONDITIONS ON THE HOME FRONT

Russia began the war in a precarious position. The working class suffered very poor working and living conditions, the middle class was still small and ineffective, the intellectual elite gave little direction, social and political tensions were near breaking point, the arms industry was weak, communications remained poor, and there was little real belief that the government would ultimately succeed against Germany. In many respects, therefore, Russians were unprepared for the crisis which now confronted them. Taxes were high, the cost of fighting the war was well beyond Russia's capabilities and agriculture and industry were vulnerable to labour shortages generated by conscription. Russian industry also suffered from poor

Russian Cossacks— although these were seen as the elite of the Russian armed forces, the Cossacks played little real part in the First World War due to the vast distances encountered on the Eastern Front

equipment. The outbreak of war brought little prospect of new machinery from overseas as the importation of resources all but ceased.

Despite all these problems it was still difficult to imagine that the 300-year-old dynasty of the Romanovs would soon be overthrown. In 1914 there was little discussion amongst the working class and the revolutionary political groups of the possibility of the overthrow of the Tsarist regime.

At the start of the war, the Russians scored a number of victories using their well known 'steamroller' tactics. The Germans responded by transferring troops from the Western Front, and thereby allowed the French to stem the German advance at the Battle of the Marne. France's reprieve proved to be Russia's death knell. Late 1914 and early 1915 were the blackest times for the Russians in the First World War. The German offensives, with vastly superior forces, sent the Russians into retreat. First at Tannenberg and the Masurian Lakes, and then along the entire Eastern Front, the Germans gained the upper hand. Only in the south-west, around Lemberg, and then only for a short period, were the Russian armies successful. Even here the Germans regrouped and sent aid to their Austrian allies and the Russian advance was halted and pushed back. The Russians lost large tracts of territory and, to make matters worse, war broke out with Turkey, thus limiting Allied supplies to Russia to the northern sea route.

TANNENBERG AND MASURIAN LAKES

The lack of these supplies from the West exacerbated the dreadful situation at home. With the armies in retreat, soldiers abandoned their weapons, units lost other critical military supplies and the government was forced to send raw recruits into the front line to fill the gaps. It has been estimated that during the first year of the war Russia lost four million men. Fortunately by the middle of 1915 the situation on the front began to

Russian soldiers in the snow on the Eastern front

stabilise, and even turn against the enemy. The Russians were able to hold the Germans to a line, munitions production increased and the training of recruits began in earnest. The heroism of the Russians had saved the French once, and throughout 1915 there were repeated calls from the Western allies for Russia to attack once again.

HOME FRONT WORSENS

On the home front the early enthusiasm for the war began to wane as news of the military setbacks became public. There were calls for the removal of inefficient ministers, many of whom were merely the lackeys of the Tsarina and Rasputin. The Duma cooled in its attitude towards the war and by the end of 1915 its opposition became open and vocal. J.N. Westwood suggests that the Duma now began to circulate rumours about the Tsar's government's willingness to win the war. Previously, he writes, they had merely suggested that it was incapable of victory because of incompetence. Now they stated that it was deliberately prolonging the war for its own purposes.

THE ROLE OF THE TSAR

In mid-1915, possibly in response to these criticisms, the Tsar decided to take personal control of the war effort from the front line. This left the Tsarina and Rasputin in control in Petrograd (the name now given to St Petersburg in order to avoid German associations) and marked the beginning of the end for the regime. The real problem with the Tsarist autocracy became clear: it was a headless administration staffed by very mediocre bureaucrats who ran a government apparatus that was out of date with the twentieth century and out of touch with the real world. The inability to coordinate the war effort, the unwillingness to set correct priorities and the seemingly cavalier attitude the military had towards the running of the war left the Tsar's government with few supporters by the end of 1915. While Russia was not the only war-torn country to suffer administrative problems, it failed to recover from the massive defeats of late 1914 and its administrative apparatus was incapable of rectifying the damage. The regime in fact succeeded in alienating every major group with an interest in stability. Even the industrialist Alexander Putilov believed that Tsarism was finished, that the revolution would come initially from the middle class but, because of its lack of strength, the initiative would then pass to the workers and more radical politicians.

Thus, while the anger of 1914 was directed at the numerous German establishments in the major cities, from late 1915 anger was directed specifically at Nicholas and his ministers. As Commander-in-Chief of the armed forces Tsar Nicholas II was now held to be directly responsible for the losses being incurred. His long absences from the capital, the appointment of incompetent ministers and the scandals surrounding the Tsarina and Rasputin brought his government into further disrepute.

At the same time the cost of living turned further against the working class. There were food shortages and price rises. Strikes became more common. Many members of the Duma, fearful of the possible involvement of the working class in a mass political movement, continued to hope that the regime would reform itself. Numerous appeals were made to the Tsar seeking changes to head off a possible revolution. At his wife's urging Nicholas II ignored each of these requests.

The Brusilov Offensive

Instead, to improve the situation at the front and to divert attention away from the economic and social conditions within the country, a major military campaign was mounted in the south-west by General Brusilov in mid-1916. At first the campaign was a great success, with the Russians

War on the Eastern Front, 1916

driving deep into Austrian territory. However, once again General Head-quarters was not up to the task of consolidating its gains. Rather than launching a follow-up offensive at the Germans, GHQ pulled troops away from its German front and sent them to join Brusilov. This gave the Germans a breathing space in which to send reinforcements to the Austrians and send Brusilov into retreat. The Brusilov Offensive may have relieved pressure on the French and helped save Verdun, but its failure added to the ever-increasing woes of the Tsar's regime.

As 1916 wore on conditions in the major cities worsened. Strikes became a more regular feature of Russian urban life and the open expression of discontent continued in the Duma.

SUMMARY

- Russia suffered major military defeats, e.g. Tannenberg and Masurian Lakes, which undermined support for the war effort and the Tsarist regime.
- The Tsar assumed personal control of the war effort in 1915.
- Internal government was left in the hands of the Tsarina and her advisers, many of whom were not equipped to deal with the increasingly difficult economic situation.
- Continuation of the war further eroded support for the regime.
- The Duma and workers' soviets became increasingly critical of the Tsarist regime.

KEY PERSONALITIES, GROUPS, TERMS

Alexandra: Tsarina of Russia; born 1872, died 1918; Princess of Hesse-Darmstadt and grand-daughter of Queen Victoria; married Nicholas II in 1894; always gravely concerned for the health of her son, Tsarevich Alexei, a haemophiliac; believed strongly in her husband's right to rule Russia without any devolution of power; turned increasingly away from her husband's ministers and sought support from Rasputin; her influence over Nicholas II, and the unpopularity of Rasputin, helped to bring down the Romanov dynasty in 1917; along with her husband and five children she was executed at Ekaterinburg in 1918.

Grigori Rasputin: Russian mystic; born 1872(?), died 1916; wandering self-styled priest (in reality he was a *starets* or 'holy wanderer'); around 1903 abandoned his family to carry out the wishes of God; came into contact with members of the royal family, and then with the Tsarina; led Alexandra to believe that he was the only one who could cure the Tsarevich's illness; became the power behind the throne; due to his meddling the royal family lost influence and power; murdered in late 1916 by members of the royal family in a belated attempt to save the regime.

Pavel Miliukov: Russian politician; born 1859, died 1943; liberal politician who pushed for constitutional change from the early years of the twentieth century; 1905, with other liberals, formed the Union of Unions; leader of the Kadets in the First Duma; during the First World War organised the Progressive Bloc, another group of liberal politicians pressuring the Tsar to make constitutional concessions; later a member of the Provisional Government.

Ivan Goremykin: Russian politician; born 1839, died 1917; old-style reactionary politician, appointed Prime Minister in 1914; failed to fulfil the Tsar's orders to stamp out revolutionary movements.

Lavr Kornilov: Russian General; born 1870, died 1918; Commander-in-Chief of the Russian Army, 1917; appointed because of his ability to maintain discipline; politically naive; at the behest of ambitious financiers in Petrograd he demanded more powers from the Provisional Government; marched on the capital but his coup attempt failed; main effect was to give the Bolsheviks more power at the expense of the government; joined Generals Alexeyev and Kaledin in setting up a Volunteer Army to try to smash the Bolsheviks; killed 1918.

Alexei Brusilov: Russian General; born 1853, died 1926; commanded the Southern Front in First World War; achieved two great victories against the Austrians, but was ultimately defeated by the Germans; failure was due to haste and a lack of reserves rather than a lack of discipline and courage; failure of his second offensive in 1917 was a severe blow to Kerensky's government and a gain for the Bolsheviks.

EXERCISES

1. What were the major problems facing the Tsar's government in the period 1914–16?
2. How did the aims and attitudes of the political groups in the Duma change between 1914 and late 1916?
3. How did the Tsar and his government attempt to deal with the growing instability within the country after the middle of 1915?
4. Research the campaigns of the First World War on the Eastern Front.
    a Find maps showing the names and locations of the major battles, the commanders, the numbers of troops involved and the outcome.
    b How did the result of each battle impact upon the internal situation in Russia?
5. a Why did the Tsar take command of the Russian forces in mid-1915?
    b List the advantages and the disadvantages associated with this decision.
    c What alternatives to this move did the Tsar have?
6. What do the photographs in this section tell you about the conditions under which the Russian troops fought in the war? In what ways would these conditions have contributed to the overthrow of the Tsar's government?
7. List the major grievances held by Russians, of all classes, against Tsarina Alexandra. Do you believe that these criticisms were in any way justified? Why?

DOCUMENT STUDY   (No. 3)

Read the following historical sources and answer the questions which follow.

The Recollections of Bruce Lockhart, British Vice-Consul in Russia during the   **SOURCE 1J**

First World War, published in his memoirs some years after the war

It was the tragedy of Russia that the Tsar, dominated by a woman who was obsessed with the one ambition to hand down the autocracy unimpaired to her son, never took the public organisations into his confidence . . . And, although his loyalty to his Allies remained unshaken to the last, it was his failure to harness the loyalty of his own people which eventually cost him his throne . . .

Moscow [was] full of rumours and depression . . . The [German] counter-attacks had already begun, and refugees were streaming into the city and taxing its housing resources to the utmost. (There were) discontent and disorders among the new conscripts in the villages, the wounded did not like going back, the peasants objected to their sons being taken away from the fields . . . In Moscow there had been bread riots . . . Confidence in the Russian army had given way to a conviction of German invincibility, and every section of the Moscow population railed bitter resentment against the alleged pro-German policy of the Russian Government . . .

Horrible rumours of Russians manning the trenches with nothing but sticks in their hands percolated through from the front to the countryside . . . At factory centres like Ivanovo-Voznesensk there were anti-government strikes attended in some areas by shooting . . .

SOURCE 1.K

Extract from A. De Jong, *The Life and Times of Grigori Rasputin*, published in 1982
True, he [Rasputin] frequented aristocratic and even lay houses, but this was a time when mysticism and the quest for God, or strange gods, was much in vogue, and many great houses had their particular starets or holy fool to visit them and hold forth on matters spiritual.

SOURCE 1.L

Extract from L. Kochan and A. Abraham, *The Making of Modern Russia*, published in 1983
The growing influence of Rasputin [after 1911], the licentious, hypnotically gifted monk, rendered the Court more and more odious.

SOURCE 1.M

Extract from Robert K. Massie, *Nicholas and Alexandra*, published in 1992
Thus, the military defeat of 1915 played a major part in all that was to happen afterward. For it was the tragic and bloody defeat of the army which weakened the grip of Grand Duke Nicholas and persuaded the Tsar to take personal command of his troops. By going to the army, hundreds of miles from the seat of government, the Tsar gave up all but a vague, supervisory control over affairs of state. In an autocracy, this arrangement was impossible; a substitute autocrat had to be found. Uncertainly at first, then with growing self-confidence, this role was filled by the Empress Alexandra. At her shoulder, his 'prayers arising day and night', stood her Friend, Rasputin. Together they would finally bring down the Russian Empire.

Questions

a From Source 1.J, list four indications of increasing discontent in Russia during the First World War.

b Using Source 1.K and your own knowledge, explain the influence of Rasputin over the Russian royal family.

c How useful would an historian find Source 1.J and Source 1.M when attempting to understand the effects of the First World War on the Tsarist regime? (Consider the nature and reliability of each source as well as its content.)

d Using all four sources and your own knowledge, explain why the Tsarist regime was on the point of collapse by the end of 1916.

Women demonstrating on the streets of Petrograd, 1917

The Winter of Discontent

FOCUS QUESTIONS

What factors contributed to the outbreak of revolution in February/March 1917?

In what ways was the outbreak of revolution in February/March 1917 a spontaneous response to continued hardship rather than a planned assault on the autocracy?

In what ways was the working class, and not the autocracy or the war, the vehicle of the revolution in Russia?

The Russian economy was never strong enough to sustain a long war effort, particularly with a total of fifteen million men being called up before the fighting ended. Russian industrial production began to slump, transportation failed, and the supplies and munitions which were produced were not always efficiently distributed once they reached the front. Dominic Lieven, in his biography of Nicholas II, claims that the Minister for Communications, E.B. Krieger-Voynovsky, and the Minister for Agriculture, A.A. Rittikh, were 'efficient professionals' who provided the necessary material and logistic support for the front right up until the outbreak of the February/March Revolution. As a general rule, however, the distribution of arms, ammunition, medical supplies and other provisions proved unreliable.

THE EFFECTS OF THE WAR

At home, agricultural output dropped as men, machines and even animals were drawn into the war effort. This produced severe food shortages in the cities and inflated prices. Between 1914 and 1916 the price of food and consumer goods increased between 300 and 500 per cent.

At the end of 1916 Russia's winter saved its armies from complete

THE DECLINE IN MORALE

annihilation by the Germans, but the onset of the very severe weather also brought on conditions which worked against the Tsarist regime. There was a wave of strikes in the capital and other cities, but this time when the soldiers were called upon to fire on the crowds many refused to do so. In some liberal circles there was even talk of removing the Tsar and replacing him with another member of the royal family. Criticism became so rife that in November the Tsar made further changes to his government. As usual these proved to be inadequate to deal with the crisis at hand.

Desertions within the ranks of the armed forces became an open scandal, the Tsar made little effort to supervise the army or its movement, there was openly seditious talk amongst the upper levels of the officer corps, and the general population continued to find it difficult to survive. Very few people continued to believe that the Russians would be victorious in the war:

> ...The war has brought out all that is worst in Russia, not the best. The enthusiasm that at one time was felt, evaporated as the war dragged on, leaving only apathy as regards the war and a feverish thirst for money. The opinion of the Army is that those left in the towns have no thought for the war, but only for money making.
> (Public Record Office: OF 371 3003. *A Report on the Russian Army*, quoted in N. Rothnie, *The Russian Revolution*, 1990.)

RASPUTIN AND ALEXANDRA

The role played by Grigori Rasputin must be examined in this context. It was largely on the advice of Rasputin and the Tsarina that Nicholas made the decision to assume personal control of the war effort. Then, with Nicholas spending more time away from the capital, Alexandra, firmly under Rasputin's influence, took control of the government of Russia. Ministers and bureaucrats were appointed, transferred or dismissed on Rasputin's advice and whim: in a sixteen-month period there were four different Prime Ministers, five different Ministers of the Interior, four different Ministers for Agriculture and three different Ministers of War. Transport, the food supply and even military appointments and strategy were thrown into chaos. All this at a time when governmental stability and efficiency were vital. Bernard Pares wrote in *The Fall of the Russian Monarchy*:

> In the midst of a world wide struggle, in a time of the closest collaboration with the best brains of Western statesmanship, the Russian ministers were selected by an ignorant, blind and hysterical woman on the test of their subservience to an ignorant, fanatical and debauched adventurer.

Rumours that Alexandra was secretly assisting the Germans began to circulate, and some of the Progressive Bloc within the Duma began speaking of a coup which would remove the Tsar and his wife.

By the start of 1917 the internal situation had become hopeless for the Tsar's government. Rasputin was murdered in December 1916, but this did little to change the attitude of those in power. Some of the governing class hoped that the death of Rasputin would prompt the Tsar to return from the front and the Tsarina to withdraw from public life. Instead, the autocracy stood firm in its convictions and exhibited little concern for the problems facing the country. The

Russian monarchy would survive Rasputin by a mere three months.

The winter of 1916–17 was so severe it halted all rail links between the war front, the major cities and the countryside. Fuel and food, already in short supply, became even scarcer. Unemployment continued at high levels and urban discontent began to impact upon the small businesses in the cities. Grain supplies for the cities remained critically low: Moscow required 120 freight cars of grain a day. In January 1917 it was receiving only twenty-one. Bread continued to be in short supply. In January 1917, to mark the twelfth anniversary of Bloody Sunday, 300 000 workers went on strike. By the end of February 1917 inflation was again increasing and the mood of the industrial working class showed further signs of disorder. Looting became commonplace after the imposition of bread rationing on 1 March 1917.

A week later, the refusal by the management of the Putilov engineering workshop to meet workers' demands regarding sacked colleagues and continuing poor conditions triggered a city-wide strike in Petrograd. Within days well over 100 000 workers were on strike in the city. This gave an indication of the mass scale of the discontent. This discontent, and the workers' frustration at not receiving a just response to their economic and political demands, provided the spark for the Revolution. The attitude of the Tsar's troops in Petrograd proved just as important. During the 1905 Revolution the autocracy had been saved by the loyalty of its military. Now, in 1917, the army, many of whom were new recruits, sided with the striking working class. Even the Tsar's Cossacks could no longer be relied upon to maintain order.

SUMMARY

- The winter of 1916–17 exacerbated the economic and social distress of the people.
- Food shortages in the cities and industrial discontent led to an increase in strikes and protests.
- The Tsar and the Duma were unwilling to compromise or co-operate to resolve the situation.
- The Tsarist regime collapsed as a result of its own inertia.

EXERCISES

1. Consider each of the following factors associated with the downfall of the Tsarist regime. Rank each factor in order, from most important factor to least important factor, and justify the decisions you have made.
Very poor leadership from the government ministers
The Tsar was totally out of touch with the situation in Russia
The independent role of the military, and its effect upon the economy
The lack of leadership from the Duma
The rejection by the Tsar of parliamentary change
The lack of cooperation between the Tsar and his ministers

The Tsar's leadership of the armed forces from 1915

The role of Rasputin in the government

Lack of support from the upper classes for the Tsar

2. How effectively was the Russian autocracy functioning at the beginning of 1917?

3. Make a list of the major socialist groups in late 1916.

   a What were the aims of each group?

   b What were their perceptions about the probability of revolution at this time?

4. a What were the major demands made by the Duma during the First World War?

   b Why did the Duma have so little influence upon the events in Russia during the war?

   c In what ways was the Duma's position further undermined by the interference of the Tsarina?

5. Trotsky wrote that 'War is the locomotive of history'. What evidence can be drawn from Russia in the years 1901–17 to prove that this was true?

DOCUMENT STUDY   No. 4

Read the historical sources and answer the questions which follow.

SOURCE 1.N

Selections from the private letters of the Tsarina to Nicholas II, March 1917 quoted in D. Shub, *Lenin*, pp.188–9

I

Yesterday there were riots on the Vasiliev island and on Nevsky, when the poor raided the bakeries. They demolished the Filipov bakery and Cossacks were sent against them. All this I learned from unofficial sources. The riots increased by ten o'clock, but by one they subsided. Khabalov is now in control of the situation. (9/3/17)

II

The strikers and rioters in the city are now in a more defiant mood than ever. The disturbances are created by hoodlums. Youngsters and girls are running around shouting they have no bread; they do this to create some excitement. If the weather were cold they would all probably be staying at home. But the thing will pass and quiet down, provided the Duma behaves. The worst speeches are not repeated in the papers, but I think that for speaking against the dynasty there should be immediate and severe punishment. (10/3/17)

III

The whole trouble comes from these idlers, well-dressed people, wounded soldiers, high-school girls etc, who are inciting others. Lily spoke to some cab-drivers to find out about things. They told her that the students came to them and told them if they appeared in the streets in the morning, they would be shot to death. What corrupt minds! Of course the cab-drivers and motormen are now on strike. But they say that it is all different to 1905, because they all worship you and only want bread. (11/3/17)

SOURCE 1.O

Letter from Mikhail Rodzianko, President of the Duma, to the Tsar, 11 March 1917, quoted in D. Shub, *Lenin*, pp. 188–9

The situation is serious. The capital is in a state of anarchy. The government is paralysed; the transport service has broken down; the food and fuel supplies are completely disorganised. Discontent is general and on the increase. There is wild shooting on the streets; troops are firing at each other. It is urgent that someone enjoying the confidence of the country be entrusted with the formation of a new government. There must be no delay. Hesitation is fatal.

SOURCE 1.P

George Keenan, an American diplomat and politician, writing about the events in Russia forty years after they took place, quoted in M. Bucklow and G. Russell, *Russia: Why Revolution?*, p. 149

The first and most decisive of the causes seems to me to have been, unquestionably, the failure of the autocracy to supplement the political system with some sort of parliamentary institution—the failure, in other words, to meet the needs of the land-owning nobility and then, increasingly, of the new intelligentsia from all classes for some sort of institutional framework that would associate itself with the undertakings of the regime, give them a sense of participation in the governmental process, and provide a forum through which they, or their representatives, could air their views and make their suggestions with regard to government policy. In the absence of any such institution, literally hundreds of thousands of people . . . possessed of no more consuming passion than the desire to contribute to its [Russian society's] correction . . . found themselves . . . repelled by the regime.. .

SOURCE 1.Q

Professor E. Trubetskoy, a moderate liberal, on the events of March, 1917, quoted in D. Shub, *Lenin*, p. 204

This revolution is unique. There have been bourgeois revolutions and proletarian revolutions, but I doubt if there ever has been a revolution so truly national, in the widest sense of the term, as the present one. Everybody made this revolution. Everyone took part in it—the workers, the soldiers, the bourgeois, even the nobility—all the social forces of the land.

Questions
a i) Name three different groups of people who, according to the Tsarina (Source 1.N), were creating trouble in Russia?

ii) According to the Tsarina (Source 1.N) what action should be taken against the outspoken members of the Duma?

b Using Source 1.Q and your own knowledge, describe the grievances held against the Tsarist regime.

c Compare Source 1.Q and Source 1.P. Which of these two sources would be more useful to an historian attempting to understand the nature of the Tsarist regime in early 1917? (In your answer you must consider the nature, audience, motive and reliability of each source as well as its content.)

d Using all four sources and your own knowledge, explain why the Tsarist regime was confronted by a spontaneous revolution in March 1917.

EXTRA READING

B. Pares, *The Fall of the Russian Monarchy*
N. Rothnie, *The Russian Revolution*
A. Wood, *The Origins of the Russian Revolution*
B. Pares, *The Russian Revolution*
J.N. Westwood, *Endurance and Endeavour*
M. Bucklow and G. Russell, *Russia: Why Revolution?*
L. Kochan and A. Abraham, *The Making of Modern Russia*
D. Christian, *Power and Privilege*
Robert K. Massie, *Nicholas and Alexandra*
M. McAndrew and D. Thomas, *Century of Change: Nineteenth Century Europe*
Richard Pipes, *The Russian Revolution*
E. Radzinsky, *The Last Tsar*
D. Lieven, *Nicholas II*

THE PROBLEMS AND ISSUES

Again, consider the Problem and Issue:

Revolution and Counter-Revolution

in the coming of revolution in February/March 1917.

The **revolutionary** forces were:
* soldiers   • peasants   • urban masses
* the Progressive Bloc in the Duma

The **counter-revolutionary** forces were:
* the Tsar • the Tsarina
* sections of the bureaucracy and the nobility

Ask yourself, **why did the revolutionary forces prevail in February/March 1917?**
* the collapse of army loyalty   • the impact of the war   • intransigence of the Tsar
* economic discontent   • social discontent   • political discontent
* disintegration of traditional institutions

WRITING THE ESSAY

After 1905, was revolution against the Tsarist regime inevitable?
When answering this question you should consider the following factors:

FOR REVOLUTION
Reforms of 1905–06 limited
Autocracy remained in control and the attitudes of Nicholas II were fixed
Continuing resentment of the opponents to the regime, especially the working class
Working class demands
Industrialisation continues
Poor conditions in agriculture and industry
War
AGAINST REVOLUTION
Autocracy had re-established control after 1905 through force/fear
Reforms of 1905
Fundamental Law, 1906 reasserted the supremacy of the Tsar
Stolypin's reforms in agriculture
Increased industrialisation
No coordinated opposition

Also consider the events of late 1916 and early 1917, along with the actions and attitudes of:
Nicholas II, Alexandra, Sergei Witte, Pyotr Stolypin, Grigori Rasputin, Mikhail Rodzianko, Pavel Miliukov, Ivan Goremykin

Then finally think about the following issues:
* What is meant by historical inevitability? Is this a relevant term to apply to the February/March revolution in Russia in 1917?
* Was revolution more likely in Russia in early 1905 or in early 1917? Try to explain the decision you reach.
* Of all the personalities mentioned so far in this study, which individual was most responsible for the coming of revolution in 1917? Give reasons for your answer.

The following two historians' ideas may also assist you in forming your ideas:

SOURCE 1.R

George Keenan on the causes of the Russian Revolution
quoted in M. Bucklow and G. Russell, *Russia: Why Revolution?*, **pp. 149–50, 152**
The denial of political expression must be clearly distinguished from the question of

physical cruelty and oppression in the treatment of the population . . . If one abstracts from the behaviour of the regime in the administration of justice and in the imposition of political discipline that element that was provided by the provocation from the revolutionary side, then the use of police terror cannot be regarded as more than a minor determinant of the alienation of great sectors of society that underlay the breakdown of 1917 . . .

Mention must be made, in conclusion, of the Russian revolutionary movement. It was, of course, not the revolutionary parties that overthrew the autocracy in 1917. Nevertheless, there were indirect ways in which their existence and activity affected the situation of the regime . . . First . . . the revolutionary movement drew many talented youths into an attitude of defiance and revolutionary disobedience to it, thereby impoverishing it in talent, energy and intelligence . . . Second there was the effect . . . on government policy . . . These revolutionary parties and groupings had, as a rule, no interest in seeing genuine progress made in the creation of the liberal institutions. Their aim was generally not to reform the system but to cause it to fall and to replace it.

. . . I am inclined to feel that had the war not intervened, the chances for survival of the autocracy and for its gradual evolution into a constitutional monarchy would not have been bad . . .

- What role does Keenan see political oppression as playing in the development of a revolutionary consciousness in Russia?
- In Keenan's view, the revolutionary movement played a small role in the downfall of the regime. Is this a realistic point of view? Give reasons for your answer.
- Does Keenan see the downfall of the Tsarist state as inevitable?

A modern historian's view SOURCE 1.S
from J.N. Westwood, *Endurance and Endeavour*, pp. 222–3.
It was only to be expected that after two years of war and sacrifice, with no apparent result, Russians would be beginning to ask themselves whether the country was being properly led . . .

The feeling that there were many in the government who wanted the Germans to win, or who were in German pay, gained sustenance from memories of the alleged chaos in the ministry of war in 1914, blamed on the war minister, Sukhomlinov.

. . . Desperately anxious to so weaken the monarchy that Nicholas would feel forced to grant them greater influence through some kind of responsible government, before the end of the war ruined their chances, the liberals appear to have changed their tactics after 1915; hitherto they had merely spread doubts about the government's competence to win the war, not about its willingness . . .

Although workers were beginning to heed anti-war agitators, and strikes were occurring in key industries, most Russians did not condemn the war as such, only the way it was being prosecuted.

- Summarise into your own words the main argument being presented in this source.
- Westwood emphasises the anti-German feeling in Russia during the First World War. From your own knowledge:
  - How strong was this anti-German feeling?
  - What role did anti-German feeling play in the downfall of the Tsarist government?
- Does Westwood view the revolution of 1917 as 'inevitable'? Why/why not?

The Two Revolutions

At the end of this topic you should attempt to answer the following question:
Why were there two revolutions in Russia in 1917?

THE PROBLEMS AND ISSUES

In this topic the relevant Problem and Issue for analysis in the HSC is:
Revolution and Counter-Revolution
Revolution may be seen as the replacement of an established system of government by an alternative system.
Counter-revolution may be reviewed as the attempts of the established system of
government to either retain its power or return to power.

TIME LINE

Note: the following dates are according to the Western calendar—until February 1918
the Russian calendar was thirteen days behind the Western calendar. Therefore in
Russia the March and November revolutions are referred to as the February and
October revolutions.

1916
November 15	P.N. Miliukov gives speech in Duma attacking government incompetence
November 24	Trepov appointed Russian Prime Minister—implementation of a policy of strong repression
December 30	Assassination of Rasputin by Prince Yusupov and others

1917
March 7	Managers of the Putilov steelworks lock out 20 000 workers after breakdown in pay talks—other factory workers go on strike in sympathy
March 8	Fifty factories close and 90 000 workers on strike in Petrograd International Women's Day brings thousands of socialist women onto streets in protest marches
March 9	Estimated 200 000 workers on strike in Petrograd
March 10	Estimated 250 000 workers on strike—all newspapers and public transport cease Cossacks refuse to fire upon march of striking workers
March 11	Soldiers in the Pavlovsky Life Guards refuse to carry out orders Mikhail Rodzianko, President of the Duma, telegrams the Tsar asking for urgent action to end the civil unrest

	Tsar orders the dissolution of the Duma
March 12	Mutiny in the Volinsky Regiment of the army—soldiers march into Petrograd
	Duma refuses to dissolve—instead it forms a twelve-man committee to take over the government of Russia: this is the Provisional Government
March 13	Tsar telegrams Duma offering to share power—Rodzianko and Duma refuse
March 14	Army generals telegram Tsar informing him of the withdrawal of support from the armed forces
	Petrograd Soviet issues Order No. 1, depriving all army officers of authority and giving military authority to elected representatives of soldiers
	Tsar leaves Army Headquarters at Mogilev to travel the 500 km to Petrograd to take control
March 15	Revolutionaries stop Tsar's train 250 km from Petrograd
	Tsar agrees to abdicate, initially in favour of his son Alexei then in favour of his brother Grand Duke Michael
March 16	Grand Duke Michael renounces the throne
	Provisional Government, led by Prince Georg Lvov, takes control of government
March 30	Provisional Government confiscates all imperial and monastic lands
April 16	Lenin, Zinoviev, Trotsky and other left-wing leaders return from exile
April 17	Lenin issues April Theses which outlines Bolshevik proposals for revolution in Russia and calls for 'All Power to the Soviets'
May 4	Bolsheviks in streets with banners proclaiming 'Down with the Provisional Government'
May 11	Lenin realises need for Bolsheviks to have own combat forces—Red Guard formed
May 14–16	Lvov reshuffles Provisional Government: Guchkov and Miliukov are dismissed, Menshevik representation is increased, Kerensky becomes Minister of War
June 16	Opening of First All-Russian Congress of Workers' and Soldiers' Deputies—Lenin announces that the Bolsheviks are 'ready at any moment to take over the government'
June 29–July 28	New military offensive commences in Galicia (Kerensky Offensive)—after initial success the Russians are forced into retreat
	General Brusilov is replaced by General Kornilov
July 15	Trotsky joins the Bolsheviks
July 16–18	Bolsheviks attempt to overthrow the government—the attempt fails—many Bolsheviks (including Trotsky) are gaoled and Lenin flees to Finland
July 20	Resignation of Prince Lvov—Alexander Kerensky becomes Prime Minister
September 9–14	General Kornilov launches coup attempt—Kerensky uses the Bolsheviks to defeat it—many Bolsheviks (including Trotsky) are released from gaol

September 19	The Bolshevik Party achieves an overall majority in the Moscow Soviet
September–October	Trotsky set free—becomes Chairman of Petrograd Soviet Lenin revives slogan 'All Power to the Soviets'
October 6	The Bolshevik Party achieves an overall majority in the Petrograd Soviet Trotsky elected Chairman of Petrograd Soviet
October 11–21	German forces occupy islands in the Gulf of Riga and threaten Petrograd
October 17	Provisional Government discusses evacuation of Petrograd
October 20	Lenin returns to Moscow Kerensky opens the pre-parliament to discuss the formation of the Constituent Assembly
October 22	Creation of Military Revolutionary Committee (Milrevcom) of Petrograd Soviet to coordinate tactics—members visit Kronsversk arsenal and seize weapons and ammunition
October 23	Meeting of the Bolshevik Party Central Committee votes in favour of armed seizure of power
November 4	The Red Guard is formally organised
November 5	Trotsky successfully appeals to garrison of Peter and Paul fortress to give their weapons to the Red Guard Workers at Sestrorektskii factory hand 5000 rifles to the Military Revolutionary Committee
November 6–7	Units loyal to Provisional Government occupy positions in Petrograd and shut down Bolshevik newspapers Bolshevik Red Guards respond by taking control of much of Petrograd
November 7–8	Kerensky calls on help from troops at the front Lenin, in disguise, re-enters Petrograd Bolsheviks complete occupation of the city
November 8	Kerensky escapes Winter Palace and goes to front in search of military support Lenin declares the deposition of the Provisional Government, with power passing to the Soviets Trotsky opens a special meeting of the Petrograd Soviet Lenin makes first public appearance Moscow Soviet forms its own Military Revolutionary Committee
November 9	Troops from the Moscow Milrevcom seize the Kremlin Battleship 'Aurora' trains its guns on the Winter Palace where the ministers of the Provisional Government are taking shelter—Winter Palace falls Bolsheviks open the Second All-Russian Congress of Soldiers' and Workers' Deputies Congress of Soviets pass Lenin's decrees on Land and Peace Congress of Soviets authorises new Provisional Government (Sovnarkom)with Lenin as Chairman

FOCUS QUESTIONS What were the major events in the February/March Revolution?
How important were the armed forces in each revolution?
What do you notice about the speed with which these events
took place?
What does this speed indicate about the nature of the Tsarist
regime and/or the Provisional Government?

B Y FEBRUARY/MARCH 1917 the autocracy had shown itself incapable of
developing a governmental system based on the participation of all
Russians. The constitutional experiment of the Dumas, begun in
1905, was in ruins and by 1917 even its staunchest supporters had lost faith
in the system. They renewed their demand for a government of national confidence. The Tsar was totally incapable of giving the leadership
demanded. With strikes strangling Petrograd he chose to return to Army
Headquarters where he received only the heavily censored reports of his generals and advisers. His only positive response was to order reinforcements into
Petrograd to control the increasing demonstrations and food riots. On 10
March the situation deteriorated with the closure of all workshops.
Almost 200 000 people were on strike. The Tsarina's message to her
husband on that day shows how out of touch the regime had become:

THE FAILURE OF POLITICAL REFORM

> This is a hooligan movement—if the weather were very cold they would all
> probably stay at home. But all this will pass and become calm, if only the
> Duma will behave itself.

Others, however, felt differently. Shulgin, an Octobrist deputy in the
Duma, wrote in his diary on 12 March:

> During the last few days we have been living, as it were, on a volcano . . . It is not,
> of course, a question of bread. The trouble is that in that large city it is impossible
> to find a few hundred people who feel kindly towards the government.

The Duma again demanded the appointment of a new ministry. In a
last desperate attempt to save the regime, Mikhail Rodzianko, the President
of the Duma, appealed to the Tsar:

> There is anarchy in the capital. The government is paralysed. It is necessary
> immediately to entrust a person who enjoys the confidence of the country with the
> formation of the government. Any delay is equivalent to death.

The Tsar ignored the plea and, instead, dissolved the Duma on 11 March. At
this critical moment the two powers capable of saving the situation—the Tsar
and the Duma—failed to combine and cooperate. It would prove the
death knell for both.

Once again, the attitude of the army held the key. When ordered by the
Tsar to restore control in the capital, the generals refused to act and withdrew
their support. Ironically, they did so on the advice of the leaders of the
Duma who assured the generals that military intervention would lead to an
unnecessary civil war and that the Duma was now in control of events. (If

they had known of the re-emergence of the socialist organisation, the Petrograd Soviet, the reaction of the generals may well have been different and their loyalty to the Tsar may have been maintained!) Troops dispatched to enforce the Tsar's hard line sided with the protesters. On 11 March members of the Pavlovsky Life Guards shot one of their officers rather than fire on the protesters. On 12 March, entire regiments deserted in support of the Volinsky Regiment's subsequent mutiny and assisted the people in seeking arms. By 14 March the city of Petrograd was in the hands of revolutionaries, for by this date two new bodies had emerged.

THE FORMATION OF THE PROVISIONAL GOVERNMENT

On 12 March, as a last defiant gesture, part of the Duma formed a provisional committee of twelve representatives. Led by Prince Lvov, it announced its intentions to restore order and authority. This committee, without referring to the entire Duma membership, declared itself to be the Provisional Government of Russia. Its ministers had been neither elected nor chosen, and the new Prime Minister, Lvov, had not previously held a government post. It was therefore immediately hamstrung by its lack of constitutional validity and lack of executive power. Whatever authority it might have had would have come from the Tsar; with the Tsar gone, what authority could it then call upon? Furthermore, it constantly referred to the yet-to-be-elected Constituent Assembly as the 'real master of the Russian land'.

ESTABLISHING THE PETROGRAD SOVIET

Also on 12 March, workers in Petrograd re-established the Petrograd Soviet of Workers' Deputies, an institution similar to the earlier Soviet of 1905. The

Prince Lvov, Prime Minister of Russia following the February/March Revolution

Petrograd Soviet was made up of Mensheviks, Socialist Revolutionaries (and two Bolsheviks) and broadly represented the interests of workers and soldiers in the capital. In these initial stages it supported the Provisional Government, believing that the bourgeois phase of the revolution had arrived. The Soviet had emerged in great haste and lacked any clear plans to assume the government of Russia at this stage. It was therefore prepared to share power with the bourgeois-dominated Provisional Government. However, the Petrograd Soviet did view itself as the body which was most truly representative of the Russian people. Over the course of 1917 it became increasingly determined to act as such.

Thus, by the afternoon of 12 March 1917 there were two 'governments' of Russia: one led by the moderate middle class-members of the Duma, and the other drawn from representatives of the radical political parties and the workers; one with a desire to maintain the interests of the 'respectable' elements of society, and the other determined to continue the revolution's momentum; both held their meetings in rooms adjoining the same corridor in the Tauride Palace. This 'dual power' and ambivalence in political philosophy did not bode well for the establishment of a stable and effective government in Russia.

THE TSAR ABDICATES

Three days later, Nicholas II abdicated and when his brother, Grand Duke Michael, declined the throne, Romanov dynastic rule and the Tsarist state ended. As indicated earlier, the Tsar had been abandoned by his generals in the face of the demands of sections of the Duma leadership. General Alexeyev, Chief of Staff, had only done so on the understanding that the Tsar would be succeeded by his son, Alexei, or his brother, the Grand Duke Michael. With Michael bowing to the pressure of the Duma leadership and also renouncing the throne, Alexeyev found himself faced with no alternative but to accept the end of the Romanov dynasty. Nicholas II had fallen victim to the political intrigues which had become characteristic of the Duma. These same politicians would eventually fall prey to these same manipulations.

The revolution which overthrew the Tsar in March 1917 had been a spontaneous outburst which was the direct result of the war and the heavy

The Tauride Palace, Petrograd. Between 1906 and 1917 it was the meeting place of the Duma. Throughout 1917 it housed both the Provisional Government and the Petrograd Soviet.

burdens the Russian people had been forced to carry. It was essentially a bour-geois revolution and was welcomed most by a middle class who had lost faith in the Tsarist system. The Provisional Government was dominated by middle-class liberals. The sole exception was Alexander Kerensky, the Minister for Justice. A moderate socialist who actively worked for a sense of accommodation between the government and the Soviet, Kerensky was the only member of both bodies.

THE ROLE OF 'THE PEOPLE'

Another key feature of this revolution was the role and position of 'the people'. The mutiny of the capital's garrisons had been so rapid and unprecedented that it was difficult to identify any individual person or group as its leader or organiser. It was comprised of soldiers, factory workers, labourers and students: a collection which Shulgin (a conservative nationalist Duma deputy) described as 'His Majesty the Russian People'.

However, while this mob was disci-plined and determined it also proved very fickle. It had no coordi-nated sense of the direction which the revolution would take—mass meetings were known to just follow the lead of the most recent speakers to address them, and with the fall of the Tsarist government, the protests in the streets did not stop. Strikes continued in the cities, while in the countryside land seizure by the peasants became the major form of anti-bourgeois protest.

REACTION TO THE ABDICATION

While the socialist and radical parties may have been taken by sur-prise at the sudden fall of the Tsar, the re-emergence of the Petrograd Soviet gave them a forum for the expression of their interests. The Soviet therefore insisted that the Provisional Government introduce immediate reforms, in particular the return of basic freedoms such as speech, press and assembly, and an amnesty for all political prisoners. All these measures were introduced and even Lenin had to admit that overnight Russia had become the 'freest country in the world'. To help promote the Soviet's position among the workers and soldiers it established its own newspaper,

The empty throne of the Tsar— St George's Hall, the Kremlin

Izvestiya ('The Truth'). In it the Soviet called for the immediate takeover of all landlord estates. This instruction, combined with the absence of an effective police force and the continuing breakdown of discipline at the front, led the peasants to do largely as they pleased. Agrarian anarchy appeared. Furthermore, news of the February/March Revolution excited the Russian revolutionaries in exile and the political amnesty allowed the great majority of them to return to Russia. Josef Stalin, a member of the Bolshevik faction, returned from Siberia; Leon Trotsky began his journey from New York; while the most celebrated revolutionary, Vladimir Ilyich Ulyanov (Lenin), was in Switzerland. After negotiations, the German government agreed to assist Lenin's return to Russia and provided a sealed train to carry him and his party across the war zone to Petrograd.

On 14 March 1917 the Petrograd Soviet issued its famous Order No. 1. **ORDER NO. 1** Addressed to the troops, it declared that they were not to obey any order from the Provisional Government unless it was countersigned by the Soviet. It instructed each army and naval unit to elect a committee from the lower ranks and to send a delegate to the Soviet; all political activity amongst the troops was to be in line with the wishes of the Soviet. This ensured that the rank and file of the armed forces became linked to the wishes and philosophy of the Soviet, and neither the officer corps nor the Provisional Government could call upon the troops to take action against it. From the perspective of the Provisional Government, people such as Shulgin viewed Order No. 1 as marking 'the end of the army'. Instead it further hamstrung the Provisional Government and strengthened the authority of the Petrograd Soviet.

Political prisoners freed in the early days of the February Revolution. The banner reads: Long Live the People who have opened the prison doors.

From these earliest days the Provisional Government and the Petrograd Soviet held discussions about the establishment of a Constituent Assembly. Both sides agreed that it should be elected by universal, direct, equal and secret suffrage and that it would take over the government of Russia from the Provisional Government. The major barrier to cooperation between the government and the Soviet was the continuation of the war.

In March 1917 the Petrograd Soviet called on belligerents of both sides to conclude a peace settlement which was not based upon any 'war aims'. The Provisional Government, on the other hand, resolved to continue the war effort, with the Foreign Minister, Pavel Miliukov, assuring Russia's allies that its war obligations would be fulfilled. Participation in the war subsequently became central to the fate of the Provisional Government. A Russian surrender may have been seen as a betrayal of the millions who had already suffered; or the Provisional Government may have been more interested in securing the support of the Western allies and the monetary and territorial benefits which would come with the defeat of Germany. Even Bolsheviks such as Lev Kamenev and Josef Stalin argued at this stage that the war should be pursued through to victory and openly stated their support for the government in this matter. This policy of 'defensism' was seen as the way by which the revolution could be strengthened. At this stage in his political career, though, Stalin was viewed as 'a grey blur' who demanded 'little attention'. Whatever of the reasons behind the decision, the Provisional Government pushed on with the war against Germany.

LENIN'S RETURN AND THE APRIL THESES

Vladimir Lenin arrived back in Russia on 16 April 1917. He immediately set to work disciplining the Bolshevik Party and altering its attitude towards the Provisional Government. Up until then the Bolsheviks had supported the Provisional Government, viewing it as part of the bourgeois rule which was envisaged by Karl Marx. The Bolsheviks believed that it was out

A section of the Petrograd Soviet in the early months of 1917. The fact that the Bolsheviks did not yet have control over this institution is indicated by the banner which reads: Down with Lenin.

of this capitalist phase that the true proletarian revolution would emerge. By 1917 Lenin had rejected this idea. Almost alone, he brought the power of his personality, intellect and drive to bear on the Bolsheviks and in a statement known as the April Theses he spelt out what would become the official Bolshevik position: the war was an imperialist conflict and support for the war effort should end; the bourgeois phase of the revolution had already occurred and the Bolsheviks must abandon all support for this government and its policies; 'the Soviet was the one possible form of revolutionary government', and though now dominated by the non-Bolsheviks, the goal of the Bolsheviks must be to win control of the soviets now emerging in all major cities and towns:

> Comrade soldiers, I greet you without knowing yet whether or not you have been believing in all the promises of the Provisional Government. But I am convinced that . . . they are deceiving you and the whole Russian people. The people need peace; the people need bread; the people need land. And they give you war, hunger, no bread—leave the landlords still on the land. We must fight for the social revolution, fight to the end, till the complete victory of the proletariat. Long live the world revolution.

In this manner the Bolsheviks would bring about, by Lenin's definition, the true socialist revolution.

The Bolshevik Party Congress adopted Lenin's argument, the Provisional Government was condemned and the slogan 'All power to the soviets' reflected the tactic by which the Bolsheviks hoped to bring about the final revolution.

Lenin was also convinced that the suffering of the working class in Europe had been deepened by the war and the 'imperialistic greed of great powers'. He also believed that 'the spilled blood of the people [be paid for] with the blood of its oppressors'. This use of violence became the Bolsheviks' 'sacred duty'. He believed that a socialist revolution was imminent in Germany where the capitalist system was well entrenched. He denounced the 'defensist' policies which supported the continuation of the war. Instead, he espoused the philosophy of 'defeatism' in which the war must be brought to an immediate end. He even went so far as to criticise defensist statements which had appeared in the Bolshevik Party's own newspaper, *Pravda* ('News'), and announced that he was prepared to destroy the Bolshevik Party rather than cooperate with the Provisional Government and moderates within the Soviet. By May 1917 Lenin had won the Bolshevik Party over to this line and had increased the Party's support base. It was a remarkable achievement.

Lenin's underlying political philosophy reeked of violence and portrayed the future as belonging to 'parties', 'masses' and 'states' and not to individuals. It struck directly at the heart of the Provisional Government, and in 'normal' circumstances in Russia could not have survived. However, these were not normal circumstances. The Provisional Government had dismantled the Tsarist apparatus which could have saved it: gone were the secret police and administrative controls on political dissidents; the Tsarist bureaucracy ceased to function as an effective government institution; in the countryside the landlords abandoned their responsibility of maintaining discipline and order. The Provisional Government turned to 'government by committee', believing that discussion and compromise were superior to compulsion. In these circumstances the war and the attitude of the armed forces would prove critical to the Provisional Government's success or failure.

THE PROBLEMS OF 'DUAL POWER'

The Provisional Government had the dual difficulty of establishing an ordered form of government in Russia and at the same time continuing the war effort. However, the continuing anarchy in the cities and the growing power of the soviets severely hampered the establishment of an effective political system. With its emphasis on order, discipline and efficient administration, the Soviet seized the initiative and was increasingly viewed by 'the people' as their truly representative body. It was the Soviet which dealt with the army, the railways, communications, employers and employees. The situation soon developed in which the Provisional Government was described as 'the authority without power', while the Petrograd Soviet was styled 'the power without authority'. J.N. Westwood suggests that the reasons for the failure of the February/March Revolution must therefore be found in the reluctance of the Soviet to use this 'power', particularly in relation to ending the war. He points out that the leader of the Socialist Revolutionary/Menshevik bloc, V.M. Chernov, was popular and trusted. However, he lacked the 'authority' to take the steps which were required. He was too prepared to resort to compromise in an attempt to keep the revolution heading in a direction which would maintain middle-class support. Chernov did not want a repeat of the lost opportunities of 1905.

BOLSHEVIK AGITATION

In contrast, Lenin's control of the Bolshevik Party following the publication of his April Theses led to further demonstrations and protests in Petrograd. Once again it was the Soviet, rather than the Provisional Government, which called for and eventually obtained some semblance of order. By May 1917 'the people' were in fact proving themselves more radical than the Soviet. It was Lenin who came to realise that by appealing to 'the people' the Bolsheviks would gain the popular support which could then be used in the Soviet to bring about the revolution he wanted. The view at the time was that such a scenario was impossible; many believed that Lenin's philosophy and ideas could never succeed in Russia in 1917 simply because the Russian people were *not* 'revolutionary'.

Bolshevik resistance and agitation continued regardless. Demonstrations in Petrograd in May and heavy Soviet pressure forced the resignation of the War Minister, Alexander Guchkov, and Alexander Kerensky, the socialist, took the post. The government itself was reshuffled and, though still headed by Lvov, it now included, apart from Kerensky, four other socialists in the cabinet, a clear indication of the growing anti-bourgeois sentiment emerging amongst the workers and soldiers. In an attempt to bolster its reputation, the Provisional Government launched a major offensive in Galicia in June/July. In response to this disastrous military campaign the Bolsheviks offered a simple powerful answer: 'Peace, Bread, Land'.

Kerensky tried desperately to rekindle the fighting spirit and sense of purpose among the army. He believed that if the troops did not continue to fight they would degenerate into a 'meaningless mob' which would threaten the internal security of Russia. General Brusilov, one of Russia's few successful generals, was appointed Commander-in-Chief and the government adopted as its goal the pursuit of a 'just peace' without 'annexations or indemnities'. Kerensky put forward the message that the troops were no longer the force of an autocratic regime but rather the arm of a new liberated Russia, endeavouring to conclude the war with no disadvantage to Russia.

Because Kerensky was seen by some as a new Napoleon Bonaparte leading his country on to victory, his appeals carried considerable weight. However, Bolshevik propaganda and the effect of Order No. 1 proved stronger. The failure of the offensive in Galicia in July 1917 saw the army fall apart. Entire units mutinied; troops refused to fight; officers were murdered; chaos and wholesale looting began. Kerensky prophesied:

> When trust in me is lost, a dictator will come and then mistrust will be suppressed with bayonets and whips. (Quoted in Brian Moynahan, *Comrades*, 1992, p. 181.)

Ultimately, however, Kerensky's own authoritarian manner and inability to command respect within the government were to work against him.

At the same time as the war effort was taking a turn for the worse, new developments emerged within the Soviet itself. In June 1917 the First All-Russian Congress of Soviets convened in Petrograd. Representatives of all the soviets of the major cities of Russia attended and Lenin and Kerensky met for the first time. Of the 822 representatives, the Bolsheviks provided only 105, the other delegates representing the Mensheviks, Socialist Revolu-

The Provisional Government's army assembles in preparation for the July protests.

Street protests in Petrograd in July were quickly dispersed by loyal troops.

tionaries and a variety of other minor political groupings. Lenin's address to the Congress reiterated the Bolshevik argument of working through the soviets. He praised it as:

> that new type of government which had been created by the revolution and examples of which can be found only in the history of the greatest rise in the revolutionary tide, for instance in 1792 in France.
>
> Power must be transferred to the Soviet, support for the Provisional Government must end. Tsereteli [Menshevik Minister of Posts and Telegraphs] said that there is no political party in Russia that would express its readiness to assume full power. I answer there is! No party can refuse this and our party does not refuse it. It is prepared at any moment to take over full power.

This argument was not yet accepted by the majority of the delegates. Instead, the Congress passed a vote of confidence in the Provisional Government. One person who did share Lenin's views was Leon Trotsky. Trotsky had arrived back in Russia in May 1917 and, though independent of both Bolshevik and Menshevik, he also saw a need for immediate action and soon moved to a position in support of Lenin.

THE 'JULY DAYS'

A demonstration against the Provisional Government as a show of support for the Bolsheviks in the working-class districts of Petrograd was planned for 9 June. The march was called off at the last moment when the Congress of Soviets, fearful of bitter street fighting, condemned it. Instead the Congress organised its own street demonstrations for 18 June, intending to show proletariat support for the Soviet. While the abandonment of its march may have seemed a political setback to the Bolsheviks, they gained some heart from the predominantly pro-Bolshevik banners which appeared amongst the workers during the Congress-organised protest.

In early July 1917, in the middle of the military failures in Galicia, further protests broke out in Petrograd and the Bolsheviks found themselves with a real opportunity to overthrow the Provisional Government. Petrograd was full of restless elements: rebellious troops, armed workers (Red Guards) and mutinous sailors from the nearby base at Kronstadt.

Lenin, who had been in Finland, returned to Petrograd and, for a few days in July at least, the fate of the Provisional Government depended on how the Bolsheviks used this outburst of mob feeling in the capital. Luckily, from the government's point of view, the movement very quickly lost its momentum and the Bolsheviks failed to harness its potential power. Reliable troops arrived from the front, sealing the fate of the popular uprisings of these so-called 'July Days'.

The Provisional Government, confident in its new support, decided to crack down on the Bolsheviks. On 19 July it ordered the arrest of Bolshevik leaders on the charge of inciting armed insurrection. The Bolsheviks were labelled as traitors and collaborators with the Germans. Trotsky was arrested; Lenin fled back to exile in Finland. There was widespread condemnation of the Bolsheviks and their popular support declined. On 20 July Prince Lvov resigned, and Kerensky took up the post of Prime Minister while maintaining his portfolio as Minister of War.

However, the setback of the July Days was not fatal for the Bolshevik movement. The socialist leaders of the government continued to be bound by their sense of common purpose. Within their wider programme of social, economic and political reform none considered the Bolsheviks to be a 'serious' threat. For example, the new Interior Minister, Tsereteli, believed that to accuse the Bolsheviks of political crimes and order their elimination 'smacked of autocracy'. Even Kerensky, despite his tough anti-Bolshevik rhetoric, took few practical steps to lessen their influence.

Other events over the next few months then returned the advantage to the Bolshevik Party. Foremost amongst these was the worsening situation at the

THE KORNILOV REVOLT

Some of the delegates at the first All-Russian Congress of Soviets – the two men to the right of the front row are the prominent Mensheviks G.V. Plekhanov and N.S. Chkeidze

Alexander Kerensky – second Prime Minister of Russia during the Provisional Government

front. In July, the Provisional Government had appointed a new Commander-in-Chief, General Kornilov. An ultra-conservative who urged a hard line against deserters and mutineers, he believed that the government must smash the Petrograd Soviet. This led to a break down in relations between Kerensky and Kornilov: Kerensky feared that any crackdown on the army would provoke a revolt in the Soviet. Fearful of a military coup, Kerensky dismissed Kornilov. This provoked a leadership crisis in the army at the worst possible moment: German forces had just taken Riga and were advancing across Russian territory, and regular troops in Petrograd had divided loyalties.

Kornilov, still determined to overthrow the Soviet, ordered several cavalry units to march on Petrograd in August. Kerensky's response was to make himself 'dictator' of Russia and take control of all ministerial portfolios. He then turned to the Soviet and to the Bolsheviks for support. Bolsheviks arrested in July were released and, along with their rearmed supporters, were used to strengthen Kerensky's position and overcome the Kornilov revolt.

The Bolsheviks' role in the Kornilov affair indicates the growing support they now enjoyed. Though Lenin remained in Finland and the Provisional Government was resolute in its decision to arrest him should he return, the Party quickly recovered from the debacle of July. In fact in the last week of July it had secretly held its national congress, attended by delegates representing 240 000 members. The Kornilov revolt and the new prestige the Bolsheviks derived from it now gave them a new resolve for action, particularly as a result of Kerensky's weakened position.

Lenin urged his followers to seize power as soon as possible. From Finland he produced the treatise *State and Revolution* in which he outlined Bolshevik tactics for the coming struggle. In it he stressed the annihilation of the bureaucracy, the continuation of repression through 'the state' and the destruction of the old state machinery and institutions. All this was for the purpose of 'overthrowing the bourgeois, destroying bourgeois parliamentarianism'. In order to remove any popular support from the Provisional Government, Lenin deliberately promised the people what they wanted. In this way, such simple Bolshevik promises as 'Peace to the people, land to the peasants, confiscation of scandalous profits' quickly found their mark.

By October 1917, Kerensky had lost support of the army leadership and the conservative groups within Russia. His government was careering towards disaster. Power shifted quickly to the Soviet as the alliance between government and army, which had previously saved it, began to disintegrate.

The authority of the Provisional Government had been completely undermined by the disastrous policy of continuing the war. Military defeat, mutiny and insurrection on the front, continued food shortages, inflation and the collapse of order and authority at home had been the result. Factory owners had used the Bolshevik defeat in July as an excuse to

THE DECLINE OF THE PROVISIONAL GOVERNMENT

The false passport used by Lenin to escape to Finland – it is made out in the name of Konstantin Petrovich Ivanov

Anti-Kornilov pamphlet distributed by the Executive Committee of the Petrograd Soviet. It reads: 'Those who are for Kornilov are against the revolution. Those against the revolution are against the people. Those against the people are against the salvation of the motherland. Without the people there is no salvation of the motherland!'

reimpose discipline on the shop floor. As a consequence strikes had occurred, productivity had declined, food had remained scarce, wages had not kept pace with price increases and fuel shortages continued. As in the winter of 1916–17, the 'bony hand of hunger' began to grip the Russian people and this phrase, by the textilist Pavel Riabushinsky, was now used against the government by Trotsky's pro-Bolshevik propaganda. Events, often not of their own making, continued to work in favour of the Bolsheviks. Nikolai Sukhanov, a Menshevik member of the Soviet Executive Committee, went so far as to state that the rise of the Bolsheviks had less to do with support for 'Bolshevism' and Lenin's ideas than with a general dislike for Kerensky and the policies of the Provisional Government.

The Provisional Government had delayed any real effort to solve the problems of Russian agriculture or the plight of the peasants. The Land Committee established in May 1917 to direct and supervise land reform degenerated into a rabble of well-meaning, but ignorant, revolutionaries. The peasants simply turned to land seizure—not out of revolutionary zeal but from self-interest. The need for strong government in the provinces was obvious to many, but the Provisional Government failed to take this opportunity to secure control.

BOLSHEVIK TACTICS

In this context the Bolshevik slogan of 'Peace, Bread, Land' proved effective. More importantly, in the urban centres the proletariat was systematically coming to embrace the Bolshevik cause. In September 1917 the Bolsheviks won majorities in the Petrograd and Moscow soviets, with Trotsky becoming chairman of the Petrograd Soviet. Kerensky's fate was sealed. Lenin argued that the time had now come for the transfer of power to the soviets. In reality he had no love for this institution. Rather he recognised that their capture would provide the institutional basis for the seizure of the entire government by the Bolsheviks. The slogan of 'All Power to the Soviets' should have read 'All Power to the Bolsheviks'.

Kerensky's announcement of elections on 25 November for the long-promised but much-delayed Constituent Assembly triggered Lenin into action. On 20 October 1917 Lenin secretly returned to Russia. After heated debate he convinced the majority of the Bolshevik Central Committee that the Bolsheviks must seize power immediately. In preparation, the Bolshevik delegates walked out of the pre-parliament for the Constituent Assembly . The Menshevik Sukhanov warned the other delegates that the only option left for the Bolsheviks was armed uprising, but the others continued to downplay the seriousness of the Bolshevik threat.

Kerensky was aware of Bolshevik plans and endeavoured to enlist military support from the Cossack regiments to support his government. He was unsuccessful, for the general mood of the soldiers had become unsympathetic. The general feeling, though, was that the Bolsheviks still were no real threat. As one Bolshevik observed, the government probably only needed an armed force of 500 men and the Bolsheviks would have been destroyed:

> Perhaps [replied Trotsky], but to do this the government would have required first of all resolution and daring. Secondly it would have needed a good detachment of 500 men. And where was that to be found?

On 2 November, Kerensky moved to impose stricter discipline within the army. The new War Minister, Alexander Verkhovsky, in an attempt to undermine the growing support for Bolshevik calls for an immediate end to the war, responded by calling for an immediate peace with Germany. Kerensky dismissed him, prompting the Welfare Minister, Dr Nikolai Kishkin, to describe the ludicrousness of a situation in which a government dismisses its War Minister on the eve of a possible coup! Tereshchenko, the Foreign Minister, described the whole scenario as a 'madhouse'. Meanwhile, Trotsky was organising Bolshevik supporters into an army of their own: the Red Guard.

The Bolshevik seizure of power was carried out by the Military Revolutionary Committee established within the Petrograd Soviet and headed by Trotsky. It included forty-eight Bolsheviks and was ostensibly to act only on the orders of the Petrograd Soviet. On 6–7 November 1917 the Committee, acting on directions from the Bolshevik Party, and not the Soviet, used loyal troops and Red Guards to systematically occupy key points in Petrograd—the railway, post office and government buildings. On 7 November a group laid siege to the Winter Palace, the headquarters of Kerensky's government. The ministers inside were

THE BOLSHEVIK COUP

Members of the Women's Death Battalion receiving a blessing in Petrograd. This unit was one of those charged with the defence of the Winter Palace against the Bolsheviks.

issued with an ultimatum to surrender or the Bolsheviks would open fire from the cruiser *Aurora* moored a short distance away in the Neva River. The *Aurora* in fact fired a few blank rounds and one live shell which exploded in a corridor of the palace. Forty armed Bolsheviks raided the palace and arrested the members of the Provisional Government. The revolution was almost complete.

At about the same time that evening, at the opening session of the Second All-Russian Congress of Soviets, Lenin reappeared in public to announce the fall of the Provisional Government and the transfer of all power to the Soviet of Workers, Soldiers and Peasants' Deputies. The Congress, following a walkout protest by Mensheviks and Socialist Revolutionaries, endorsed the Bolshevik action. A new Bolshevik-dominated government, the Council of People's Commissars, was immediately established, with Lenin as its head. Trotsky became Commissar for Foreign Affairs and Stalin became Commissar for Nationalities. A new Central Committee was elected consisting of Bolsheviks and left-wing Socialists. In all major cities power passed swiftly to the soviets.

The failure of the Provisional Government to maintain power was a reflection of its inability to gain support from all sections of the population: it proceeded with the war; it failed to act upon the urgent social and economic problems; it was emasculated by the actions and authority of the Petrograd Soviet. And yet the Petrograd Soviet also refused to take power throughout 1917. Why? One possible explanation was that the majority of the Soviet's delegates believed firmly in the 'Marxist dialectic': there needed to be a long bourgeois phase before the workers could take power and this had not yet happened in Russia. A further explanation may be found in the intellectual basis of the Petrograd Soviet—they were at no stage truly representative of the working class!

Also, the Bolshevik success was not just a result of the failures of the Provisional Government and the continuing economic dislocation of the Russian people. From the dark days of July 1917 and after, the Bolshevik Party worked hard among the working classes to educate them for the task which lay ahead. The Bolsheviks preached politics, and fostered literacy and a culture whose sole aim was the successful waging of a class war. This so-called 'Prolekult' set the Bolsheviks apart from their socialist brothers and sisters. Their hard-line approach in this area enabled them to

① Winter Palace   ④ Smolny Institute
② Peter Paul Fortress   ⑤ Head Post office
③ Tauride Palace   ⑥ Putilov Works

■ Railway Station

Map of Petrograd showing the major sites involved in the Bolshevik coup

attract the support of the working classes away from the soft-line attitude to education and popular culture adopted by the Mensheviks and others. Furthermore, those who could have opposed the Bolsheviks continued to disregard them as a real threat. The October/November Revolution therefore became a coup founded on the indifference of the people towards the Kerensky government, the inability of the government to provide effective leadership and the ability of a small group of people (the Bolsheviks) to exploit a situation to its own ends.

SUMMARY
- The war exacerbated the domestic difficulties of Russia and highlighted the structural problems in the Russian government and economy.
- The actions of Grigori Rasputin and Tsarina Alexandra alienated the Tsar from the people.
- The February/March Revolution was a spontaneous outburst of popular dissent against the war and the Tsar's government.
- The Provisional Government existed in a constitutional vacuum and was consistently reluctant to seize the initiative for change.
- The re-emergence of the Petrograd Soviet created a duality of power and authority which was exploited by the Bolsheviks.
- The Provisional Government came to be seen as the tool of the middle class, while the workers turned to the Petrograd Soviet as their 'representative government'.
- The Bolsheviks deliberately targeted the Petrograd Soviet as the instrument for their takeover of power.
- The Bolsheviks sought power for themselves, not for the socialists or the soviets or the Russian people.

KEY PERSONALITIES, GROUPS, TERMS

Provisional Government: Temporary civilian government formed from the State Duma following the February/March Revolution; saw its major function as maintaining stable government until elections could be held for the Constituent Assembly (set down for November 1917).

Petrograd Soviet: Representative body of workers and soldiers in Petrograd; re-emerged in 1917 and came to challenge the Provisional Government for control of the Russian state.

Dual Power: The situation which existed in Russia throughout most of 1917—i.e. the civilian government was essentially in the hands of the Provisional Government, while the Petrograd Soviet also claimed the right to govern; Order No. 1 gave the Petrograd Soviet jurisdiction over the armed forces.

Vladimir Ilyich Lenin: Russian revolutionary, real name Vladimir Ilyich Ulyanov; born 1870, died 1924; from a middle-class, educated family; 1887, brother hanged for assassination attempt on Tsar Alexander III;

entered Kazan University to study law; expelled for taking part in demon-strations against student freedom; completed legal studies in St Petersburg; practised law for brief time before becoming involved in politics of social democrats; 1893, moved to St Petersburg and became active revolutionary; 1897, gaoled and exiled to Siberia for subversive activities; 1898, married Nadezhda Krupskaya; 1898, Russian Social Democratic Party founded; 1900, freed and went abroad; founded Party newspaper, *Iskra* ('The Spark'); 1902, wrote *What is to be done?* describing the future state as being run by professional revolutionaries; 1903, split in the RSDP over question of membership—Lenin became leader of the Bolshevik (majority) faction; arrived back in Russia too late to take effective part in 1905 Revo-lution; 1905–17, abroad writing and discussing future of Russia; during the First World War he argued for 'defeat' in order to bring on the revolution; April 1917, returned from Switzerland via a 'sealed train' with assistance from the German government; wrote April Theses outlining an end to the war, gov-ernment ownership of all land and the overthrow of the Provisional Gov-ernment—won other Bolsheviks to his point of view; July 1917, attempted overthrow of Provisional Government failed and he fled to Finland; wrote *State and Revolution* in which he maintained his opposition to parliamentary democracy and argued that the dictatorship of the proletariat would not lead to the immediate withering of state institutions; seized power from the Provisional Government and established the Council of People's Commissars (SOVNARKOM), with himself as Chairman—initial actions were to secure peace with Germany, nationalise the land and secure his control over the state; established the CHEKA (Extraordinary Commission to Combat Counter-Revolution, Sabotage and Speculation) in December 1917 to rule by force and terror; worked with Trotsky to form Red Army to combat White forces in the Civil War; destruction of economy by 1920 led to formulation of the New Economic Policy to raise production; continued to work to entrench Bolshevik/Communist rule; suffered a series of strokes following 1918 assassination attempt; died 1924.

Leon Trotsky: Russian revolutionary of Jewish origin, real name Davi-dovich Bronstein; born 1879, died 1940; born in prosperous peasant family in the Ukraine; well educated; became professional revolutionary in 1897; 1898, arrested and exiled to Siberia; joined Social Democratic Party while in exile; 1902, escaped, went abroad and met Lenin; sided with Mensheviks after the 1903 party split; returned to Russia to participate in 1905 Revolution; became a leading member of the St Petersburg Soviet of Workers' Deputies; again arrested and exiled; wrote *Results and Prospects,* a pamphlet which advocated a state of permanent revolution in which the urban workers would be the backbone of the revolutionary order—this takeover of power would inspire other working classes of the world to follow suit; escaped 1907 and abroad until 1917; writings in this period reflected his belief that the organised working class could bring about revolution; returned to Russia mid-1917; joined Bolshevik Party; elected to Central Committee and later elected Chairman of Petrograd

Soviet; assumed leadership of the Party's preparation for the revolution with Lenin either in hiding or abroad; as Chairman of Milrevcom he removed the Provisional Government from power in October/November 1917; appointed Commissar for Foreign Affairs in new government and helped defeat Kerensky's counter-revolution; Soviet Russia's chief negotiator at the peace talks with Germany at Brest-Litovsk; 1918–25, Commissar for War; organiser and leader of the Red Army during the Civil War; enlistment of former Tsarist officers and abandonment of militia-style force introduced at the start of Bolshevik rule led to criticism; 1919, became member of the Politburo and helped establish Comintern; caught up in the democratic debate within the Party and supported government-controlled trade unions, suppression of Kronstadt revolt and Lenin's introduction of New Economic Policy; early 1920s onwards, pushed for rapid industrialisation of Soviet economy—this led to conflict with other leading members of the Party; sought greater democracy and central planning of the state; 1923 published *The New Course*, an open letter aimed at re-establishing support within the Party—criticised as supporting factionalism and opportunism; 1925, lost position of Commissar of War; 1926, removed from Politburo; 1927, dropped from Central Committee and deported from Soviet Union; wrote numerous articles against Stalin's regime; murdered by Stalinist agents in 1940.

Alexander Fyodorovich Kerensky: Russian lawyer and politician; born 1881, died 1970; eloquent anti-Tsarist speaker in the State Duma and leader of the Socialist Revolutionaries; after the February/March Revolution he became Minister of Justice, then Minister of War; leader of the Provisional Government from July 1917; decision to continue the war with Germany undermined his popularity; overthrown by the Bolsheviks in October/November; spent the rest of his life in exile.

Mikhail Rodzianko: President of the State Duma; born 1859, died 1924; pro-Tsarist who attempted to convince Nicholas II to make reforms in order to preserve the monarchy in some form; chaired the discussions which led to the formation of the Provisional Government in February/March 1917.

Lavr Georgyevich Kornilov: Russian soldier; born 1870, died 1918; served in Russo-Japanese War; in First World War was a divisional commander in Galicia; captured by the Austrians but escaped; after the February/March Revolution was appointed Commander-in-Chief of the Russian Army; when Alexander Kerensky ignored his demands that army discipline be restored, he attempted to seize power and establish a military dictatorship; coup attempt failed and he was arrested; escaped during the October/November Revolution to join Anton Denikin's anti-Bolshevik action; killed in action during the Civil War.

Grigori Evseyevich Zinoviev: Russian revolutionary, real name Ovsel Radomylsky; born 1883, died 1936; spent his time in exile working with Lenin from 1908; founding member of the Communist Politburo, President of the Third Communist International and the party chief in Leningrad (Petrograd); joined with Kamenev in advocating the inclusion of all non-Bolshevik socialist deputies in the new revolutionary government; criticised for the Comintern's failure to bring about world-wide revolution; eventually allied himself with Trotsky in an attempt to counter Stalin's influence and was expelled from the Communist Party; later readmitted to the Party but his position was never secure; executed for treason in the purge of 1936.

Lev Borisovich Kamenev: Russian revolutionary politician, real name Lev Rosenfeld; born 1883, died 1936; a founding member of the Bolshevik Party; argued against the Bolshevik seizure of power in 1917, claiming that the Party was not yet ready and that defeat would be the result; Chairman of the first Communist Politburo and acted as Lenin's deputy; continued to advocate the inclusion of all socialist deputies within the new government; 1917–24, supported the notion of party unity and following Lenin's death he joined with Stalin and Zinoviev to oppose Trotsky; later outmanoeuvred by Stalin and expelled from the Communist Party; tried for treason during the purge of 1936 and executed.

Prince Georg Yevgenyevich Lvov: Russian statesman; born 1861, died 1925; prominent liberal member of the Duma; responsible for the development of the zemstva; position as Chairman of the All-Russian Union of Zemstva meant he became head of the Provisional Government following the February/March Revolution; moderation and dislike of violence made him unsuited to the revolutionary situation; resigned in favour of Kerensky; escaped to France during the Bolshevik Revolution.

EXERCISES

1. What role was played by individuals in the coming of the two revolutions in Russia in 1917?
2. a   What problems were faced by the Provisional Government?
   b   How effectively were these problems handled by the Provisional Government?
3. a   In what ways did the aims and nature of the Petrograd Soviet change during 1917?
   b   What was the effect of these changes?
4. Why did the Bolsheviks fail in their attempt to seize power in July 1917?
5. What was the significance of the Kornilov Revolt?
6. How important was Lenin to the Bolshevik cause?
7. How extensive was support for the Bolsheviks when they took power at the end of 1917?

DOCUMENT STUDY   (No. 5

Examine the four historical sources and answer the questions which follow.

Telegram from Tsar Nicholas II to General Khabalov, Commander of the Petrograd Military District, 10 March 1917   SOURCE 2.A

I command you to suppress from tomorrow all disorders on the streets of the capital, which are impermissible at a time when the fatherland is carrying on a difficult war with Germany.

SOURCE 2.B

A report by an agent of the Okhrana (the Tsarist secret police), 11 March 1917
The movement which has started has flared up without any party preparing it and without any preliminary discussion of a plan of action . . .
Now everything depends on the behaviour of the military units; if the latter do not join the proletariat, the movement will quickly subside; but if the troops turn against the government, then nothing can save the country from a revolutionary upheaval.

SOURCE 2.C

Leon Trotsky, *The History of the Russian Revolution*, 1932–33
The fact is that the February revolution was begun from below . . . the initiative being taken on their own accord by the most oppressed and downtrodden of the prole-tariat—the women textile workers, among them no doubt many soldiers' wives. The overgrown breadlines had provided the last stimulus. About 90 000 workers, men and women, were on strike that day. The fighting mood expressed itself in demonstrations, meetings, encounters with the police . . . on the following day the movement not only failed to diminish but doubled. One half of the industrial workers of Petrograd were on strike on the 24th February [9 March]. The workers came to the factories in the morning; instead of going to work they held meetings; then began processions towards the centre. New districts and new groups of population were drawn towards the movement. The slogan 'Bread' was crowded out or obscured by louder slogans: 'Down with autocracy!' 'Down with the war!' . . . Around the barracks, sentinels, patrols, and lines of soldiers stood groups of working men and women exchanging friendly words with the army men.

SOURCE 2.D

Extract from newspaper article by British journalist
J. Pollock, 'The Russian Revolution: A Review by an Onlooker', published May 1917
It is at present impossible to arrive at an exact figure of the numbers killed in and after the fighting [in Petrograd] but . . . the truth probably lies between four and five thousand killed . . . In the provinces the revolution was of a paper character, being mostly executed in the telegraph offices. Normal life was scarcely interrupted for more than one day in Moscow, and even less in other cities . . .
The new government is displaying enough ability to justify the belief that if it had a fair chance it would find its way towards a stable and democratic republic . . . Ministers have to take up the reins where they were dropped in blood and dirt and treachery by Nicholas the Second's government . . . [I have] not a doubt that the former government would have succeeded in selling Russia and the Allies to the Germans, and would have left Russia miserable, ashamed, semi-Asiatic, and economically ruined instead of the great and splendid democratic nation that she has won the new chance to become . . .

Questions
a i) According to Source 2.C who were the most oppressed and downtrodden of the proletariat?
ii) According to Source 2.B, why did everything depend upon the armed forces?
b Using Source 2.A and your own knowledge, outline the events which led to the abdication of the Tsar in February/March 1917.
c Examine Sources 2.B, 2.C and 2.D. What difficulties would an historian encounter when attempting to use each of these sources as evidence of developments in Russia in 1917? (In your answer consider the nature, origin, motive and audience of each source as well as its content.)
d Using all four sources and your own knowledge, explain why the Tsarist regime collapsed in February/March 1917.

STUDYING AN HISTORICAL SOURCE   No. 2

Examine each of the following photographs of aspects of Russia in 1917.

a In what ways are photographs useful as historical evidence?
b What difficulties exist in using photographs as historical evidence?
c What does each of these photographs tell you about the nature of the Bolshevik Revolution and the people involved in it?

Soldiers from the Petrograd Garrison,
February 1917

Soldiers and workers exchange banners at the
Putilov works, 1917.

*Alexander
Kerensky's
Provisional
Government*

*Women's Death
Battalion—a
pro-government
force*

Soldiers in Petrograd reading Isvestiya

Pro-Bolshevik soldiers

The Petrograd Soviet

Lenin addressing a crowd— Trotsky is standing on the platform to the right

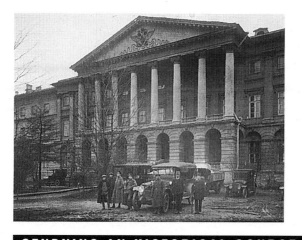

Smolny Institute, Bolshevik head-quarters in Petrograd

STUDYING AN HISTORICAL SOURCE No. 3

The following source is a literary review of a secondary source. Carefully read this source and answer the questions which follow.

SOURCE 2.E

Review of *The Russian Revolution 1899–1919* by Richard Pipes—written by Nicholas Richardson and published in the *Sunday Times*, 13 January 1991

A Very Russian Coup

'Another damn thick square book!' the Duke of Gloucester remarked to its unfortunate author. 'Always scribble, scribble, scribble! Eh! Mr Gibbon?' Like Gibbon, Richard Pipes has written a damn thick (but marvellously readable) book, the second in a proposed trilogy. Like Gibbon, he is dealing with the decline and fall of the greatest empire of its time, with the added and ironic twist that he is writing as its even more formidable successor falls apart. And like him, Pipes is describing something very similar to the triumph of barbarism and religion: the revolutionary struggles since 1789, he believes, 'are not over politics but over theology'. The Bolsheviks did not set out to topple a regime. They intended to recast humanity itself.

It may be significant that it is the set-piece political murders in this book that stay in the mind. But it is certainly crucial to Pipe's purpose that his account ends, not with the Bolsheviks' seizure of power in October 1917, but with the 'war on the village' in the summer of 1918, and the red terror: 'the French Revolution culminated in terror, whereas the Russian one began with it'. This was no accident. Political terror was not, as Soviet historians like to pretend, a back-to-the-wall reaction to allied intervention and civil war. It was an integral part both of revolutionary tradition and of Lenin's programme.

Like their predecessors and rivals, the Bolsheviks used terror as a surrogate for the mass support they never had. It also stems from their doctrine . . . The party, for all its minuscule following even among the working class it purportedly led, always knew best. If necessary, the people must be forced to be free.

Pipes argues, in a remarkably unflattering cameo, that this was in fact a matter of Lenin's own make-up as of anything else. He saw politics as warfare, and class war as just that. His rivals paid lip service to the concept. Lenin put it into practice, and that was why he won.

The Bolsheviks had played no part in the 1905 revolution in St Petersburg: they were involved instead in the disastrous uprising in Moscow. They had nothing to do with the February revolution in 1917 either. But in October, a handful of men, some 1,000, seized power in the capital of a country of 150m. It was a model coup. But in no sense did it seem the start of 10 days that would shake the world. As Pipes shows, the West paid almost no attention.

The February revolution was the result of working-class anger at food and fuel shortages, along with rising prices; of a mutinous garrison of peasant soldiers; and of the discontent of the political opposition. In Pipe's eyes the latter was crucial. For his is a primarily political view of the revolution; it was, he says, not a result of 'insufferable conditions but of irreconcilable attitudes'.

This accounts for Pipes's otherwise surprising starting-point: the university disturbances of 1899. Here, in microcosm, was the process that would lead to revolution. The regime treated the student demonstrations as sedition. The opposition blew specific student complaints up into a matter of political principle. There was no centre ground, and no compromise.

The 1905 revolution and the October Manifesto, which ushered in Russia's only—timid—experience of constitutionalism, merely hardened divisions. The government had offered concessions unwillingly. It tried hard to pretend that they did not exist. The opposition saw concession as a proof of weakness (they were right). Their concern was not to exploit them but to go for broke. The liberals (and 1905 had been their triumph) were reduced to the dangerous game of using the threat of a revolution they dreaded to extract further concessions from the crown. In practice, this meant their becoming hostages to the extremists: hostility to the monarchy ensured that there would be 'no enemies to the left'. So the liberals condoned political terrorism in the years before 1914, the Provisional Government set up after the February revolution treated the self-appointed socialist intellectuals who ran the Petrograd soviet with kid gloves, and both government and soviet turned a blind eye to Bolshevik subversion. Even after the Bolsheviks had seized power, and subsequently closed down the democratically elected Constituent Assembly, their rivals sat back on their hands.

A good deal was due to the widespread fear of counter-revolution. Pipes has no trouble in showing this to be a case of the curious behaviour of the dog in the night-time. When counter-revolution came, it was not from any general on horseback, but from the Bolsheviks. But this timidity seems characteristic of the radical intelligentsia as a whole. Here was a class whose awesome ability to peddle abstractions went along with a fear of responsibility and a fundamental gutlessness. Pipes quotes the Russian proverb, 'he who grabs the stick is corporal'. The Bolsheviks not only grabbed it but used it unmercifully.

Seizing power in Russia, Lenin marvelled, had been as easy 'as picking up a feather'. Losing it, as the unfortunate Mikhail Gorbachev's experience seems to show, is more like having those feathers plucked. If this remarkable book has a contemporary moral, it must be taken from those few months after February 1917, when democracy flourished—and the Russian state fell apart.

Questions

a What does the author mean by 'the Bolsheviks did not set out to topple a regime. They intended to recast humanity itself'?

b According to this source, how important was terror to Lenin's programme?

c According to the author, why did Lenin win while his rivals lost?

d **i)** From this source, what caused the February Revolution?
  ii) Why do you think Pipes sees the discontent of the political opposition as so crucial?

e Why is it appropriate to see the university disturbances of 1899 as the starting point for the Revolution?

f Why did the liberals become 'hostages to the extremists', condone political terrorism, cooperate with the Petrograd Soviet, and ignore the actions of the Bolsheviks?

EXTRA WRITING

Essays

A revolution may be spontaneous, but if a revolution is to succeed it must be planned. What evidence can you find in the two revolutions in Russia in 1917 to support or refute this statement?

A revolution is the work of a small group of people. What evidence can you find in the two revolutions in Russia in 1917 to support or refute this statement?

In what ways was the Tsarist autocracy responsible for its own collapse in February/March 1917?

How important was the First World War in bringing about the overthrow of the Tsarist regime in February/March 1917?

Why did the Provisional Government fail to solve the problems facing Russia in 1917?

How important was Lenin to the successful Bolshevik seizure of power in Russia in October/November 1917?

EXTRA READING

A. Wood, *The Origins of the Russian Revolution*
B. Pares, *The Russian Revolution*
J.N. Westwood, *Endurance and Endeavour*
M. Bucklow and G. Russell, *Russia: Why Revolution?*
L. Kochan and A. Abraham, *The Making of Modern Russia*
David Christian, *Power and Privilege*
Robert K. Massie, *Nicholas and Alexandra*
M. McAndrew and D. Thomas, *Century of Change: Nineteenth Century Europe*
Richard Pipes, *The Russian Revolution*
E. Radzinsky, *The Last Tsar*
Michael Lynch, *Reaction and Revolutions: Russia 1881–1924*
Dominic Lieven, *Nicholas II: The Last Tsar*
Brian Moynahan, *Comrades*
Brian Moynahan, *The Russian Century*
Jonathan Sanders, *Russia 1917: The Unpublished Revolution*

THE PROBLEMS AND ISSUES

Consider the Problem and Issue:
Revolution and Counter-Revolution
in the coming of revolution in October/November 1917.
The **revolutionary** forces were:
• soldiers • urban workers • Lenin and the Bolsheviks • the Petrograd Soviet
The **counter-revolutionary** forces were:
• the Provisional Government • Kerensky
Ask yourself, why did the revolutionary forces again prevail in October/November 1917?
• the role of Lenin and Trotsky • the role of Kerensky

WRITING THE ESSAY

Why were there two revolutions in Russia in 1917?
When answering this question you should consider the following factors

THE REASONS FOR THE FIRST REVOLUTION (FEBRUARY/MARCH)
The failure of the Tsarist government to recognise the need for change
The actions and attitudes of the Tsar, the Tsarina and their advisers

The nature of the Tsarist state: bureaucratic incompetence etc.
The context of events: the changing nature of the twentieth-century world—the inability of the regime to continue to remain isolated
Increasing industrialisation and the associated rise of urban protest
The war: military disasters, troop morale, lack of effective leadership
Economic hardship: food shortages and the 'Winter of Discontent'

THE REASONS FOR THE SECOND REVOLUTION (OCTOBER/NOVEMBER)
The spontaneous nature of the first revolution: the absence of any plan for the assumption of power or reform of the country
The power vacuum associated with the Provisional Government: its lack of constitutional validity and its reluctance to act before the election of the Constituent Assembly
The continuation of the war
The rise of the Petrograd Soviet
The ambitions of individuals, notably Kerensky and Kornilov
The failure of those in authority to acknowledge the strength or potential of the Bolshevik threat
The continuing hardships of the Russian people
The organisational ability of Trotsky
The presence, leadership and skills of Lenin

Also consider the actions of the following personalities:
Nicholas II, Alexandra, Grigori Rasputin, Prince Lvov, Alexander Kerensky, General Kornilov, Lenin, Trotsky

Finally consider the views of the following two historians:

Extracts from American historian Richard Pipes, *The Russian Revolution, 1899–1919*, published 1990

SOURCE 2.F

I
The February Revolution had many striking features that distinguish it from other revolutionary upheavals. But the most striking of all was the remarkable rapidity with which the Russian state fell apart. It was as if the greatest empire in the world, covering one-sixth of the earth's surface, were an artificial construction, without organic unity, held together by wires all of which converged in the person of the monarch. The instant the monarch withdrew the wires snapped and the whole structure collapsed in a heap. (p. 336)

II
The fall of the Provisional Government caused few regrets: eyewitnesses report that the population reacted to it with complete indifference. This was true even in Moscow, where the Bolsheviks had to overcome stiff opposition: here the disappearance of the government is said to have gone unnoticed. The man in the street seemed to feel that it made no difference who was in charge since things could not possibly get any worse. (p. 505)

Extract from Australian historian David Christian, *Power and Privilege*, published 1989

SOURCE 2.G

It [the Provisional Government] alienated its supporters equally rapidly. The aim of ruling with the support of all sections of the population led the government to adopt policies aimed at pleasing both the upper-class supporters of the Provisional Government, and the working-class supporters of the Soviet. The result was to alienate both groups. The reason, in retrospect, is obvious. The interests of upper-class and working-class Russians conflicted at so many points that policies that pleased one group inevitably alienated the other. (p. 140)

The Bolshevik Consolidation of Power

At the end of this topic you should attempt to answer the following questions:
**What methods were used by the Bolsheviks to maintain their power to 1924?
How successful were they in consolidating their position?**

THE PROBLEMS AND ISSUES

In this topic the relevant Problems and Issues for analysis in the HSC are:
**Revolution and Counter-Revolution
Ideology in Theory and Practice
The Role of the Party and the State**
Revolution should again be seen as the replacement of an established system of government by an alternative system.
Counter-revolution should be viewed as the attempts of the established system of government to either maintain its power or return to power.
The **ideology** should be seen as Marxism, and how this is altered by Lenin.
The **party** is the Bolshevik Party (later the Communist Party), while the **state** is the system of government and the institutional structures which allow that government to function.

TIME LINE

1917

November 9	Establishment of Sovnarkom, with Lenin as Chairman
November 10	Second Congress of Soviets adjourns
	Press Decree outlaws opposition press
November 11	Pro-government forces recapture the Kremlin
November 12	Strikes by unions protesting at the refusal of the Bolsheviks to widen the basis of the government
November 13	Railway unions demand that the Bolsheviks give up government
November 14–15	Pro-government forces surrender in Moscow
	Bolshevik Central Committee rejects demands of union movement—Kamenev resigns in protest
November 17	Meeting between Lenin, Trotsky and Central Executive Committee of Soviets—vote manipulated to give Sovnarkom (and Lenin) the right to rule by decree

November 22	Allied governments reject Bolshevik proposals for an armistice
November 25	Elections begin for the Constituent Assembly—Socialist Revolutionaries gain largest proportion of the votes
November 27	Bank employees refuse to hand over money to Sovnarkom
November 30	Bolshevik troops break into the State Bank and seize five million roubles
December 3	Peace negotiations with Germany begin at Brest-Litovsk
December 5	Decree dissolving courts and the legal profession—establishment of Revolutionary Tribunals
December 11	Constitutional Democratic Party banned and its leaders arrested
December 14–16	Vesenkha (Supreme Council of National Economy) created
December 15	Armistice with Central Powers ends Russia's involvement in First World War
December 20	Formation of the CHEKA (Extraordinary Commission to Combat Counter-Revolution, Sabotage and Speculation)
December 27	Decree on Workers' Control Decree on Banking

1918

early January	Commencement of Civil War between 'Reds' and 'Whites' Trotsky forms the Red Army
January 14	First assassination attempt on Lenin
January 18–19	Constituent Assembly meets, condemns the usurpation of power by the Bolsheviks—dissolved by Lenin
March 16	Treaty of Brest-Litovsk signed—ratified on 27 March
March 22	First allied troops land at Murmansk
March 27	Left Socialist Revolutionaries leave Sovnarkom
April 13	Kornilov killed—Denikin assumes control of the volunteer army
April 20	Bolsheviks begin nationalisation of industries
May	Bolsheviks lose their majorities in all soviets—reimpose their control by force 'War Communism' replaces 'State Capitalism'
May 13	Sovnarkom declares war on rural areas
May 20	Decree creating Food Supply Detachments
May 22	Czech legion rebels
early June	British forces land at Archangel
June 11	Decree ordering the formation of Village Committees of the Poor
June 12	Grand Duke Michael assassinated
June 16	Reintroduction of capital punishment
July 4	All-Russian Congress of Soviets adopts new Soviet constitution
July 16	Tsar Nicholas II and his family assassinated at Ekaterinburg
July 28	Compulsory military training introduced—all former Tsarist officers required to register
August	Lenin calls for the workers to eliminate the kulaks
August 29	Fanny Kaplan shoots Lenin
September 5	'Red Terror' officially launched
October 21	Control of labour introduced
December 2	Committees of the Poor dissolved

1919

early January	Tax in kind (*prodrazvertska*) imposed on peasants
February 17	Dzerzinsky calls for creation of concentration camps
March 2–7	Comintern established
March 9	Bolshevik Party renamed Russian Communist Party
April	French troops withdrawn
May 28	Devaluation of currency begins
June 12	Kolchak acknowledged as supreme ruler of White forces
August 31	White forces capture Kiev
October	Final delivery of British aid
November 17	White forces begin their retreat
November 26	Decree on liquidation of illiteracy

1920

January 9	Labour Obligation Commission (under Trotsky) begins militarisation of labour
February 2	Kolchak executed
April 2	Wrangel takes command of southern White army
Spring	Peasant rebellions begin—these last for a year
November 14	Wrangel evacuates White forces from the Crimea

1921

February 9	Anti-Communist peasant rebellion
late February	Mass strikes in Petrograd
February 28	Kronstadt Naval Base rebels against Communists
March	Tenth Party Congress—factions and public debate outlawed 'New Economic Policy' replaces 'War Communism'
March 15	Abolition of prodrazvertska
Summer–autumn	Famine at its peak

1922

February 2	CHEKA renamed GPU (State Political Administration)
March	Lenin orders an all-out assault on the Church
April 3	Stalin appointed General Secretary of the Party
April-July	Show trials of dissident clergy
April 16	Treaty of Rapallo signed with Germany
May 25	Lenin suffers first stroke
June–August	Show trials of Socialist Revolutionaries
December	Lenin suffers second stroke

1923

January	Lenin dictates his Testament
March 10	Lenin paralysed
October 23	Trotsky criticised by Party
December	Trotsky issues *New Course*

1924

January 21	Death of Lenin

The Nature of the Bolshevik State

FOCUS QUESTION What methods were used by the Bolsheviks to establish control of the Russian state?

KERENSKY'S AUTHORITY was so shattered that on the morning of 7 November he fled the city. Resistance within Petrograd continued for some time that day, but when the battleship *Aurora* fired on Provisional Government supporters in the Winter Palace most of the resistance ended.

THE PROVISIONAL GOVERNMENT FALLS

The Bolshevik Party had staked their claim for power in October/November 1917 by attempting to fill a vacuum that had been created by the crumbling authority of the Provisional Government and by the stalemate on the German front. Trotsky points out that the Bolshevik takeover was supported by no more than 25 000 people in a country of 150 000 000. The smallness of this number was outweighed, though, by the nature of the people it included—army regiments, members of the intelligentsia and disillusioned peasants proved to be a vigorous and committed revolutionary force.

While these events were occuring, the All-Russian Congress of Soviets continued to meet. It had voted for change, but the decision of the moderate socialists (the Mensheviks and Right Socialist Revolutionaries) to walk out in protest at the coup carried out by Lenin and Trotsky left it dominated by the Bolsheviks and Left Socialist Revolutionaries. The moderates believed that real change and reform would come in time; Lenin was not, however, prepared to wait for things to fall into place for him. He moved quickly to introduce change and impose dictatorial rule upon the country.

THE PARTY VERSUS THE STATE

In response to criticisms of the Bolshevik takeover, Lenin allowed a structure to develop which distinguished between the party and the state: the 'party' was the Bolsheviks, the 'state' was the new government drawn from the All-Russian Congress of Soviets. Lenin realised the need to maintain the facade of Soviet power—the reality was that the Bolshevik Party was slowly achieving supremacy. The small number of Bolshevik representatives and their lack of skilled personnel necessitated the tactic of transferring criticism to the 'state' and its associated bureaucracy. The heroic and selfless image of the Bolsheviks could then be maintained.

Faced with a situation where their own structures and institutions had not yet been established, the Bolsheviks allowed, and indeed encouraged, the destruction of the traditional institutions of the Tsarist regime. It was a deliberate tactic of buying time, and resulted in increased chaos throughout the country. Spurred on by the slogan 'All Power to the Soviets', thousands of local and district councils of soldiers and workers sprang up. They appeared in cities, villages, towns, even individual suburbs, and everywhere they acknowledged no authority other than their own. It was this attitude which Lenin and the Bolsheviks would exploit to their own ends. In November 1917 Lenin said about the urgency of the situation:

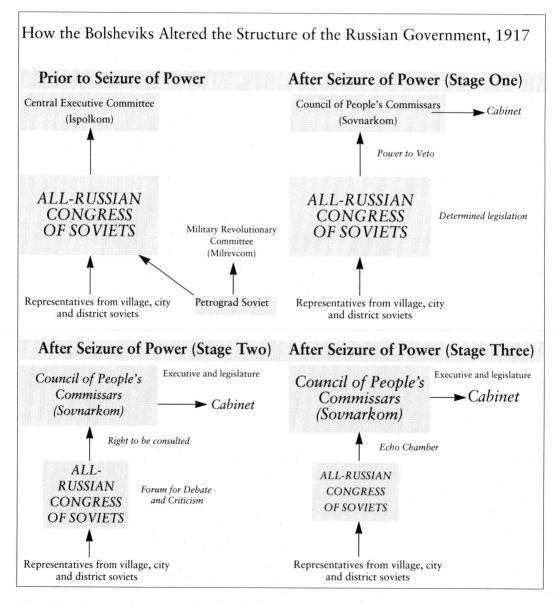

These four diagrams show the rapid alteration of the structure of the government under the Bolsheviks. Notice the decline in influence of the Congress of Soviets and the growth in power of the small group of people in the Cabinet.

> As the state is only a transitional institution which we are obliged to use in the revolutionary struggle in order to crush our opponents forcibly, it is a pure absurdity to speak of a Free People's State. During the period when the proletariat needs the state, it does not require it in the interests of freedom, but in the interests of crushing its antagonists. (Shub, *Lenin*, p. 310)

Lenin's control over events must therefore be stressed. Although he had been against the war with Germany, he was a better 'general' than his opponents in the area of class warfare. All opponents were seen as evil and deserving elimination.

Action had to be swift and uncompromising, and this speed is clearly illustrated in the decisions taken at the Congress of Soviets in the first hours of the Bolshevik coup. Three decrees were passed immediately. Firstly the Decree on Land: this confiscated all private land and placed it in the hands of the peasants. This process had already been in progress for some months and the decree simply legitimised the actions which the peasants had taken of their own accord. The second decree was the Peace Decree: immediate steps were to be taken to end the war against Germany. The decree stated that peace was to be made without loss of land or the payment of indemnities. The third decree set up the formal organisation of the new government. At the top was SOVNARKOM, or the Council of People's Commissars; at its head was Lenin as Chairman (or Prime Minister). These three decrees established the Bolshevik position in control of the government. It should be noted that while the promises in the first two decrees were honoured, the third decree created an institutional structure which the new government quickly manipulated for its own ends. As he had done in the lead-up to the coup, Lenin again played the role of the consummate politician: he promised whatever the people wanted so long as it enhanced his own power and position.

Other decrees were passed by this Congress of Soviets, many of them directly benefiting the people. Some of these included the confiscation of church lands, the introduction of civil marriages, the use of female labour in greater numbers and a declaration of the equality of all people. An eight-hour day was instituted along with a 48-hour week with guidelines for holidays and overtime. All large industries were taken over by the state, workers were given control over individual workplaces and Russia's international debt was repudiated. Peoples' courts were established in place of the old legal system; the class system of ranks and privileges was abolished; the police and the bureaucracy were dismantled.

David Christian argues that these first moves indicate that the Bolsheviks were attempting to introduce the promised socialist utopia. He points out that, at this stage at least, the Bolsheviks were not interested in introducing coercive measures of social, political and economic control. The truth is that the Bolsheviks were determined from the start to introduce such

THE DECREES

punitive measures in order to secure their power—it was just that in these early days they lacked the ability and structures to do so at the local and district levels.

THE CHANGING STRUCTURE OF THE GOVERNMENT

Pressure soon mounted to widen the government base to include representatives of all workers' organisations. These moves were supported by a minority element within the Bolshevik Party (notably Kamenev). They resigned when Lenin and Trotsky refused to countenance any changes. The Bolshevik Party achieved its domination of the government on 17 November when Lenin and Trotsky manipulated a vote which gave Sovnarkom the right to rule by decree. The Central Executive Committee now became a forum for debate rather than lawmaking. By early December the Bolsheviks had taken legitimate power away from the soviets, made their own organ (Sovnarkom) the only executive and legislative body and manipulated the appointment of delegates to commissions and congresses.

As mentioned at the start of this chapter, at the Congress meeting some of the moderate Socialist Revolutionaries and Mensheviks had resigned because of the violent nature of the Bolshevik takeover and also because they were not represented in the new government. Lenin used these resignations to further cement the Party's authority. Only the Left Socialist Revolutionaries spent time as members of the government—and even this association with the Bolsheviks was short-lived.

THE RESORT TO TERROR

Most of the Socialist Revolutionaries agreed that all socialists should take part in the lead-up to the promised elections for the Constituent Assembly. Lenin believed that his government would only survive if it remained in the hands of a small band of dedicated revolutionaries: his Bolshevik government. While his opponents argued for a return to parliamentary-style government, Lenin resorted to terror. He instructed the police in Petrograd to eliminate any opposition to the revolution. He said:

> I will be merciless with all counter-revolutionists, and I shall employ Comrade Uritsky (chief of the Petrograd Secret Police) against all counter-revolutionists, no matter who they are. I do not advise you to make his acquaintance. (Shub, *Lenin*, p.305).

Despite the precarious situation, with the Congress of Soviets still dominated by anti-Bolshevik delegates and the majority of the population indifferent to the Bolshevik exhortations to action, Lenin felt secure of ultimate success. The support of garrison troops and armed urban workers ensured that he had control of the towns and cities. These areas were the key to his final goal: power.

THE CONSTITUENT ASSEMBLY

Lenin, and others, continued to oppose the elections for the Constituent Assembly on the grounds that the Party would not poll well. However, pressure from within the Party, including the resignation of some of the top-ranking members, persuaded him to allow the elections to take place in late November 1917. As Lenin predicted, the Bolshevik Party polled only 9.8 million votes (24 per cent of the vote, or 29 per cent when the votes of the left-wing Socialist Revolutionaries were included).

Election Results for the Constituent Assembly, November 1917

	% of the vote
Socialist Revolutionaries	40.4
Bolsheviks	24
Mensheviks	2.6
Left Socialist Revolutionaries	1
Other socialist parties	0.9
Constitutional Democrats (Kadets)	4.7
Other liberal and non-socialist parties	2.8
National minority parties	13.4
Results not known	10.2

(figures quoted in Richard Pipes, *The Russian Revolution, 1899–1919*)

The largest vote went to the right-wing Socialist Revolutionaries, with its main support coming from rural voters. The total vote for socialist parties was close to 70 per cent and there were immediate calls for the non-Bolshevik socialists to form a government. The Bolshevik Party was very much against such moves, and it had many of the rightists arrested. Once again, as Christian points out, the opponents of the Bolsheviks failed to adopt a common campaign against Lenin and his followers. The perception of 'Bolshevik fragility' (which had earlier undermined Kerensky) was still widely believed.

Lenin then attempted to stop the Constituent Assembly from meeting. He was not committed to democracy, even in a Marxist form, and stridently argued that the Bolshevik Party was the only truly representative organisation in Russia. However, he failed to prevent the Assembly from convening. Although they were able to call upon support from right across the political spectrum, the elected representatives suffered from one major drawback: a belief that the removal of the Bolsheviks would involve violence, and a fear that this violence would play into the hands of the 'counter-revolutionaries'. The spectre of counter-revolution overthrowing the gains which had been made therefore led them to adopt a soft line towards their Bolshevik tormentors.

The Constituent Assembly met briefly in December, and planned to meet again in January. Lenin immediately ordered that all remaining anti-Bolshevik newspapers be closed, further arrests were made and intimidatory tactics were employed using groups of sailors and Red Guards. The Constituent Assembly formally met for one day only (18 January 1918). On the next day the Executive Committee of the Congress of Soviets dissolved it. Lenin justified this action on the grounds that the Congress of Soviets was more representative of the people than the Assembly, that the rural masses were too ignorant to understand fully how to run the state and that the professional revolutionaries had to do it for them.

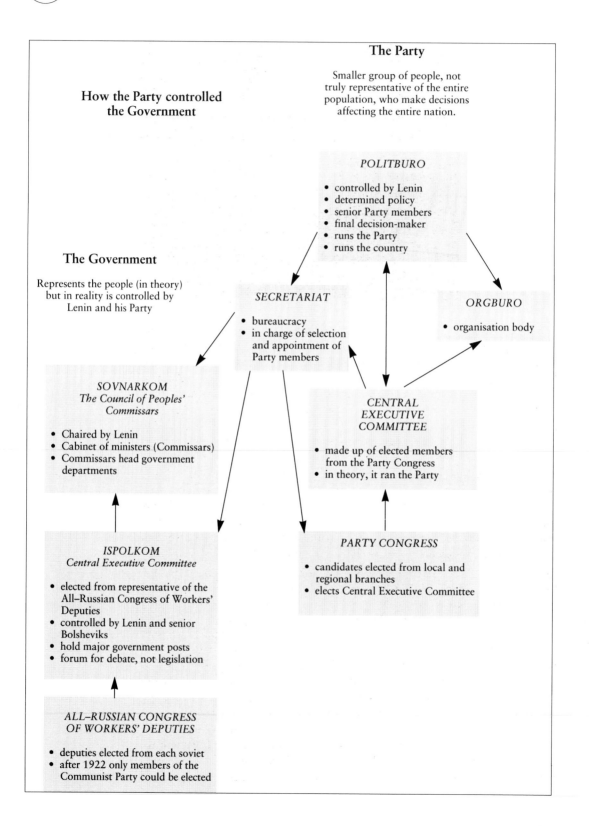

The Party

Smaller group of people, not
truly representative of the entire
population, who make decisions
affecting the entire nation.

**How the Party controlled
the Government**

POLITBURO

- controlled by Lenin
- determined policy
- senior Party members
- final decision-maker
- runs the Party
- runs the country

The Government

Represents the people (in theory)
but in reality is controlled by
Lenin and his Party

SECRETARIAT

- bureaucracy
- in charge of selection
  and appointment of
  Party members

ORGBURO

- organisation body

SOVNARKOM
The Council of Peoples'
Commissars

- Chaired by Lenin
- Cabinet of ministers (Commissars)
- Commissars head government
  departments

CENTRAL
EXECUTIVE
COMMITTEE

- made up of elected members
  from the Party Congress
- in theory, it ran the Party

ISPOLKOM
Central Executive Committee

- elected from representative of the
  All–Russian Congress of Workers'
  Deputies
- controlled by Lenin and senior
  Bolsheviks
- hold major government posts
- forum for debate, not legislation

PARTY CONGRESS

- candidates elected from local and
  regional branches
- elects Central Executive Committee

ALL–RUSSIAN CONGRESS
OF WORKERS' DEPUTIES

- deputies elected from each soviet
- after 1922 only members of the
  Communist Party could be elected

*Felix Dzerzinsky,
head of the
CHEKA*

In the meantime Lenin had continued to force through his reforms. By bolstering support from the sailors, industrial workers and sections of the landless peasants, Lenin strengthened the Bolshevik control of the local and regional soviets. Most of the population simply ignored the new rulers—because of ignorance, apathy and disorganisation—and thus potential opponents proved no match for the Bolsheviks. At this critical time in Russia's history action was required: Lenin was acting, the opposition was dithering. For example, on 21 January the Third Congress of Soviets proclaimed the establishment of the Russian Soviet Socialist Republic—a constitutional structure which legitimised the position of the Party—and Sovnarkom was swiftly put into place.

The majority of the populace was neither conscious of nor interested in the events unfolding around them. They simply wanted their ongoing grievances, particularly in relation to the use and ownership of land, rectified immediately. In the days following the Bolshevik coup, they had sought to redress these problems by unilaterally seizing land. This action by the peasantry was then given tacit approval by the Bolsheviks through their Land Decree. However, it is clear from the government's actions during these weeks that the Bolsheviks were driven more by political expediency than by purely socialistic principles. Support had been either bought or elicited through a strange mixture of incentive and force. Richard Pipes in his study of the Russian Revolution points out that the majority of the peasantry and the industrial working class were oblivious to the ideological basis of Bolshevik rule. At the same time the Bolsheviks were blinkered by their ruthless pursuit of power.

Apart from the organised political opposition from the other socialist parties, there existed mobs of agitators on the streets of Petrograd, many of whom demanded further reforms. There was also antagonism between the Red Guards and sections of the army. All this strengthened

Lenin's resolve to maintain his reforms and his hold upon the reins of power.

The mechanism used to achieve these aims would initially be the garrison troops and the Red Guards. During the weeks leading to the Constituent Assembly elections, Lenin moved towards a more systematic method of control. He reintroduced the death penalty and established the CHEKA (the Extraordinary Commission against Counter-Revolution, Sabotage and Speculation) in December 1917. These actions marked a return to an internal security organisation in line with the Third Section and Okhrana during the autocratic rule of the Tsars. Lenin also banned all middle-class political parties, censored the press (including the other socialist presses), curtailed free speech and the right of free assembly, and resorted to the use of forced labour in areas of immediate economic need. The Bolsheviks also resorted to murder. By the middle of 1918 all anti-Bolshevik parties had been forced to disband. Formally, the opposition had ceased to exist.

THE BOLSHEVIKS AS AN URBAN PHENOMON

The events of late 1917/early 1918 show to what extent the Bolshevik Party was an urban phenomenon with little commitment to rule by 'democracy'. It could be argued that the Bolshevik Party never had a commitment to popular participation in government. In 1902 Lenin's pamphlet *What is to be done?* had outlined the importance of a small dedicated band of revolutionaries who would act as the vanguard of the proletariat. He stated that this was necessary because of the political immaturity of the working class. It was up to others to assume the leadership and force through the changes which the proletariat 'needed'. By the middle of 1918 the only truly parliamentary body to be elected in Russia was dead. The Bolsheviks had openly denied the people's democracy and had publicly shown the real purpose behind their coup of November 1917—revolutionary dictatorship and the pursuit of power were more important than the will of the people.

While it may be suggested that Lenin's genius was in being able to exploit a situation that enabled the Bolshevik Party to survive the traumas of 1917–18—and it is certainly true that he manipulated the situation that faced the country during these first few months—he hardly gave the people what he had promised: 'Peace, Bread and Land'. In fact, he gave them 'famine and civil war'. His pragmatic, militaristic approach won the initial battles for the Bolsheviks.

THE DEBATE OVER THE FIRST SIX MONTHS OF BOLSHEVIK RULE

intro

It is true to say that there were features of the Bolshevik government in its first six months which indicated movement towards those ideas upon which socialism was based: land was given to the peasantry; the armed forces had become militias without insignia, officers were elected and soldiers' councils made decisions; people's courts were elected to deal with justice; the traditional class system and its institutional supports (police and bureaucracy) were swept away; private property rights were established for all people; and women's rights were recognised and extended. There is some argument, however, about the way in which these changes took place. David Christian maintains that while the Bolshevik Party did use force to gain and retain power, it did not in these early months establish a 'machinery of power' (such as institutionalised terror and bureaucratic control). Instead he argues that popular support was enough to keep it in power. The truth is that Lenin simply replaced one autocratic power base with another of his own making. The tactics he and the Bolsheviks employed from their first days in office were based upon brutality and coercion. Circumstances, allied with political ambition, created a regime which by the middle of 1918 was strikingly similar to the Tsarist autocracy in the way in which it was unswervingly convinced of its 'rightness' and would brook no opposition or criticism.

SUMMARY
- The Provisional Government fell with little resistance.
- The Bolshevik Party support was urban, and therefore it was a minority party.
- The new government passed various reforms.
- The Bolsheviks used force to establish and maintain their control.
- The election results for the Constituent Assembly showed the lack of widespread support for the Bolsheviks.
- The Bolsheviks created a structure of government which ensured that the Bolshevik Party was dominant.

KEY PERSONALITIES. GROUPS, TERMS

CHEKA: Extraordinary Commission against Counter-Revolution, Sabotage and Speculation; its aim was to find and eliminate 'enemies of the state'; reported to have dealt with 50 000 people in its first year—most victims were from the Tsarist regime or from the well-to-do, but there was no specific political target; first leader was Felix Dzerzinsky and its headquarters was in the Lubyanka; during the Civil War its activities became so notorious it was referred to as 'the Red Terror'; its primary purpose was intimidation and the creation of a climate of conformity and fear; the heir of the Tsarist Third Section and Okhrana, it was the forefather of the KGB; its influence grew to such an extent that all people were caught in its calls for 'participatory terror'; it was shut down in 1922 and replaced by the GPU (State Political Administration).

Constituent Assembly: Body promised by the Provisional Government; its role was to draw up a new constitution for Russia; at elections held for this body in November 1918 the combined socialist vote was 68.9 per cent, with the Bolsheviks gaining only 24 per cent; the Bolsheviks allowed it to meet once and then closed its doors because it did not return a Bolshevik majority; in 1905 Lenin had written of its necessity in a pamphlet entitled

Two Tactics; by 1917 he had become convinced of its irrelevance to his vision of a proletarian revolution.

Felix Dzerzinsky: Fanatical Polish communist; born 1877, died 1926; spent 15 years in Tsarist prisons and was released from exile in Siberia following the February/March Revolution; appointed by Lenin to head the CHEKA, the organisation charged with maintaining the security of the Bolshevik state and preserving the revolution; completely ruthless and 'incorruptible', he is quoted as saying, 'We don't want justice, we want to settle accounts.'

Sovnarkom: The Council of People's Commissars; in theory the executive and legislative organ of the Soviet state, this institution was actually controlled by the Bolshevik (later Communist) Party.

Politburo: Controlling committee of the Bolshevik (later Communist) Party; made up of senior Party members, it ran the Party and determined government policy on internal and international matters; in 1925 the Communist Party Congress was told the Politburo was the highest institution in the country.

Central Executive Committee: Elected from the Bolshevik/Communist Party Congress, it was in theory the major policy-making body of the Party; in reality its functions and direction were taken over by the Politburo; lost its real influence over Bolshevik policy within four days of the October/November coup.

EXERCISES

1. What methods did the Bolshevik Party use against its opposition between the seizure of power in 1917 and the closure of the Constituent Assembly in 1918?
2. Why were the opposition parties unable to remove the Bolsheviks from office?
3. **a)** How much popular support did the new Bolshevik government possess during its first year in power?
   b) What does this tell you about the Bolshevik Party and the tactics it adopted?
4. **a)** What was the CHEKA?
   b) What does the formation of this organisation tell you about Lenin and the Bolsheviks?
5. **a)** How did Lenin justify the closure of the Constituent Assembly?
   b) Based on the election results for the Assembly, were his reasons acceptable?
6. What elements of the Tsarist regime assisted in securing the Bolshevik position?
7. It is now accepted that the Bolshevik Party received financial support from the Imperial German Government to help it overthrow the Provisional Government.
   a) Why do you think the Bolsheviks resorted to this tactic?
   b) How would Lenin have justified this outside help from an imperialist, capitalist power?

8. David Thomson, in *Europe Since Napoleon,* has suggested that Lenin inherited a country that was already in a state of chaos. What evidence can you produce to support or refute this view?
9. Use the information and the two diagrams in this section to explain the relationship between the 'party' and the 'state' which developed in Russia under the Bolsheviks.
10. How did Lenin succeed in securing the position of the Bolshevik Party in Russia by early 1918?

DOCUMENT STUDY No. 6

Read and examine the sources and answer the questions which follow.

Extract from the diary of Maxim Gorky, a Russian revolutionary and novelist, in which he describes the early days of the Bolshevik Revolution, 21/11/1917
Quoted in D. Shub, *Lenin*, p. 301 SOURCE 3.A

Blind fanatics and unscrupulous adventurers are rushing headlong towards 'social revolution'—as a matter of fact it is the road to anarchy, the ruin of the proletariat and the Revolution.

Along this road Lenin and his aides think it possible to commit all crimes, such as the bloody fight in Petrograd, the devastation of Moscow, the annulment of the freedom of speech, the senseless arrests—all the monstrous doing of Von Plehve and Stolypin.

True, Stolypin and Von Plehve acted against the democracy, against all that was sound and honest in Russia, while Lenin has at present the backing of a considerable portion of the workmen, but I trust that the common sense of the working class, the realisation of their historical mission will soon open their eyes to the impossibility of fulfilling the promises made by Lenin and the depth of his madness and his anarchistic tendencies, of the Bakunin and Nechayev kind.

Extract from a pamphlet on the early days of the Bolshevik Revolution written by German Socialist, Rosa Luxemburg, published in 1918
Quoted in D. Shub, *Lenin*, p.329–30. SOURCE 3.B

To be sure, every democratic institution has its limits and shortcomings, things which it doubtless shares with all other human institutions. But the remedy which Lenin and Trotsky have found, the elimination of democracy as such, is worse than the disease it is supposed to cure; for it stops up the very living source from which alone come the correction of all the innate shortcomings of social institutions. The source is the active, untrammelled, energetic political life of the broadest masses of the people . . .

Freedom only for the supporters of the government, only for the members of one party—however numerous they may be—is no freedom at all. Freedom is always and exclusively freedom for the one who thinks differently . . . its effectiveness vanishes when 'Freedom' becomes a special privilege . . .

Without general elections, without unrestricted freedom of press and assembly, without a free struggle of opinion, life dies out in every public institution, becomes a mere semblance of life, in which only the bureaucracy remains as the active element.

SOURCE 3.C

Photograph of election posters for the Constituent Assembly, Petrograd 1917

SOURCE 3.D

Extract from Felix Dzerzhinsky's first address as chief of the Secret Police, 1917 quoted in D. Shub, *Lenin*, p.347.

This is no time for speech-making. Our revolution is in serious danger . . . Do not think that I am on the look-out for forms of revolutionary justice. We have no need for justice now. Now we have need of a battle to the death! I propose, I demand the initiation of the Revolutionary sword which will put an end to all counter-revolutionists. We must act not tomorrow, but today, at once.

Questions

a **i)** According to Source 3.A and Source 3.D, how did Lenin and Dzerzhinsky justify the actions which were taken by the Bolsheviks?

  ii) According to Source 3.B, what is the real meaning of 'freedom'?

b Using Source 3.D and your own knowledge, describe how the Bolsheviks dealt with their opposition between 1917 and 1918.

c Examine Sources 3.B, 3.C and 3.D. How useful would an historian find each of these sources when attempting to understand the events in Russia following the Bolshevik seizure of power? (In your answer consider the nature, motive, audience and reliability of each source as well as its content.)

d Using all four sources and your own knowledge, explain how the Bolsheviks were able to take control of the government of Russia?

The Civil War

FOCUS QUESTIONS What attempts were made to overthrow the Bolshevik regime? What evidence is there to suggest that the Civil War was 'lost' by the Whites rather than 'won' by the Reds?

THE BOLSHEVIK PARTY had based much of its early propaganda on the need to end the war with Germany. The Peace Decree of 1917 went some way towards fulfilling this promise, but the formal peace treaty with Germany was not signed until March 1918. The Treaty of Brest-Litovsk imposed upon the Russians a number of conditions which were universally rejected and denounced: Russia had to give up Poland, Finland, Estonia, Latvia, Lithuania and Transcaucasia (an area equivalent to twice the size of the German Empire and including 26 per cent of the Russian Empire's population, over a third of its urban population, 28 per cent of its industries and 75 per cent of its coal and iron reserves); and the Soviet Government agreed to honour its economic debts to the Central Powers, plus interest!

THE TREATY OF BREST-LITOVSK

Lenin was determined to have peace at any cost, and thereby save his revolution. Trotsky, the chief negotiator at the peace talks, was of a like mind. The price was paid by the Russian people. Was this the peace without annexations and indemnities they had been promised? For what purpose had so many millions given their lives?

Anti-German and anti-Bolshevik feeling ran high after the signing of this treaty. For example, the German Ambassador to Russia was assassinated by members of the Left Social Revolutionary Party in July 1918. Street fighting broke out in some centres between disgruntled workers and squads of the Red Army. The legacy of Brest-Litovsk was to haunt the Bolsheviks for years to come. It also provided the impetus for the first real attempt to remove the Bolsheviks from office.

Many pockets of resistance to the Bolsheviks still remained in 1918, and it was resistance founded on many grievances. Some resented the closure of the Constituent Assembly and the growing severity of the Bolshevik regime. Others, from the middle class and intelligentsia, had been members of the Kadets or the Right Socialist Revolutionaries and were now angry at the loss of their livelihood. Deputies who had been elected to the Constituent Assembly sought redress for their summary dismissal. Many of the nationalities from within the old Empire took seriously the Bolshevik declaration that all subject peoples could be free and declared their independence.

OPPOSITION TO BOLSHEVISM

Counter-revolutionary forces therefore began to gather with the aim of removing the Bolsheviks. The fall of the Tsar's government had not been widely mourned and few had sought its return. However, many now actively campaigned for the removal of the Bolsheviks. This signalled the start of the Civil War: Russia's sovereignty, whatever the government, was at stake.

THE 'WHITE' FORCES

Trotsky and other Soviet delegates at the peace negotiations at Brest-Litovsk

Richard Pipes argues that this was in fact a deliberate and necessary part of the Bolshevik programme. The leaders of the Party were convinced that it would be impossible to achieve, then maintain, power without a period of civil war.

In early 1918 German and Austrian troops occupied Russian territory beyond the ceasefire line. In the south, Generals Alexeyev and Kornilov raised a volunteer army and joined up with the Cossacks. In the east and Siberia, many semi-independent states, with authority limited only by their physical boundaries, arose. Some of the leaders in this region included Semeonov and Horvath while the influence of the Socialist Revolutionaries (under Chernov) was also considerable. There were Czech units in Siberia (prisoners of war when the war ended who had initially been allowed to move east to Vladivostok to meet up with the Allies) and Trotsky ordered their arrest. Fighting broke out between this Czech legion and the Bolsheviks, and as a result the Bolsheviks were denied access to the east.

ALLIED INTERVENTION

On 2 July 1918 the Supreme Allied War Council decided to intervene in Russia in an attempt to distract the Germans from the Western Front, create a new Eastern Front, protect Allied interests in Russia and overthrow the Bolshevik government. French troops were landed at Odessa in November 1918, British forces at Batum in December 1918 and other Allied forces entered through Murmansk, Archangel and Vladivostok. (Ironically, the British were actually permitted to land at Murmansk with the approval of the local soviet who believed they were going to assist them in an assault against the Germans.) The Allied leaders were also worried about the activities of the German communists at the end of 1918 and the possibility that they would cooperate with the Russians. This perception was reinforced by the Bolshevik calls to export revolution throughout the world. By occupying areas of Eastern Europe the Allies hoped to form a wall against the spread of communism. As Lenin said in November 1918:

> If we have never been so close to international proletarian revolution as now, our position has never been so dangerous as now . . . The imperialists of the Anglo-French-American group are thinking of building a Chinese wall, to protect themselves from Bolshevism, like a quarantine against plague . . . The bacillus will pass through the wall and infect the workers of all countries.

The Soviet regime faced two major military threats in the Civil War: the offensive from Generals Alexeyev and Kornilov, and, after their deaths, a further offensive led by General Denikin in the south and from Admiral Kolchak in Siberia. By the early part of 1919 both these commanders were in a position to make an assault upon Moscow. However, the end of the war in Europe and the continuing inability of the White forces to cooperate led to their eventual defeat.

In mid-1920 the Poles took the opportunity to break away from Russian rule. The failure of the Red Army to effectively suppress this uprising, and particularly its failure to secure Warsaw, had important consequences. The long and brutal campaign further soured relations between Russia and Poland, and Stalin would seek to redress the defeat in 1939. More importantly, it marked the actual end of practical Bolshevik attempts to 'spread communism world-wide'—a fact of which, however, the Western nations were not aware.

THE POLISH UPRISING

Allied intervention was therefore seen by the Bolsheviks' Russian opponents as their best chance for success. However, the Allied effort proved to be less than total: it was limited in scope and was viewed as being for the benefit only of the Allies. While the limited aim of safeguarding the Eastern Front was achieved—and they did make contact with the White armies—the half-hearted approach of the Allies and the disjointed effort by the Whites played into the hands of the Communists. As early as April 1919 all French forces had been withdrawn. While Japanese forces remained on Russian soil until 1922, the total impact of Allied aid to the White forces proved negligible. The Allies viewed the safeguarding of munitions and their own nationals as being more important than launching an all-out assault upon the Reds. Furthermore, peasant support for the White forces was undermined by their fear that the landlords would return should the Bolsheviks be defeated. The result was that the peasants moved to the Bolshevik side, not out of a belief in the rightness of the Red ideology but out of economic selfishness.

THE COLLAPSE OF ANTI-BOLSHEVIK FORCES

In this context the Red Army proved to be well drilled, possessed of a

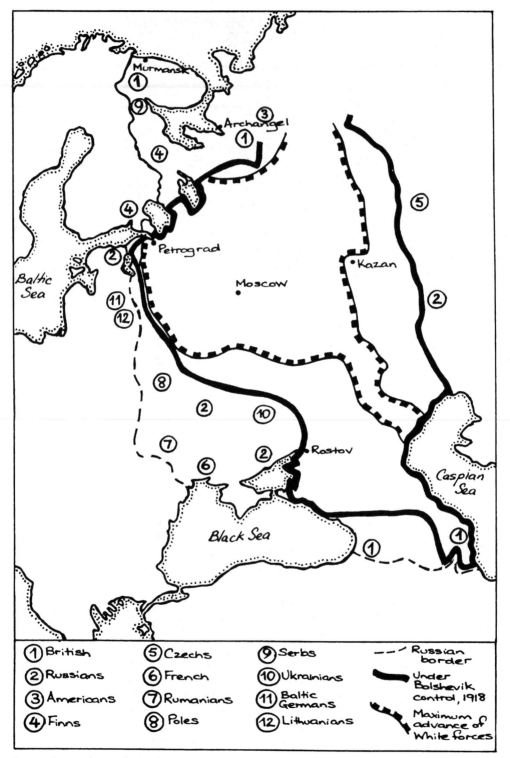

①British ⑤Czechs ⑨Serbs —–⁄ Russian border

②Russians ⑥French ⑩Ukrainians ▬ Under Bolshevik control, 1918

③Americans ⑦Rumanians ⑪Baltic Germans ▬▬ Maximum advance of White forces

④Finns ⑧Poles ⑫Lithuanians

Russia during the Civil War, 1918–1921

Corpses of some of Kolchak's White forces, shot by Reds in Siberia 1919

purpose and infused with a determination that was lacking in the White armies. To deal with the growing military problem, a more professional army was created. To make certain of its 'socialist correctness' Communist commissars were attached to each military unit to monitor discipline among the troops. Compulsory military service was reintroduced in mid-1918 and by 1920 over five million men were serving in the Red Army. Rigid discipline and control was the hallmark of this institution, with the abandonment of the original Bolshevik concept of a 'rankless militia' and the return to a strict hierarchy of officers and ranks under the control of the central government.

The crisis of the Civil War allowed the Bolshevik regime to centralise its power and helped rally support it had hitherto been unable to command. Most of its commanders were ex-Tsarist officers and its troops were conscripts. The result was the survival of the regime. The intervention of the Whites and the Allied forces also drove Lenin to take the more drastic action against his internal opponents which was referred to earlier.

Thus the Bolsheviks survived this first major threat to their hold on power. Imbued with the notion that they were fighting in defence of 'a cause', the Red Army operated as an army of the government. This was in contrast to the disparate White forces who were operating as an army and a government. Also, although the Red Army was driven back into the area approximating the boundaries of Greater Russia, this actually worked to their advantage. This gave them control of the major industrial areas of the country, provided them with a ready supply of troops and gave access to its most efficient transport networks, notably the railways. These were advantages with which the Whites could not compete. It is, perhaps, surprising that it took the

Corpses of some of the Red Army, killed by Japanese at Vladivostok, 1920

Reds so long to win! The reason may possibly be found in the observation of Peter Struve, an ex-Duma politician who supported the Whites:

> Psychologically, the Whites conducted themselves as if nothing had happened, whereas in reality the whole world around them had collapsed, and in order to vanquish the enemy they themselves had to undergo, in a certain sense, a rebirth . . . Nothing so harmed the 'White' movement as this condition of *psychologically staying put in previous circumstances*, circumstances which had ceased to exist . . .
>
> (from Pipes, *Russia Under the Bolshevik Regime, 1919–1924*, p.14)

SUMMARY

- Civil War broke out in mid-1918 between the Bolsheviks and their internal opponents.
- The Allied powers sent forces into Russia to protect their interests and to try to remove the Communists.
- The White forces lost the war as a result of:
  —conflicting interests
  —lack of organisation
  —lack of commitment
  —half-hearted Allied support
  —lack of popular support
  —the discipline of the Red forces under Trotsky.
- The Red Army was successful because:
  —it was more committed
  —it was better led
  —of the fanatical beliefs and brutality of the Red leaders
  —the people did not actively oppose them
  —it could exploit the human and material resources of Greater Russia.

Red Army: Army of the Bolsheviks during the Civil War period; initially a rabble, with the enthusiasm and organisational genius of Trotsky it became more disciplined and efficient.

Whites: Forces that opposed the Bolsheviks during the Civil War; lacked a common purpose and leadership, were scattered throughout Russia and often fought amongst themselves.

Admiral Alexander Kolchak: White general; born 1873, died 1920; established a right-wing government in western Siberia in late 1918; by early 1919 he was considered the leader of the anti-Bolshevik forces; using Czech troops in support, he launched a major offensive against the Bolsheviks in early 1919 but by June his troops were in retreat and his government had collapsed; early 1920 he was handed over to the Communists and executed.

General Anton Denikin: White General; born 1872, died 1947; ex-Tsarist officer who fled after the overthrow of the Provisional Government; formed an anti-Bolshevik Volunteer Army of Cossacks on the River Don; by mid-1919 had been successful against the Bolshevik forces; by October 1919 his forces had moved to within 400 km of Moscow but Trotsky's defensive tactics turned the tide; resigned his command in April 1920.

General Mikhail Tukhachevsky: Red general; born 1893, died 1937; led the counter-offensive against the Polish forces in mid-1920; appointed Chief of Staff 1925–28 and Deputy Commissar for Defence 1931–37; victim of the purges in January 1937.

Baron Peter Wrangel: White general; born 1878, died 1928; succeeded Denikin in command of the White forces in southern Russia; led one of the major offensives against the Red forces in mid-1920; troops were routed and he was forced to evacuate from the Crimea.

EXERCISES

1. What advantages did the Red Army have over its opponents in the Civil War?
2. How important was the work of the CHEKA in maintaining Bolshevik control during the Civil War?
3. What disadvantages faced the Allied armies during this period of Civil War in Russia?
4. To what extent was Bolshevik victory in the Civil War attributable to mistakes made by the White forces?
5. Make a detailed study of the Civil War. Use a map to place the opposing armies and show the various movements of the two sides. Clearly indicate the position and direction of the Allied armies.
6. What role did the following Bolshevik leaders play in the Civil War?
   Trotsky, Lenin, Stalin.
7. What role did terror and brutality play in the ultimate victory of the Bolsheviks in the Civil War?
8. Consider each of the following factors as possible reasons for Bolshevik victory in the Civil War. What evidence can you produce in support of each factor?

Reasons for Bolshevik Victory	Evidence

- The role of Lenin as revolutionary leader
- The role of Trotsky as founder and leader of the Red Army
- Use of 'terror' by the CHEKA
- The lack of organisation, commitment and cooperation by the White forces
- The attitudes of the peasants
- The war with Poland to 1921
- A lack of sympathy for former Tsarist officers/politicians
- A half-hearted effort from the Allies
- Geography—the resources and infrastructure of Greater Russia
- The inability of the White leaders to adjust to the changed circumstances
- The disciplined nature of the Red Army

Rank each of these factors in order of importance, and then justify your ranking.

9. Considering the war-weariness of the Allied troops, why did the Civil War last for so long?

10. Are there any other factors that you would consider important in an analysis of the Bolshevik victory? Explain these in full and give evidence to support your opinion.

DOCUMENT STUDY (No. 7)

Read the sources and answer the questions which follow.

SOURCE 3.E

Examples of Lenin's orders during the Civil War

It is necessary to organise an extra guard of well-chosen, trustworthy men. They must carry out a ruthless mass terror against the kulaks, priests and White Guards. All suspicious people should be detained in a concentration camp outside the city. The punitive expedition should be sent out at once. (9 August 1918)

In Nizhni Novgorod there are clearly preparations for a White Guard uprising. We must gather our strength, set up a dictatorial troika and institute mass terror 'immediately'; shoot and ferret out hundreds of prostitutes who get the soldiers drunk, former officers, etc. Not a moment of delay. Mass searches, execution for concealment of weapons. Mass seizures of Mensheviks and other unreliables. (9 August 1918)

Congratulations on the energetic suppression of the kulaks in the district. It is necessary to forge while the iron is hot, and not lose a minute in organising the poor of the district, confiscate all the grain and property of the rebellious kulaks, hang the instigators among the kulaks, and take hostages among the rich . . . (29 August 1918)

SOURCE 3.F

Lenin on the use of terror in a letter to Zinoviev, 26 June 1918

Only today we heard in the Central Committee that in Petrograd the 'workers' wanted to answer the assassination of Volodarsky with mass terror and that you . . . restrained them. I protest decisively. We compromise ourselves. Even in the resolutions of the Soviet we threaten mass terror, and when it comes to action, we put brakes on the revolutionary initiative of the masses, who are 'absolutely 'right'. This is impossible! Terrorists will consider us rags. This is an arch-war situation . . .

Photograph of a protest march in Moscow 1918. The banner is in support of the 'Red Terror'.

Extract from Australian historian Gordon Greenwood, *The Modern World*, published 1973

Much was due to the driving initiative, the disciplined order, and the ruthlessness of the Bolsheviks themselves. They possessed in Lenin a leader of great strength and astuteness, and in Trotsky an organiser of extraordinary capacity. The policy of terror subdued opposition and aided their cause, but the victory was not due to terrorism. The Bolsheviks were faced by a motley array of oppositionists, who had little in common. It was difficult to maintain effective co-operation between Socialist Revolutionary leaders and army generals of the old regime. There was little co-operation of policy or strategy between the White leaders, and this lack of unity was to prove fatal to the counter-revolutionary cause.

Questions

a **i)** From Source 3.H, list three reasons why the White forces were unsuccessful in the Civil War.

ii) From Source 3.E, list three groups who were to be the targets of the Terror.

b Using Source 3.G and your own knowledge, outline the use of terror as a Bolshevik/Communist tactic in the period 1918–21.

c Examine Sources 3.E, 3.F, 3.G and 3.H. How useful would an historian find each of these four sources when attempting to understand the reasons for the Red victory in the Civil War? (In your answer you must consider the nature, origin, motive, audience and reliability of each sources as well as its content.)

d Using all four sources and your own knowledge, explain why the White forces were unsuccessful in their attempt to overthrow the Bolshevik/Communist regime.

War Communism

FOCUS QUESTIONS In what ways did the Bolshevik Party in the years 1918–21 attempt to win control of the country?
To what extent did it succeed/ fail?

THE GROWTH OF THE ONE-PARTY STATE

THE POLITICAL HISTORY of the Soviet state over the period 1918–21 was marked by increasing centralisation and the denial of individual freedoms. In early 1918 the economic situation was chaotic and orders issued from the centre were frequently disobeyed or ignored. The needs of the state were increasingly guided by the urgency of ending the war with Germany and the repression of the real (and imagined) enemies within. Under Lenin's direction, the political opposition was targeted. Even though some of his closest supporters (Kamenev and Zinoviev) had briefly resigned from the Party in protest at Lenin's unwillingness to accept other socialist partners in a political coalition, Lenin remained obdurate in his desire for a one-party state.

This one-party state began to emerge from mid-1918 with the coming of the Civil War. The rise of a new threat to their authority led the Bolsheviks to take strong and decisive steps to maintain their control. The processes of coercion and control which had begun within hours of the seizure of power in November 1917 were further strengthened. New machinery to fight counter-revolution was established and a more disciplined army was set up to enforce the government's rules and decrees.

Political dissidents were dealt with ruthlessly. Mensheviks, Right Socialist Revolutionaries and Left Socialist Revolutionaries were expelled from the soviets and the CHEKA was permitted to carry out the purging of the body politic in any way it saw fit. Even Bolshevik Party membership came under stricter control from the central organisation. Debate and discussion of major issues, which had been a feature of early Bolshevik proceedings, were put aside under the pretext of the need for common action against the anti-revolutionary forces. A new constitution was promulgated. It appeared to be democratic, but in reality it was a facade for the establishment of the one-party state—see the diagram earlier in this chapter. It should be realised, though, that many so-called 'enemies of the regime' continued to be publicly active and vocal well into the 1920s. For example, the Menshevik F.I. Dan continued to push with impunity for the loosening of government controls over trade.

'STATE CAPITALISM'

It was in the area of the economy that control proved more difficult to achieve. The initial moves towards a controlled economy are referred to as the period of 'State Capitalism' and lasted from late 1917 until mid-1918. Under this policy, Lenin argued that the transition to a true proletarian economy would take time and that in the interim the skills and cooperation of the bourgeoisie would be necessary. Thus, while the state was issuing 'decrees', it was the workers—often without any reference to these government directives—who were seizing control of industries or individual workplaces. The same was also happening in agriculture. And the Bolsheviks were powerless to stop it! For example, although the Bolsheviks had issued a Decree on Workers' Control in 1917 it is estimated that for every one factory which was nationalised according to its criteria, four were taken over by workers with no reference to the government.

Throughout his political life Lenin was pragmatic in his approach to economic matters. From 1905 he accepted that a takeover of power would have to involve peasants as well as proletariat (his so-called *smychka*) and that this cooperation would be used to keep the peasants in line. For some months after the coup in 1917 the economy was in chaos and Lenin was criticised by the left wing of the Party as moving away from Marxist dogma in his cooperation with the bourgeoisie. They claimed that Lenin was too disciplined in the area of politics and too ready to compromise over economics. His reply, in a pamphlet titled *Left-wing Childishness*, claimed that such cooperation was necessary on the road to socialism. He stated that, at any rate, the new situation was an advance on the past! As usual, Lenin's beliefs held sway, particularly as the economy continued to be unable to produce enough food for the population. One solution was the establishment of the Council of Workers' and Peasants' Defence in 1918. This organisation was designed to coordinate the production and distribution of resources. In 1921 it was restructured as the Council of Labour and Defence. However, in both of its guises it was hamstrung by the continuing absence of an overriding economic plan and the persistent lack of cooperation at the grass-roots level. Similarly, in December 1917 the government had established Vesenkha, the Supreme Council of National Economy. Its aim was to assume control of the economy and to plan for the future. The irony was—and this is perhaps one of the root causes of the chaos which was to follow—Lenin, as late as December 1917, had written that 'there was not, and could not be, a definite plan for the organisation of economic life'. Consequently, the direction exerted by Vesenkha was also limited. While it did oversee the nationalisation of the banks and the railways and carried out the removal of Russia's foreign debt, its influence in creating the centralised, planned economy was minimal.

The absence of a carefully thought out plan is also shown in monetary policy. Nikolai Bukharin, who took the lead in this area, held economic views which were founded upon an interpretation of Marxist dogma which called for the complete eradication of all the institutional structures of capitalism. The primary target, therefore, was the use of currency as the medium of exchange. The 1919 Party Programme called for the abolition of money, and the mechanism for achieving this was to be the systematic flooding of the country with as much paper money as was possible—Pipes points out that by mid-1919 the printing of this 'coloured paper' was Russia's only growth industry! Inflation was rampant and workers were forced to accept 'payment in kind' for their services. In both city and countryside people turned to barter and the 'black market' in order to survive.

In the middle of 1918, however, the government did decide on a more deliberate economic policy. The production and distribution of food were still at critically low levels. The Civil War had broken out. There was a desperate need for the Bolsheviks to maintain food supplies to the urban workers in order to shore up their power base. Control over the economy became paramount. 'State Capitalism' was replaced by 'War Communism'. Through the placement of party managers and the establishment of party-organised workers' committees in each industry the Bolsheviks extended their influence over the workplace. The nationalisation of all industries was announced in June 1918. By late 1918 heavy industrial goods were being allocated and distributed according to government directive rather than market need. In practice, however, many of the smaller industries remained free of government intrusion.

Industrial production remained low, despite the efforts at centralised control. Priority was given to military hardware, labour was conscripted rather than voluntary, the value of money continued to fall and, with the transport network given over to troop movements, the distribution of goods continued to be dislocated. The net result was not the industrial expansion desired by the Bolshevik government. Instead, in many ways, Russian industry went backwards:

Comparison of Levels of Industrial Production

	1913	1921
Coal (million tons)	29	8.9
Oil (million tons)	9.2	3.8
Electricity (million kW.h)	2039	520
Pig iron (million tons)	4.2	0.1
Steel (million tons)	4.3	0.18
Bricks (millions)	2.1	0.01
Processed sugar (million tons)	1.3	0.05
Rail freight carried (million tons)	132.4	39.4

(from Michael Lynch, *Reaction and Revolutions: Russia, 1881–1924*, pp.132–3)

Of greater impact was the government's programme of grain requisitioning. Instead of creating the desired *smychka*, this action further alienated the peasants, who surrendered their crops only under duress and who often cut production levels or destroyed crops rather than hand them over. The level of grain production throughout the country by 1921 was less than half that achieved in 1913, while in the Ukraine (the breadbasket of the state) production had fallen to 20 per cent of its pre-1914 level. The economic problems were exacerbated by the scarcity of, and high prices demanded for, industrial goods. In order to coerce the peasantry to produce grain for the urban workers price controls were introduced and the requisitioning programme became more dogmatic. To try to overcome peasant resistance Lenin encouraged the formation of cooperatives to work the land on a collective basis and the formation of Committees of the Poor. Peasant intransigence, however, limited the extent of this development at this stage. There were few Party officials permanently stationed in the villages and the peasant farmers, when not under direct threat or surveillance, did largely as they pleased. All of this was to be a major cause of division between the central Soviet government and the village populations for the next decade. Similarly, many of the government's attempts at control were continually undermined by a burgeoning 'black market' economy. A new group emerged in rural society—the *meshochiniki*. These 'men with sacks' were private traders who roamed the countryside and cities providing food and goods for the population. The importance of these people eventually led even the Communist leadership to accept them as part of the economic system.

Even the basis of the Bolshevik's support in 1917 suffered terribly as a result of these economic policies. Kochan and Abraham estimate that between 1917 and 1920 over half of the urban working class actually disappeared, either through death in the Civil War, as a result of famine, or by returning to their villages. Many major industries, such as steel and sugar, ceased to operate effectively. The impact of these developments was to prove critical to the future of the Communist Party, with its 'traditional'

Starving children in the Don River basin, 1921— victims of the famine created by War Communism

members being replaced by self-serving bureaucrats and intelligentsia who put great value in the importance of 'manual labour' while ensuring that they themselves had nothing to do with it!

Strikes and open rebellion broke out both in the countryside and in the factories. Within the Party itself there developed a Workers' Opposition faction (headed by Alexandra Kollontai and Alexander Shliapnikov) which argued vehemently for a change in Party policy and a return to the practical and doctrinal demands of the working class. For example, Kollontai and Shliapnikov called for compulsory labour from non-working-class members of the Party. The resolution against factionalism and public debate over policy which was passed at the Tenth Party Congress in 1921 was, in part, an attempt to stifle criticism of this kind. The Party was moving increasingly away from its working-class roots and towards the bureaucracy-driven apparatus it was to become—in its fully-fledged form—under Stalin and his successors.

'War Communism' was therefore a time of complex military, political, social and economic change in which each of the following factors must be taken into consideration:

The Constituent Assembly and political parties

The Constituent Assembly had been dissolved in 1918. Formally, no legal opposition to the Bolsheviks was then allowed and later systems of political representation were weighted in favour of the urban working class. The Left Socialist Revolutionaries continued to operate within the political system until the early 1920s because the Bolsheviks feared that further reprisals against this group would lead to the complete alienation of the peasantry. There was partial disenfranchisement of those who had hired the labour of others or lived on interest, dividends or rent. Businessmen, clerics, ex-policemen and Romanovs were treated in a similar manner. In an attempt to distance themselves from the excesses of the 1917 coup and the weeks which followed, the Bolsheviks renamed themselves the Russian Communist Party in March 1919. The aim was to present a more all-encompassing image to the people.

Soviets

By June 1918 the Bolsheviks had lost their majority in each soviet in Russia. They reimposed their will upon these institutions by force.

Factories

The Bolsheviks decreed the nationalisation of all factories within the area controlled by the Red Army. Ration cards were issued and workers paid in kind instead of currency. Factories were forced to be run along military lines. Managers in the factories had to be Communist Party members.

Labour

Many workers were forced to join the labour gangs for the construction of roads, canals and munitions. Strikes incurred the death penalty. Trade Unions were forced out of existence, amid great debate within the Party. There was little choice with job selection and working conditions. In this climate of forced socialism each citizen was expected to make the same sacrifices as the soldiers.

Agriculture

To feed the workers in the urban areas, peasants had to hand over provisions. This was met with resentment and led the government to forced requisitioning. The result was clashes with peasants and a breakdown of law and order. Less grain was sown, livestock were killed by the peasants but the government continued its policy of requisitioning. Despite falls in production, the amount seized increased. Vesenkha was established to coordinate agricultural production.

The Party

From the outset Lenin directed and controlled the Party. The CHEKA was used to maintain control while the early reorganisation of the Party apparatus made it more centralised and controlled from the top. The Party was highly organised into cells in each factory or workplace. The cells watched and controlled local elections and production levels, reported people to the CHEKA (the GPU after 1922) and either criticised or approved factory management. Children were encouraged to join the 'Young Pioneer' organisation. Similarly, the government came under the control of the Party. Members of the Communist Party had to be atheists, and loyalty to the Party came before everything. At the Tenth Party Congress in 1921 a resolution on Party unity was passed—this outlawed all factions within the Party and stifled public debate of Party policy.

Armed forces

The military was used by the Bolsheviks to maintain order and control. Strict discipline was reintroduced into military life, while the army was used to impose government directives, such as grain requisitioning.

SUMMARY

- According to the Bolsheviks, War Communism was introduced to meet the economic, political and military crises of the Civil War.
- War Communism has been seen by many to be a deliberate attempt to swiftly impose 'Communism' upon Russia.
- War Communism involved the centralisation of economic control and the eradication of the traditional features of a market economy where possible.
- The policies imposed by War Communism were resented by the rural classes and the city workers and created tension between these groups and the Bolsheviks.
- War Communism paved the way for the bureaucratisation of the nation and the Party.
- The nature of the membership of the Communist Party changed greatly during War Communism.

Left Communists: Faction of the Central Committee of the Communist Party during the Civil War; led by Bukharin and others; pushed for immediate action on the international front to spread revolution and socialism abroad; opposed by Lenin as he pushed for peace with Germany and a slow move to socialism.

Democratic Centralists: Faction of the Communist Party; supported the theory that ordinary members of the Party influenced policy; believed in using Party Congress (democracy) and the Central Executive Committee (authoritarian bureaucratisation).

Workers' Opposition: Faction of the Communist Party; believed that non-working-class elements had become too influential within the Party; called for a return to original Marxist principles and revolutionary tactics.

Prodrazverstka: Russian term for the system of formal requisitioning of grain during War Communism; use of force was an essential feature; units sent into the countryside were rewarded with part of the produce they collected.

Vesenkha: Government body; the Supreme Council of National Economy; established in 1918 to administer and plan the economic life of the Soviet state; slowly nationalised major industries and by late 1919 it had taken control of about 3500 enterprises; as part of this planned economy, Gosplan was established in 1921 to create and maintain a policy of long-term planning.

Alexandra Kollontai: Russian revolutionary; born 1872, died 1952; daughter of a Tsarist general; 1906, joined the Mensheviks; 1914, switched to Bolsheviks in admiration of Lenin's anti-war stance; emissary/agent/courier of Lenin to Bolshevik Central Committee in March 1917 delivering message of non-cooperation with Provisional Government; used by German government to pass on money to Lenin and Bolsheviks; gaoled for her part in attempted July coup; released in early August; member of Left Communist faction; believed in workers' control in industry as against Lenin's idea of individual management; part of the faction which over-ruled Lenin in 1918 and imposed War Communism; 1917–18, Commissar for Public Welfare; 1919 published *The New Morality and the Working Class*; believed that women should be free economically and psychologically; advocated free love; mistress of Shliapnikov; became one of the leaders of the Workers' Opposition faction; 1921, wrote pamphlet in which she argued that the Party hierarchy had lost touch with the rank and file, and that petit bourgeois elements had taken over the Party; dismissed for 'dereliction of duties'; 1923–25, 1927–30, Ambassador to Norway; 1925–27, Ambassador to Mexico; 1930–45, Ambassador to Sweden; died 1952.

Alexander Shliapnikov: Russian revolutionary; born (?), died 1937; highest Bolshevik functionary of a working class background; during First World War, directed Party underground in Petrograd; did not believe that the events of February 1917 were real and scoffed 'What revolution? Give the workers a pound of bread and the movement will peter out'; March 1917, sponsored measure in Petrograd Soviet which gave each socialist party the right to have three representatives on Ispolkom—believed in cooperation of socialists; viewed Order No. 1 as an attempt by the intellectuals to secure control over the garrison rather than being for the benefit of the soldiers; March 1917, part of a three-man sub-committee to get the party up and running; this sub-committee produced the first edition of the new series of *Pravda* ; lost power and prestige with the return of Stalin and Kamenev to St Petersburg in 1917; appointed Commissar of Labour in Lenin's government; along with his mistress, Alexandra Kollontai, became a leader of Workers' Opposition faction; executed 1937.

Council of Workers' and Peasants' Defence: Administrative body; established mid-1918; war emergencies and collapse of transport system led the Party to impose tighter central control over the economy—this Council was established to collect and utilise resources for the waging of the war; 1920, became the Council for Labour and Defence, chaired by Lenin; became the economic cabinet that issued decrees on all aspects of the economy; grew to become more important than Vesenkha.

EXERCISES

1. What were the aims of the Bolshevik Party to 1921? Did they achieve them?
2. What was the role of each of the following groups in the Bolshevik/Communist consolidation to 1921?
   a urban workers
   b agricultural workers
   c bureaucrats and Party functionaries
3. How did Lenin retain control of the Party during this period?
4. In 1918 the Bolshevik Party changed its name to the Communist Party.
   a Why did it make this change?
   b What effect did the change of name have on the Party's role in Russia?
5. a What was the difference between 'State Capitalism' and 'War Communism'?
   b In what ways was War Communism in line with Marxist ideology?

DOCUMENT STUDY   No. 8

Read the sources and answer the questions which follow.

Instructions issued by a leader of the CHEKA in 1917,
Recorded by a member of the CHEKA and published in his memoirs in 1927

SOURCE 3.I

We are not waging war against individuals. We are exterminating the bourgeoisie as a class. During the investigation, do not look for evidence that the accused acted in deed or word against Soviet power. The first questions that you ought to put are: To what class does he belong? What is his origin? What is his education or profession? In this lies the significance and essence of the terror.

Extract from Australian historian David Christian, *Power and Privilege*, published in 1994

SOURCE 3.J

More than anything else, the Communist victory [in the Civil War] reflected the successful mobilisation of resources by a determined and highly militarised ruling group. However, success in the Civil War set a fateful precedent for it meant a return to traditional strategies of direct mobilisation, and the autocratic political culture that had sustained them. Eventually, the Communist party would fall back on these traditions to solve the even greater problems they faced once the Civil War ended. In this way, the Civil War marked a return to the past rather than a leap into the future.

SOURCE 3.K

A Soviet political poster of 1918, depicting the sword of the Red Army cutting off the advancing White forces

SOURCE 3.L

Extract from the statement issued by the Kronstadt sailors explaining the reasons behind their rebellion, 1921

In carrying out the October Revolution, the working class hoped to achieve its liberation. The outcome has been even greater enslavement of human beings.

Power has passed from a monarchy based on the police and armed forces into the hands of the usurpers—the Communists—who have given the toilers not freedom but the daily bread of ending up in the torture chambers of the Cheka, the horrors of which exceed many times the rule of tsarism's police.

But the basest and most criminal of all is the moral slavery introduced by the Communists: they have also laid their hands on the inner world of the working people, compelling them to think only as they do.

By means of state-run trade unions, the workers have been chained to their machines, so that labour is not a source of joy but a new serfdom. To the protests of peasants, expressed in spontaneous uprisings, and those of the workers, whom the very conditions of life compel to strike, they have responded with mass executions and an appetite for blood that by far exceeds that of Tsarist generals.

Questions

a **i)** According to Source 3.I, who were the chief targets of the CHEKA?
  ii) According to Source 3.L, what was the most criminal act committed by the Communists?
b Using Source Source 3.J and your own knowledge, why did the Communists win the Civil War?
c Examine Source 3.J, Source 3.K and Source 3.L. In what ways would an historian find each of these sources useful when attempting to understand developments in Russian between 1918 and 1921? (In your answer you must consider the nature, origin, motive and audience of each source as well as its content.)
d Using all four sources and your own knowledge, explain why the Communists were still in power in Russia at the end of 1921.

War Communism—an Assessment

FOCUS QUESTION Was 'War Communism' a response to economic and military circumstances, or was it a deliberate attempt to implement communist theory in Russia?

Was the period of 'War Communism' a period of Marxist theory in action or was it a period of political necessity? In order to fully answer this question it is necessary to examine the areas of bureaucracy, Party, military and the economy. It may also be worthwhile considering the fact that the term 'War Communism' was never actually used by the Bolsheviks until after they had announced its abandonment. Alec Nove describes War Communism as having the following characteristics:

WHAT WAS 'WAR COMMUNISM'?

1 An attempt to ban private manufacture, the nationalisation of nearly all industry, the allocation of nearly all material stocks, and of what little output there was, by the state, especially for war purposes.
2 A ban on private trade, never quite effective anywhere, but spasmodically enforced.
3 Seizure of peasant surpluses (*prodrazverstka*).
4 The partial elimination of money from the state's own dealings with its own organisations and the citizens. Free rations, when there was anything to ration.
5 All these factors combined with terror and arbitrariness, expropriations, requisitions. Efforts to establish discipline, with party control over trade unions. A siege economy with a communist ideology. A partly-organised chaos. Sleepless, leather-jacketed commissars working around the clock in a vain effort to replace the free market.

(*An Economic History of the USSR*, p.74)

Lenin pictured among soldiers who had just assisted in crushing the rebellion of the Kronstadt sailors

THEORY VERSUS PRACTICE

In the bureaucracy it was envisaged by the Bolsheviks that the state would 'wither away' according to Marxist theory. Lenin believed that this would occur only when exploitation was eradicated. Following their coup the Bolsheviks dismantled the old Tsarist administrative structures, but remnants were maintained in order to keep the state functioning. Indeed, the very nature of the Bolshevik system of government soon meant the growth of a new bureaucratic system which was every bit as convoluted and corrupt as that which it had replaced. The Bolsheviks argued that during times of extreme stress the governmental structures had to be flexible. However, with the ending of the crisis the Bolsheviks remained inflexible. The structures they had set up remained in place, and became stronger.

The control of the means of production was centralised, the Communists introduced an eight-hour day and insurance cover for all workers with disabilities and for those who were unemployed. All productive workers (soldiers, sailors, collective workers and industrial workers in large firms) were given the vote. The corrupt and wasteful political and economic system existing under the Tsars was eradicated and replaced by a system which was supposedly 'freer' and 'fairer'. In reality the majority were worse off. This was not the 'dictatorship of the proletariat' envisaged by Marx—the military and political situation quickly overran the Bolsheviks and the strength of their adherence to Marxist theory was tested and found wanting.

At the Tenth Party Congress, Lenin summed up the period 1918–21 as follows:

> The poverty of the working class was never so vast and acute as in the period of the dictatorship. The enfeeblement of the workers and peasants is close to the point of complete incapacitation of work.

Lenin had tried a series of measures to stimulate economic development while maintaining central control; each had failed. International trade had been nationalised, the larger industries had been placed under state control, a moneyless economy had been introduced, labour had been organised into gangs, abolition of inheritance had taken place, agricultural requisitioning had been instituted and the Supreme Economic Council had been established for the coordination of economic policy at all levels. Yet, without exception, production levels fell to well below those of pre-1914.

Although Lenin was aware of the economic chaos which these measures created he pushed on regardless. The securing of his vision of the revolution was uppermost in his mind, and he was prepared to adopt (and then convincingly justify) any change in policy which might be required. The Party's economic policy was therefore in the hands of people who held strongly to the 'rightness' of their actions and ideas. Unfortunately, while these people were strong on Marxist (or Leninist) rhetoric, they had little or no experience of practical economics. It was only after things had gone terribly wrong that they began to claim that War Communism had been forced upon them by circumstance. In fact it had been a deliberate policy.

This deliberate policy plunged the Russian countryside into a famine which cost at least five million lives. Even *Pravda* admitted that by 1921 one in five people was starving and that the situation was desperate. The government accepted foreign aid from bodies such as the American Relief Administration headed by Herbert Hoover but most of it came too late. Disease, such as typhus, was rife and there were even those who resorted to cannibalism in order to survive.

The desire for greater central control was at the heart of all of these developments. In the early days of the revolution the 'Party' had been a fairly nebulous concept. There had been open debate and discussion and little formal direction of provincial cells by those in the cities. Similarly, the traditional military hierarchies had been quickly swept away. All this changed from November 1917 as Lenin imposed tighter and tighter controls from the central Party organisation—with power emanating particularly from those people in his immediate circle. Debate was stifled and even the membership of the Party was placed under greater scrutiny. In the armed forces ranks and discipline were returned. Again, if all this had been 'due to

TIGHTENING OF CONTROL

circumstances', why were these measures maintained once 'the circumstances' had been removed?

Lenin was criticised at the time as deviating from accepted revolutionary doctrine. Pronouncements he had made in *State and Revolution*, such as his opposition to the use of bourgeois specialists and the need for workers' control over industry, were used against him by members of the left opposition within the Party (notably Bukharin, Radek, Obolensky, Shliapnikov and Alexandra Kollontai). His statement that 'under socialism *all* will govern in turn and quickly become accustomed to no one governing' was also used against him. Lenin, however, was unmoved. In his characteristically pragmatic fashion he justified every move in terms of the rightness of the eventual cause. The state and its associated bureaucracy were simply part of the movement towards the proletarian utopia.

Strikes, demonstrations and violence became a familiar pattern towards the end of the period of War Communism. There was, though, one protest which even Lenin could not ignore, and it came from that group which had provided some of the staunchest original supporters of the Bolshevik cause—the armed forces. In March 1921 sailors at the Kronstadt naval base revolted. Thousands of sailors at the base mutinied against the Bolshevik government. They believed that Lenin and his supporters no longer represented the will of the people and called for 'Soviets without Communists'. Lenin sent in the Red Army to quell the mutiny. It took three weeks to do so.

Such a wide range of developments, all of which resulted in the strengthening of central control by the Bolshevik elite, could not have just been a result of 'circumstances'. This period in Russian history saw the Party further entrench itself as it continued to operate in its own interests rather than in the interests of the people it was supposed to represent.

SUMMARY

- War Communism was a deliberate attempt to introduce communist principles into Russia.
- Only after the measures had failed and changes had to be made did the Bolsheviks claim that War Communism had been a response to circumstances.

EXERCISES

1. In what ways did Lenin's ideas change with the onset of the Civil War in 1918?

2. Were the measures introduced during the Civil War in line with Marxist theory or were they simply decisions of political expediency? Give evidence to support your ideas.

3. Describe the political situation in Russia in 1921.

4. To what extent can it be said that the period of War Communism marked a failure for the Communists?
5. What alternative policies do you believe the Communists could have introduced?
6. Why was the response to the Kronstadt revolt so important?
7. How did the Civil War period change the character of the Bolshevik/Communist Party? Give evidence to support your conclusions.
8. Consider the following pamphlets written by Lenin. How consistently was Lenin actually putting his own ideas into practice in the years 1917–21?

What is to be done? (1902)
Stressed the need for a revolutionary theory, and a revolutionary party to implement it.
One Step Forward, Two Steps Back (1904)
Outlined the essential role of the party and specified the importance of the inner party leadership.
Two Tactics (1905)
Viewed the 1905 Revolution as bourgeois in character, based on bourgeois principles and stated that a Constituent Assembly must be convened to ensure the full development of the capitalist government. Argued that the working class would need to become fully conscious of its position before its revolutionary potential could be reached.
The State and Revolution (July, 1917)
The Bolshevik state would be replaced by the dictatorship of the proletariat, and the withering of the state apparatus would take time. The state would be needed in the transitional stage. Lenin also maintained his opposition to parliamentary democracy.
The Impending Catastrophe and How to Combat It (September 1917)
Foreshadowed nationalisation of the banks and some of the larger monopolistic industries. There was no mention of the nationalisation of private property. He also stressed that anyone could help run the state: the workers were capable of completing all jobs and taking all positions.
Immediate Tasks of the Soviet Government (April 1918)
Stressed how important technicians were to the state, even if it meant using the skilled workers and managers from Tsarist times.

9. In *Europe Since Napoleon*, David Thomson asserts that the period of War Communism trampled down the rights of the peasants and the workers simply to help the Bolsheviks win the Civil War. How accurate is this analysis?
10. Consider each of the following points in relation to War Communism:
    The forced requisitioning of grain, 1918–21
    Famine 1921–22—approximately five million dead
    Peasant uprisings as a result of falling prices and grain requisitioning
    Decline of the moneyed economy
    Strikes in industry and the introduction of the death penalty for strikers
    Removal of the Trade Union movement
    Centralisation of power by the Bolshevik Party
    The decline in food production and industrial output
    The decline in the value of the rouble
    The absence of direct Communist Party control in most areas
    The Kronstadt uprising 1921
    The factionalism within the party 1918–21
Why were the Bolsheviks/Communists still in power in 1921?

The NEP (New Economic Policy)

FOCUS QUESTIONS What were the major features of the New Economic Policy?
Why did Lenin introduce the NEP?
In what ways did the NEP mark a departure from Communist ideology?

THE CRISIS OF 1921

GOVERNMENT SOVIET POLICY throughout the period of War Communism had been predicated on the use of force and terror to gain political control and economic stability. Peasants and industrial workers alike had been treated poorly in order to provide for the needs of the Party. The government's use of grain requisitioning and forced labour created tension between it and the people. In the towns, support for the government declined as a result of lowering wages, heightened inflation, long hours, food shortages and a general lack of open debate over economic and political policy. While most of the population had not been keen to encourage the White forces, by 1921 they openly resented the exactions of the government. One group of striking workers in Petrograd in 1921 issued a statement claiming that:

> A complete change is necessary in the policies of the Government. First of all, the workers and peasants need freedom. They don't want to live by the decrees of the Bolsheviks; they want to control their own destinies. Comrades, preserve revolutionary order! Determinedly and in an organised manner demand: liberation of all the arrested Socialists and non-partisan working-men; abolition of martial law; freedom of speech, press and assembly for all who labour. (Quoted in M. Lynch, *Reaction and Revolutions: Russia 1881–1924*, p. 123.)

Production of most articles and foods fell below pre-1914 levels. Strikes and violent disturbances were common. The ultimate rejection of the government was the Kronstadt uprising in 1921. The sailors at Kronstadt had been traditional supporters of the regime and their outbreak marked the low point of Bolshevik fortunes after 1917.

THE 'TACTICAL RETREAT'

As was the case throughout these first years, the dominant issue was the provision of enough food to sustain the population. War Communism and the use of coercion had failed to meet these needs. By 1921 the counter-revolutionary forces and foreign troops had either left Russian soil or been defeated. The Party leaders then sought a new direction. Many inside the Party wanted to eradicate the interference from powerful party cadres and return to open discussion. Lenin was the force and the controlling agent throughout these years, and his word was law. As usual, his response to criticism was repression. At the Tenth Party Congress in 1921 all public debate was stifled with the passing of a resolution on 'Party unity'. Lenin then turned to a new direction within the economy, the New Economic Policy.

Under this policy the requisitioning of foodstuffs and the division of the peasantry into two groups were abandoned. This brought an immediate easing of the tensions within Russian society. Agricultural workers now had to send only part of their produce to the state; the remainder could be sold as they wished. Peasants now had to pay a tax to the government which was, in some areas, higher than it had been under the Tsars—the economy now favoured the wealthier peasants. There were new laws governing land ownership and the granting of grain loans to help with production.

To encourage the movement of goods, private trading was allowed. This led to the growth of a new class, the Nepmen. These private traders (the descendants of the *meshochniki*) eagerly pursued their occupations and by 1922 more than three-quarters of retail trade was being carried out by them. For the poorer workers, however, all this did was create another group of people for them to resent.

Lenin also realised that planning through Vesenkha had failed to raise industrial production, with costs remaining high and techniques continuing to be inefficient. To reverse these trends, small-scale commercial industries

FEATURES OF THE 'NEP'

Soviet poster depicting the desired 'smychka' between rural and urban workers

(those employing fewer than twenty people) were privatised. Loans were more readily available, in line with a change in Party policy which reintroduced money as the medium of exchange. In 1922 a new rouble was introduced to facilitate these developments.

Despite these changes under the New Economic Policy the majority of the workers continued to be employed by the state. Furthermore, the government maintained its grip upon the economy through its control of what Lenin described as the 'commanding heights': banking, heavy industry, transport and foreign trade were all strictly directed by central government authorities.

Lenin was criticised for taking socialism back to capitalism with this change in direction in 1921, but it was stressed to the Party that this was not the case. It was merely a 'tactical retreat'. It was stated that errors had been made, and to overcome these it was necessary to go back a little way, correct the situation, and then move forward again. Lenin maintained that there was little use in preserving an economic system which had so obviously failed. To do so would spell the death of the Party, especially since the hoped-for world-wide revolution had failed to materialise. Therefore an intermediate capitalist stage had to be introduced before the final stage of communism was reached. He stated in October 1921:

> I regret it . . . because our experience, which is not very long, proves to us that our conception was wrong. Our NEP means that in applying our former methods we suffered defeat and had to begin a strategic retreat. Let us retreat and construct everything in a solid manner; otherwise we shall be beaten. The defeat we suffered in the spring of 1921 on the economic front was more serious than that we had ever before suffered when fighting against Kolchak . . . The system of distribution in the villages and the immediate application of Communist methods in the towns held back our productive forces and caused the great economic and political crisis in the spring of 1921. (Quoted in David Shub, *Lenin*, p. 412.)

By bolstering its control of the urban economy, and loosening its influence in the countryside, Lenin's belief was to establish a 'smychka', or alliance, between industrial workers and peasants. The smychka would then become the basis for future economic development. Lenin instituted the New Economic Policy as a tactical measure to save his Communist rule. He did not intend it to be a permanent feature of the Bolshevik state's economic development.

Much propaganda was used to sell this move to the party. Trotsky had first raised this policy in 1920, arguing that the peasants would only increase production if offered an incentive. He argued that there be a set production level which would be taxed. Any excess production would then be available for sale on the open market. At the time this idea had been denounced as ideologically unacceptable. However, by early 1921 Lenin had come to see that political necessity and the need for Party unity was more important than ideological purity.

SUMMARY

- Economic hardship and military devastation caused major difficulties for the Bolshevik state by 1921.
- There were increasing calls for a change in economic policy and for a freeing of debate and discussion.
- Future public debate was stifled at the Tenth Party Congress in 1921.
- Lenin introduced the NEP to reinforce the Party's hold on power.
- The NEP included some capitalist features, with the state retaining control of the major economic institutions.

Smychka: Alliance of industrial workers and peasants which Lenin saw as the basis of the New Economic Policy.

Nepmen: Private traders and middlemen; took advantage of the reintroduction of private trading and profit-making under the New Economic Policy; came to control the majority of the retail trade.

KEY PERSONALITIES, GROUPS, TERMS

EXERCISES

1. a What were the major features of the New Economic Policy?
   b In what ways did the New Economic Policy mark a change in Communist ideology?
2. What reasons were given for the introduction of the New Economic Policy?
3. a What groups within the Party were opposed to the New Economic Policy?
   b How did Lenin overcome this opposition?

DOCUMENT STUDY   (No. 9)

Read the sources and answer the questions which follow.

SOURCE 3.N

Graphs showing changes in production levels, 1913–26,
from 'various Soviet sources', reproduced in John Laver, *Russia 1914–41*, p.30

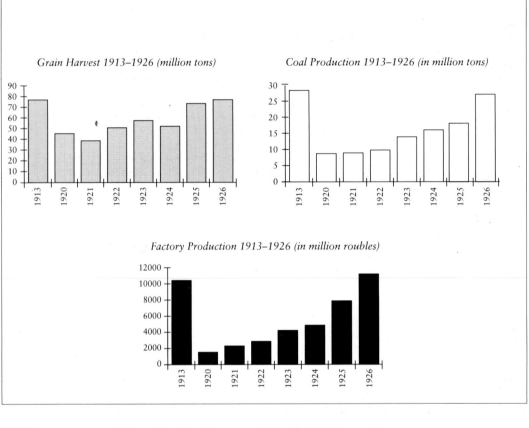

Grain Harvest 1913–1926 (million tons)

Coal Production 1913–1926 (in million tons)

Factory Production 1913–1926 (in million roubles)

SOURCE 3.N

A view of the New Economic Policy by R.N. Carew-Hunt,
The Theory and Practice of Communism, published in 1966
Lenin himself had held it to be no more than a tactical retreat which necessity
alone justified, and it is unlikely that the party as a whole would have long acquiesced
in an economy so divergent from its principles . . .

SOURCE 3.O

Another view of the New Economic Policy
by S.W. Page, *Russia in Revolution*, published in 1965
Lenin's retreat came not a moment too soon . . . [but] by 1923, the Russian
economy was in the process of rapid recovery . . . Many of the Communists saw all
but the proletariat getting richer every day. The very bourgeoisie, whom the revolu-

tion had supposedly disposed, were brazenly flaunting their newly gained wealth. Bitter arguments raged about this . . .

Part of the speech presented by Stalin at Lenin's funeral, 1924

SOURCE 3.P

We Communists are people of a special mould. We are those who form the army of the great proletarian general, the army of Comrade Lenin. There is no higher honour than belonging to this army. In leaving us, Comrade Lenin ordered us to hold high and keep pure the great title of 'Member of the Party'. We vow to thee Comrade Lenin, that we shall honourably fulfil this, thy commandment.

Questions

a i) From Source 3.M, in what year was the grain harvest at its lowest level?
  ii) From Source 3.M, in what year was factory production at its lowest level?
  iii) From Source 3.P who was 'the great proletarian general'?
b Using Source 3.0 and your own knowledge, describe the changes introduced by the New Economic Policy.
c Examine Source 3.M and Source 3.P. What difficulties would an historian encounter when attempting to use each of these sources as evidence of developments in Russia to 1924? (In your answer consider the nature, origin, motive and audience of each source as well as its content.)
d Using all four sources and your own knowledge, how important was the introduction of the New Economic Policy to the survival of the Communist regime?

The Consequences of the New Economic Policy

FOCUS QUESTION To what extent was Communist Russia a socialist state by 1924?

A T THE Tenth Party Congress of 1921, Lenin believed that by giving Russia a breathing space the peasantry would be won over to the government and that the Party would cement its rule. The much-disliked CHEKA was replaced in 1922 by the GPU (State Political Administration), and in many quarters there was a move to impress the people with a show of legality by the government in its dealings with them. Economic stability was given priority, but Lenin made it plain to the Party that the New Economic Policy was not just an economic palliative. The Soviet Union—the new name for the region following the 1924 Constitution—was now a one-party state with all people and institutions within it working for the common cause. Members of the Left Communists, such as Bukharin, therefore abandoned their opposition to the new policy direction, believing that it was a necessary part of the development to a proletarian state.

ECONOMIC RESULTS

Grain harvest and pig-iron production levels regained, or surpassed, their pre-1914 levels. Widespread electrification was introduced. The decentralisation of the market system and the reintroduction of money allowed, and encouraged, production levels to increase. In some areas the ravages of famine remained, but on the whole, agriculture began to meet the food needs of the people and industries began to produce the goods required by an expanding market. The land under cultivation increased by 50 per cent between 1921 and 1927 and numbers of live-stock rose. Coal and textile production both doubled. By 1923 well over 85 per cent of firms were in private hands, with the remainder run by the government who still employed over 80 per cent of the workers. Transport and communication also slowly improved, helped by the importation of over 1000 new engines from Germany and Sweden.

THE 'SCISSORS CRISIS'

The New Economic Policy also sparked what has become known as the 'Scissors Crisis'. This term referred to the widening gap between agricultural and industrial prices. As agricultural production increased in the early 1920s there was a consequent fall in the price offered for the goods. Conversely, the prices for industrial goods rose because of shortages caused by inefficient production methods and the disruption of the Civil War. The 'crisis' that ensued was generated by the fact that the peasants had to pay more for manufactured goods yet had a lower income from their own produce. Many feared that this would again lead the peasants to abandon their support (however tenuous) for the regime, and it was left to an upturn in the economy in the mid-1920s to stabilise the situation.

SOCIAL RESULTS

The introduction of the New Economic Policy further generated ideals that were against the very ethos of communism: greed, self-interest, independence and exploitation. With official sanction, thousands of small traders (the Nepmen) appeared and began to organise and develop an internal market. In the agricultural areas, Bukharin's order to 'enrich yourselves' was taken up enthusiastically. As a consequence, a richer group of peasants, the 'kulaks', re-emerged. The peasants were given tenure of their land, and were allowed to hire labour and rent land. As well, they were able to sell their surplus produce wherever they could and use the produce as they liked. These new freedoms applied more to the workers in agriculture than to those in industry, with the proletariat still being seen as the leaders on the road to the classless society. However, divisions also appeared in their ranks. The use of 'bourgeois specialists', technicians and the use of wage differentials undermined any notion of proletarian unity. J.N. Westwood writes that the Bolsheviks had styled themselves as the 'vanguard of the proletariat' and were now finding themselves in the van with no proletariat to guard!

PRACTICE VERSUS THEORY

While it seemed to many that the government was reneging on its communist principles with the introduction of the New Economic Policy, it must be remembered that the state continued to employ the majority of the workforce. The state also tightened its control over banking and credit facilities, transport, foreign trade and large-scale domestic enterprises. Add to this list all large-scale heavy industry. The state remained in firm control and Lenin was adamant that the Communist Party would retain control of the state.

The New Economic Policy did not solve the economic problems facing Russia. Its reliance upon small-scale farms, most of which were uneconomic units, simply could not produce the levels required for the transition to the desired communist state. The problem of feeding the masses may have been temporarily solved, but the question of the free operation of the market system in agriculture was not ideologically sound to most Party members. Within the economic chaos and deprivation of the early 1920s Lenin had engineered a strategic retreat in Party policy, but it created more problems in the long run. The crux of the problem lies at the heart of Marxist ideology itself. Production levels and distribution networks must be sufficient to meet the needs of all people before the move to collective or cooperative ownership can take place. In the Russian context, however, improvements in production and distribution created a mentality in which collectivisation and cooperation would be resisted. The state response therefore became increased coercion. Both the agricultural and industrial workers would feel the brunt of this force under Stalin.

SUMMARY

- The New Economic Policy slowly stabilised the Soviet economy.
- The New Economic Policy created new groups within the society, notably the kulaks, who were to prove an obstacle to future developments.

Ideology in Theory and Practice

1917–1924

FOCUS QUESTION What were the consequences of the introduction of the NEP?

THE BOLSHEVIK PARTY had seized power in 1917 with the intention of passing this power to the industrial working class. Some decades earlier Karl Marx had observed the changing industrial landscape in Britain in the 1840s and 1850s. What he saw appalled him. He believed that the working class was being exploited by the owners of capital and that they were becoming progressively poorer. The end result for Marx was a violent struggle in which the working classes (the proletariat) would be victorious over the owners of capital. The workers would then own the means of production and they would eventually share it evenly with all the people. Over time the people would come to appreciate the benefits of this new system and make it work. Because of this increased knowledge, in time the state itself would wither away. All state institutions would disappear.

THE MARXIST DIALECTIC

LENIN'S CHANGES

Obviously the possibility of creating such a revolution in a peasant society was very small. Even Marx had little faith that it would occur in Russia. Lenin, however, strongly believed that such a revolution could occur in the Russian context. He argued that once a revolutionary party had been formed to lead the masses then the need for parliamentary democracy would disappear. Over time, this party-state would itself be replaced by the 'dictatorship of the proletariat' and, again much later, the state itself would wither away. The state would be needed to maintain order and discipline in the transitional stage. From the time of the 1905 Revolution Lenin expressed a recognition of the need for a cooperation between workers and peasants if this was to occur. As a consequence he was prepared to be flexible with his movement's doctrinal demands.

Lenin's primary aim in 1917 was the consolidation of power in the hands of the Bolshevik Party. He supported the internationalisation of communism as a means of protecting his new government (and in part because he believed the communist ideal). All business was put into the hands of the industrial workers instead of private owners; the state alone was to have the knowledge to direct labour and its use; and attempts were made to coerce the Russian people into accepting socialist principles. Once the Bolshevik Party had assumed power, Lenin justified the imposition of Marxist principles on a predominantly peasant society by stating that he personally felt the actions taken were acceptable. In this way any change to Marxist thought became acceptable to the party, simply because it was agreeable to Lenin. Lenin had overruled opposition within the Party in the seizure of power in 1917. He had proved correct then (because the Bolsheviks had succeeded when the doctrine said they should not have). Therefore, in the future, Lenin must still be right, even if the doctrine said he was wrong!

IDEOLOGICAL THEORY VERSUS POLITICAL REALITY

Within a very short time Lenin's ideological theory gave way to political reality. Russia came to be dominated by the Communist Party. No other parties were tolerated, very few of the Party hierarchy were from the proletariat and the Party itself was limited in its membership. In its original conception the Party had been an open and democratic organisation, with regional cells having autonomy and little central control. This soon changed. Under the pressures of Civil War and personal ambition, the Bolshevik Party (renamed the Communist Party) came to be completely dominated by the Central Executive Committee. In this way the leaders of the 1917 Revolution became the guardians of the state. By the time the New Economic Policy was introduced the ruling organisation, Sovnarkom, was only a rubber stamp for the decisions of the Central Committee of the Communist Party. The men who sat in the Central Committee were the elite of a very hierarchic organisation. All opposition was crushed during these years using the systematised terrorism of the CHEKA, and at the Tenth Party Congress of 1921, wider powers were given to the Central Committee and factions were outlawed. To control the Party even further, Lenin in 1919 created a party bureaucracy (named the People's Commissariat of State Control), headed by Stalin, to keep the members in line. Rather than withering away, the state was in fact burgeoning and becoming more intrusive.

In economic policy the Bolsheviks initially attempted to impose a strict ideological line. Their early attempts to destroy the capitalist institutions
proved successful, but little attention was given to establishing stable commercial structures in their place until Vesenkha was established in 1918. War
Communism was itself an attempt to take the ideological hard line. Its
failure led Lenin to rethink his economic priorities. The introduction of
the New Economic Policy only confirmed that the Party was moving well
beyond the broad guidelines of Marxism. The introduction of individual
enterprise in agriculture and small industries, the opening up of international
trade and the purchase of machinery and expert advice from other countries
were signs that the hard-line ideology of War Communism had gone.

Of course much of this was misleading. The government continued to
maintain a firm control over every aspect of the country's everyday decisions. In
large-scale industry, and in its relations with foreign countries, the Central
Committee increased its control. There were other signs that all was not well in
the communist utopia. Russia was by no means becoming a classless society as
had been advocated by Marxist theory. The creation of the new bourgeoisie (the
Nepmen and the kulaks) sparked heated debate within the Party, especially as
the kulaks took advantage of the relaxed situation to press home their newly won
freedom from state control. Relations within the peasant community deteriorated,
although the move to cooperatives did strengthen the Party's control.

By late 1922 many Communist Party officials had had enough of the mixed
economy and called for its removal. Only Lenin's leadership maintained the
New Economic Policy for as long as it lasted. In 1924 Lenin died.

SUMMARY

- Marxism advocated:
  —the withering of the state apparatus
  —the dictatorship of the proletariat
  —the development of a classless society with communal control of
     the means of production.
- Marxism did not see these developments as being possible in
  Russia. Intermediate cap stage must dev. first.
- Leninism advocated: VANGUARD
  —the use of a strong party to implement Marxist theory
  —the need for a state apparatus to operate in the transitional
     period.
- Lenin saw this as all being possible in Russia.
- When Leninism was put into practice, the results were the
  strengthening of the Party, the growth of the state apparatus
  and the introduction of measures which actually fostered the
  development of social classes.

Research

Assess the policies and achievements of Lenin between 1917 and 1924. In your assessment examine each of the following:

- Leadership
- Policy direction
- Policy continuity
- Treatment of opposition
- Use of terror to enforce decisions
- Control over the Party
- Constitutional changes
- Security of the Revolution
- External relations

EXTRA WRITING

Structured Essay

a What measures were introduced as part of the New Economic Policy?

b How did the Communists attempt to deal with the problems which faced them in the period 1917–24?

c Why were the Communists still in power in Russia in 1924?

Essays

- How important was Lenin to the Bolshevik consolidation of power to 1924?

- To what extent was communist ideology being put into practice by the Bolsheviks as they consolidated their position between 1917 and 1924?

EXTRA READING

David Christian, *Power and Privilege*
J.N. Westwood, *Endurance and Endeavour*
G. Gill, *Stalinism*
Alan Wood, *Stalin and Stalinism*
I. Deutscher, *Stalin: A Political Biography*
I. Deutscher, *Trotsky*
T.A. Morris, *European History, 1848–1945*
P. Baker and J. Bassett, *Stalin's Revolution*
L. Kochan and A. Abraham, *The Making of Modern Russia*
R. Pipes, *Russia Under the Bolsheviks, 1919–1924*

THE PROBLEMS AND ISSUES

Consider the Problems and Issues:

Revolution and Counter-Revolution
Ideology in Theory and Practice
The Role of the Party and the State

in relation to the period 1918–24

Revolution is represented by: the Bolshevik Party, the Left SRs, Lenin and Trotsky, elements of the state (some factory workers and some of the armed forces).

Counter-revolution is represented by: the Whites, the Allies, kulaks, remnants of the old political parties, the Constituent Assembly.

The **theory** is the Marxist model: bourgeois period, the dictatorship of the proletariat followed by the withering of the state.

The **practice** is: there is no bourgeois period, there is the dictatorship of the Party rather than of the proletariat, and the state flourishes—there is a use of coercion/terror and the need to maintain control at all costs. Political pragmatism takes precedence over ideological purity (e.g. in the NEP).

The **Party** is represented by: the increasing power of the Central Executive Committee, the blurring of the division between Party positions and those in government and military as Party affiliation comes to dominate.

The **state** is theoretically in the hands of the All-Russian Congress of Soviets and its associated institutional structures. The state institutions are to control/direct the armed forces, the economy is dominated by bureaucrats who are increasingly the servants/members of the Party

---

Essay: WRITING THE ESSAY

What methods were used by the Bolsheviks to maintain their power to 1924? How successful were they in consolidating their position?

In answering this question you should consider the following:

BOLSHEVIK METHODOLOGY
Centralisation of control
SOVNARKOM and the Central Executive Committee
The CHEKA and the use of force
The Red Army
War Communism
The New Economic Policy
The growth of the bureaucracy
The growth of central Party control—the Tenth Party Congress

BOLSHEVIK SUCCESS
Make a judgement based on the following:

Elimination of all formal opposition
The withdrawal of Western and counter-revolutionary forces
The destruction of the Tsarist administrative state
State control of major industries, banking, foreign trade and transport
International acknowledgment of the regime's legitimacy
Versus
The growth of new middle-class groups
The continuing backwardness of agriculture
The continuing division between urban and rural
The movement away from strict Marxist ideology

Consider the actions of the following people:
Lenin, Trotsky, Stalin, Bukharin, Kamenev, Zinoviev, Tukhachevsky, Denikin, Kolchak

Finally consider the following two historians' views:

from J.N. Westwood, *Endurance and Endeavour*, pp. 281–2   SOURCE 3.Q

Not only had the Revolution occurred in a nation lacking the developed capitalistic society which Marx had envisaged, but the small proletariat had disappeared during the Civil War. True, there were urban workers, but few of them were the experienced and politically conscious men of 1917. The latter had been killed while fighting for or against the Bolsheviks in the Civil War, or had become Bolshevik officials and army officers, or had left the factories in favour of the countryside. The factory workers of the early twenties were largely ex-peasants, ill-educated, ill-disciplined, and not particularly interested in the party. Thus the Bolsheviks, who had regarded themselves as the vanguard of the proletariat, found themselves in the van with nothing to guard.

SOURCE 3.R

from L. Kochan and A. Abraham, *The Making of Modern Russia*, p. 340

The overall consequence [of the New Economic Policy] was an economy in which the State virtually monopolised industrial life, acted as the arbiter of commercial life, and left agricultural production under the control of an ever growing number of small producers. This was an inherently unstable mixture, as was shown by wild fluctuations in prices. It seemed that the peasant producer held the whip hand over the industrial proletariat. The peasant had only the obligation of a taxpayer to the State. The town worker, on the other hand, was exposed to all the hazards of food rationing and unemployment. At this time the quip was current that the initials N.E.P. denoted 'New Exploitation of the Proletariat'. By early 1924 there were nearly one and a quarter million unemployed, the result of a ruthless drive to re-establish sound money and the profitability of individual enterprises. At its height the total was to reach two million, over a quarter of the Russian proletariat. Other casualties of the new market rationality were Lunacharsky's efforts at providing universal free education on progressive lines, Semashko's attempts to provide a universal free health service, and Kollontai's efforts at replacing women's domestic labour by providing communal facilities for housework. All this came as a terrible shock to many Communists; the disillusionment suffered by the rank and file workers must have been as great. Driven by unemployment to set themselves up in small businesses, they were naturally drawn to ask whether the capitalist mode of production was such a bad thing after all.

Stalin's Struggle over Power

At the end of this topic you should attempt to answer the following question:
Why did Stalin win the struggle over power in the period 1924–28?

THE PROBLEMS AND ISSUES

In this topic the relevant Problems and Issues for analysis in the HSC are:
Ideology in Theory and Practice
The Role of the Party and the State
The **ideology** may be seen as Marxism, and how this is altered by Lenin and then by Stalin.
The **party** is the Communist Party, while the **state** is the system of government and the institutional structures which allow that government to function.

TIME LINE

1917	Stalin appointed Commissar for Nationalities (a position he holds until 1923)
1919	Establishment of the three executive organs of government: Politburo, Orgburo, Secretariat—the General Secretary of the Communist Party was the only full member of all three bodies
	Stalin appointed Commissar of State Control
1920	Stalin appointed Commissar of Workers' and Peasants' Inspection
1922	
April	Stalin appointed General Secretary of the Central Committee of the Party
May	Lenin suffers first stroke
December	Lenin suffers second stroke
	Lenin's Testament written (also known as Lenin's Letter to the Congress)
1923	
March	Lenin suffers third stroke
1924	
January	Death of Lenin—succeeded by Alexei Rykov as Premier of USSR
	Stalin begins manoeuvres to isolate and block Trotsky in the Politburo: Zinoviev and Kamenev form triumvirate with Stalin to rule USSR— Rykov and Tomsky also anti-Trotsky
May	Lenin's Testament read to a closed session of selected delegates to

	Thirteenth Party Congress
1925	Zinoviev, Kamenev and Trotsky attack moderates in Politburo (Bukharin, Rykov and Tomsky) over pace of industrialisation in NEP—Stalin supports moderates
	Fourteenth Party Congress—all left-wing motions defeated by large majorities
	Stalin and Bukharin form duumvirate to rule USSR
	Size of Politburo increased from 6 to 9: new members all supporters of Stalin
1926	Trotsky, Zinoviev and Kamenev combine for first time to denounce lack of debate in Party—they are condemned as 'traitors of the revolution' by Stalin
	Zinoviev removed as Chairman of Leningrad Soviet
	Kamenev removed as Chairman of Moscow Soviet
	Zinoviev expelled from Communist Party
	Trotsky and Kamenev removed from Politburo
1927	Kamenev expelled from Communist Party
	Trotsky expelled from Communist Party
	Stalin has control of majority of Politburo
	Stalin turns against Bukharin—Bukharin and supporters labelled 'right-wing deviationists'
1928	Purge of Moscow branch of Party
	Bukharin resigns as editor of *Pravda*
	Bukharin, Rykov and Tomsky removed from Politburo
	Trotsky exiled to Central Asia
	Stalin sole surviving member of Lenin's original Politburo
1929	Trotsky expelled from Soviet Union

FOCUS QUESTIONS

Who were the major players in the struggle over power following Lenin's death?

What advantages did Stalin possess over his opponents?

What methods did Stalin use to consolidate his position?

Were the events of 1924–28 a struggle 'for' power, or a struggle 'over' power?

STRUGGLE 'OVER' POWER

THE TRADITIONAL NOTION of 'a struggle for power' is inaccurate when applied to the Soviet Union following Lenin's death. Instead, it was a case of individuals and/or factions who already had power manipulating events and situations in order to ensure that other individuals and/or factions did not gain more power. In this game of move and counter-move it was Stalin who proved himself the consummate player.

BARRIERS TO STALIN'S RISE

Stalin's rise to the top of the political ladder had to overcome a large obstacle from the start: the negative opinion of Stalin that was Lenin's legacy to the Party. While Lenin had supported Stalin's appointment as Commissar of Nationalities (1917), Commissar of State Control (1919), Commissar of Workers' and Peasants' Inspection (1920), his membership of the Politburo, and his position as General Secretary of the Party (1922), by 1924

Alexei Rykov, Chairman of Sovnarkom, Premier of the USSR

Leon Trotsky, Commissar of War

Nikolai Bukharin, in charge of propaganda

Lev Kamenev, Chairman of Politburo

Grigori Zinoviev, Chairman of Comintern

Mikhail Tomsky, in charge of trade unions

Lenin was in fact calling for Stalin's removal. This was set out in a document officially known as Lenin's Letter to the Congress (usually referred to as Lenin's Testament). This statement was written in 1922 after Lenin suffered the first of a series of strokes that culminated in his death:

> By stability of the Central Committee . . . I mean measures against a split. I have in mind stability as a guarantee against a split in the future, and I intend to deal here with a few ideas concerning personal qualities. I think that from this standpoint the prime factors in the question of stability are such members of the C.C. as Stalin and Trotsky. I think relations between them make up the greater part of the danger of a split, which could be avoided, and this purpose, in my opinion, would be served, among other things, by increasing the numbers of the C.C. members to 50 or 100.

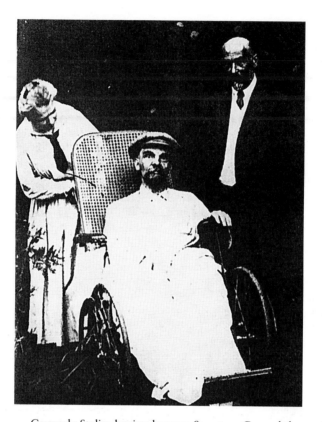

Lenin, pictured in 1923

Comrade Stalin, having become Secretary General, has unlimited authority concentrated in his hands, and I am not sure that he will always be capable of using that power with sufficient caution. Comrade Trotsky, on the other hand . . . is distinguished not only by his outstanding ability. He is personally perhaps the most capable man in the present C.C., but he has displayed excessive self-assurance and shown excessive preoccupation with the purely administrative side of the work. These two qualities of the two outstanding leaders of the present C.C. can inadvertently lead to a split, and if our Party does not take steps to avert this, the split may come unexpectedly.

I shall not give further appraisals of the personal qualities of other members of the C.C., [but] recall that the October episode with Zinoviev and Kamenev was no accident, but neither can the blame for it be laid upon them personally, any more than non-Bolshevism can upon Trotsky. Speaking of the young C.C. members, I wish to say a few words about Bukharin and Pyatakov. They are, in my opinion, the most outstanding figures (among the youngest ones) and the following must be borne in mind about them: Bukharin is not only a most valuable and major theorist of the Party; he is also rightly considered the favourite of the whole Party, but his theoretical views can be classified as Marxist only with great reserve . . . As for Pyatakov, he is unquestionably a man of outstanding will and outstanding ability, but shows too much zeal for administrating and the administrative side of the work to be relied upon in a serious political matter.
25 December 1922

Postscript
Stalin is too rude and this defect, although quite tolerable in our midst and in dealings amongst us communists, becomes intolerable in a General Secretary. That is why I suggest that the comrades think about a way of removing Stalin from the post and appointing another man in his stead who in all other respects differs from Comrade Stalin in having only one advantage, namely that of being more tolerant, more loyal, more polite and more considerate to the comrades, less capricious etc. This circumstance may appear to be a negligible detail. But I think that from the standpoint of safeguards against a split and from the standpoint of what I wrote about the relationship between Stalin and Trotsky it is not a detail, or it is a detail which can assume decisive importance.
4 January 1923

However, Lenin's final thoughts and instructions remained a secret until the Thirteenth Party Congress in May 1924. Here Lenin's Testament was read to representatives of the Party in a closed meeting. Kamenev and Zinoviev (the two most senior Communists following Lenin's death) allied themselves with Stalin to neutralise the letter. They did so not because they supported Stalin but because they opposed Trotsky. They feared that the release of the Testament would bring Trotsky to power as Lenin's successor.

Stalin's position as General Secretary of the Communist Party also gave him power that he could use for his own advancement. The General Secretary was the only full member of the three executive arms of the Communist Party administration: the Politburo, the Orgburo and the Secretariat. He was uniquely placed to control the passage of business in the Politburo and the appointment of people to responsible positions. He could even manipulate the membership of the Communist Party itself. This is usually seen as crucial in Stalin's success: the Politburo was made up of people who were extremely powerful within the Party in their own right. Each had his own channels of

Lenin's mausoleum in Red Square, Moscow

THE STRUGGLE OVER POWER

STAGE 1: STALIN ATTACKS THE LEFT

THE LEFT OPPOSITION
Trotsky
Zinoviev
Kamenev
Strongly disagreed with continuation of NEP – urged rapid and immediate industrialisation, along with collectivisation of farms and use of force to ensure the peasants produced enough food to feed the cities – urged use of 'shock brigades' to build factories, power stations, railways – argued that money be obtained by taxing peasants

STALIN

THE RIGHTISTS
Bukharin
Rykov
Tomsky
Urged the continuation of NEP for at least twenty years – this was seen as the way to encourage peasants to produce more food which they could sell to the towns for profit; the town population would grow and move into factories to produce consumer goods for peasants to buy: the result was to be prosperity for both peasants and townspeople

- 1923: Stalin purged Party membership of 'lukewarm members'
- 1924: influx of new members ('Lenin enrolment') – the 'Stalin-admitted' members outnumbered the old Bolsheviks
- Stalin, Zinoviev and Kamenev formed TRIUMVIRATE to block Trotsky
- Lenin was 'deified' – any criticism of Party policy denounced as heresy and led to explulsion from Party – discipline and obedience became more important than revolutionary zeal
- Trotsky:
  - criticised the cult of Leninism
  - criticised Stalin
  - failed to attend Lenin's funeral
– his support was undermined + Stalin reminded the Party that Trotsky had only been a Bolshevik since mid-1917
- 1925: Zinoviev and Kamenev sided with Trotsky re NEP – Stalin moved to support the moderate Rightists – at 1925 Party Congress all left-wing motions were defeated – Zinoviev and Kamenev were removed from Moscow and Leningrad Soviets – Stalin increased the size of the Politburo – Zinoviev and Kamenev were denounced as 'traitors to the revolution' – Zinoviev and Kamenev, along with Trotsky, expelled from Party by 1927

STAGE 2: STALIN ATTACKS THE RIGHT

STALIN

Stalin:
'We have internal enemies. We have external enemies. This, comrades, must not be forgotten a single moment.'

THE RIGHTISTS
Bukharin
Rykov
Tomsky
Urged the continuation on NEP for at least twenty years – this was seen as the way to encourage peasants to produce more food which they could sell to the towns for profit, the town population would grow and move into factories to produce consumer goods for peasants to buy: the result was to be prosperity for both peasants and townspeople

- 1925: DUUMVIRATE of Bukharin and Stalin – controlled Politburo following disgrace of Zinoviev and Kamenev (with Stalin able to dominate if he so wished)
- end of 1927: Stalin abandoned Bukharin's economic policy using the argument that two good years of harvest had actually led to a fall in grain supplies as the peasants withheld grain to force up prices – Stalin saw this as capitalism at the expense of the cities – felt that industrialisation must take precedence over agriculture
- 'Extraordinary Measures' introduced to force kulaks into line:
  - Article 107 of Criminal Code: concealing grain a crime
  - all grain hoards liable to confiscation
  - soldiers sent into countryside to find grain and punish hoarders
  – this led to panic in countryside and fighting in some areas
- Stalin announced sabotage at Shakty Mines on Don – he declared war against 'internal enemies' – Bukharin denounced Stalin as a tyrant – Bukharin and his followers were condemned as 'right-wing deviationists'
- end of 1928: purge of Moscow branch of Party – Bukharin resigned as editor of *Pravda* – Bukharin, Rykov, Tomsky expelled from Politburo by 1929

communication and influence. Stalin's ultimate victory lay in the influence he gained over the Party's personnel.

From the establishment of Bolshevik Party rule in Russia in 1917, appointment had been seen as more important than election in the filling of important posts. The Orgburo and Secretariat had wide-ranging powers to make direct appointments and positions held in local-level bodies were subject to scrutiny from these two central bodies. Stalin was able to ensure the appointment of his own supporters to positions of responsibility throughout the political structure. Even when positions were not filled by established supporters the system was such that the appointee developed a sense of gratitude and obligation to Stalin. He gained great influence over the regional Party apparatus and with this came control of delegate selection for the annual Party Congress. The Congress thus became a large, pliable assembly which unquestioningly supported Stalin. It was this process which was at the heart of the vilification and heckling which met all who spoke against Stalin from the Thirteenth Congress (1924) onwards.

The Party delegates, however, still retained some autonomy and were technically free to speak and vote as they wished. Stalin had to use other methods to reinforce his support base. One method was to associate himself with the authority and philosophy of Lenin. Stalin set about creating and strengthening the 'cult of Lenin': the placing of Lenin's body in a mausoleum in Red Square, and the renaming of Petrograd as Leningrad are two examples. All aspirants for top offices in the Soviet Union attempted to

Josef Stalin, General Secretary of the Communist Party

associate themselves with the dead leader. They continually invoked Lenin's name and cited his writings when seeking support for a particular policy line. They believed that whoever was perceived to be the best Leninist would be the one best placed to inherit Lenin's authority. Initially Trotsky and Zinoviev, as well as Stalin, attempted to do this, but there was a clear difference in the image they projected. Trotsky and Zinoviev portrayed themselves as Lenin's colleagues, co-workers and equals. In contrast, Stalin presented himself as Lenin's disciple. With the growing deification and veneration of Lenin, it was Stalin's approach which gained support within the Party. First Trotsky, then Zinoviev, and finally Bukharin fell victim to this pressure from Stalin, and when the 'cult of Stalin' burst onto the scene in 1929 it was the logical extension of what had gone before. Stalin was able to link himself inextricably with the cult of Lenin and thus assume unimpeachable authority—because he was the continuer of Lenin, as well as his best pupil, he thereby inherited Lenin's authority.

The appointment procedure operating within the Party assisted Stalin in another way. Opposition groups within the Party called for greater democratisation, a return to open debate, and criticised the increasing centralisation of power into the hands of the Party secretaries and bureaucrats. However, any replacement of 'appointment' with 'election' for Party positions would call into question the power and privileges of those already in these positions. These incumbents were therefore encouraged to throw their weight behind Stalin.

Stalin's position was also strengthened by changes in Party membership during the 1920s. At the Tenth Party Congress in 1921, the Party had 732 000 members; by 1930 this had grown by nearly a million. In 1924 and 1925 Stalin had supervised the 'Lenin enrolments' into the Party, while also instigating a number of 'purges' of less desirable members. The result was that the large numbers of people who joined the Party were less ideologically aware and were less well educated than the 'traditional' Bolsheviks. The original members had joined the Party when there had been a 'cause' to fight for and were driven by the Marxist ideology of world revolution; these new members were joining when the Party was already in power. They responded to Stalin's more practical and understandable directives rather than the scholarly, ideologically driven arguments of his opponents. He spoke to the ill-educated Party masses in a way they understood and they responded by giving unquestioning support.

Another source of support for Stalin was the philosophy which he espoused. Stalin's notion of 'socialism in one country' argued that the Soviet Union could successfully build socialism without having to rely on outside assistance. This gave a sense of meaning to those who had recently joined the Party: unlike the doctrine of world revolution which seemed to promise nothing but waiting for rescue by the proletariat of Western Europe, this doctrine promised success through their own efforts. It tapped directly into the nationalist sentiments of the Russians. Similarly, Stalin's rejection of the NEP at the end of the 1920s would strike a responsive chord. The gradualism and moderation of this economic policy was seen by many as only strengthening the hold of capitalism. Smashing the reliance upon the petit bourgeois peasantry by introducing state-directed industrialisation and collectivisation rekindled the sense of commitment and enthusiasm.

The entire notion of Party also worked in Stalin's favour. At the Tenth Party Congress in 1921 all 'factions' (internal opposition groups) were banned—Party solidarity was seen as paramount. Thus Trotsky, Zinoviev and others—because of their sense of loyalty to the 'Party'—attempted to work against Stalin through the Party's own apparatus and structure. As has been pointed out, this was where Stalin's own strength lay! Similarly, none of his opponents made full use of his own power base as each was outside the bounds of the Party: Trotsky did not use the army, Zinoviev did not use the Communist International, Tomsky did not use the trade unions. Yet, by remaining within the bounds of the Party the opposition further breached the anti-factional decision of 1921. Stalin could present himself as positive and constructive while the opposition always appeared as negative and destructive.

Finally, Stalin's great skill as a politician must be acknowledged. He was able to outwit his opponents by attacking when the time was opportune and biding his time if necessary. His timing, his building of alliances of convenience and his use of the political resources available showed a skilled political practitioner at work. In contrast, his opponents appeared clumsy and politically naive. They made mistakes, failed to take advantage of any opportunities that offered and eventually fell victim to their own inadequacies.

THE TENTH PARTY CONGRESS

SUMMARY

- Stalin's rise to power in the Soviet Union was a complex process with many causes. Some of the more important are:
- He was a tireless worker and his early career had been supported by Lenin
- His skills in politics and administration were highly relevant to the tasks of the 1920s
- His position as General Secretary of the Communist Party enabled him to promote his own supporters and control crucial votes
- His economic and political pragmatism enabled him to outmanoeuvre the Left and then the Right, while always staying with the majority in the Politburo
- He was ruthless in his treatment of his opponents
- His opponents played into his hands and underestimated the threat from Stalin until it was too late to act effectively against him
- He manipulated events to create a sense of crisis or emergency so that his opponents could be accused of being lukewarm about the revolutionary cause

- As General Secretary, he always claimed to speak for the Party, and his opponents were therefore hesitant to attack him as to do so would be to attack the Party—thus no public debate took place
- He had the support of ruthless, shrewd men with strong power bases of their own
- His contempt for the old Bolshevik Left and his impatience with the moderate Right was shared by many other leading Communists
- His 'deification' of Lenin and his deliberate association of himself with Lenin meant other members of the Party were reluctant to criticise Stalin for fear of therefore being seen to be critical of Lenin.

KEY PERSONALITIES, GROUPS, TERMS

Josef Stalin: Communist leader; born 1879, died 1953; real name Josef Vissarionovich Djugashvili; native of Georgia; educated in a seminary; expelled for spreading Marxism; joined the underground political movement in late 1890s; arrested and sent to Siberia; escaped 1904; rearrested and escaped five times prior to 1914; 1907, supervised the robbery of the State Bank of Tiflis and dismissed from Social Democratic Party; released from exile in 1917; returned to Petrograd in March 1917; edited *Pravda* and called for immediate commencement of peace negotiations; passed a motion calling for all revolutionary groups to combine against the Provisional Government; supported Lenin in his call for a coup in July 1917; worked closely with Lenin in the organisation of the Bolshevik Revolution of October/November 1917; appointed Commissar for Nationality Affairs—signed Declaration of the Rights of the Nations of Russia; instrumental in the closure of the Constituent Assembly, 1918; annoyed Trotsky with his involvement in the Civil War; March 1919, appointed to Politburo; April 1922, appointed General Secretary of the Party; used his positions within the Party to undermine Trotsky and other opponents following Lenin's death in 1924; 1928, introduced First Five Year Plan; 1930s, instituted the purges and show trials; 1936, introduced new Constitution; 1941, became Chairman of Council of Peoples' Commissars and took command of Soviet armed forces; 1942, made first of many calls for the opening of a 'second front'; died 1953.

Nikolai Ivanovich Bukharin: Bolshevik revolutionary; born 1888, died 1938; friend and associate of Lenin; returned to Russia from exile in 1917 and became editor of *Pravda*; moderate in his beliefs, advocating slow and gradual progress of the revolution through methods such as the New Economic Policy; ousted from the Politburo in 1929; continued to operate as a member of the Right Opposition; editor of *Izvestiya*, 1934–37; executed during the purges 1938.

Mikhail Tomsky: Bolshevik revolutionary; born 1880, died 1936; Politburo member and head of the trade union organisation; with Bukharin and Rykov he made up the moderate Rights in the Politburo; 1922, assisted in organising the show trials of the Socialist Revolutionaries; opposed to the centralisation of wages; 1928, joined Bukharin and Rykov in protesting at Stalin's Urals–Siberian method of grain requisitioning; dismissed when he criticised Stalin's abandonment of the New Economic Policy; continued to try to protect the union movement; his demands were swept aside during the period of industrialisation; committed suicide 1936.

Alexei Ivanovich Rykov: Bolshevik revolutionary; born 1881, died 1938; originally a Social Democrat, he joined the Bolsheviks in 1905; became a fanatical supporter of Lenin but sided with Zinoviev and Kamenev in opposing Lenin's calls for a revolution in October/November 1917; appointed Commissar for Internal Affairs; 1917–24, head of Supreme Economic Council (Vesenkha); argued for inclusion of other socialist parties in the government; one of the architects of War Communism despite lack of business/economics background; called for compulsory grain deliveries and close contact with rural cooperatives; 1921, appointed Deputy Chairman of Special Committee for Famine Relief; 1924–30, succeeded Lenin as Premier of the Soviet Union—dismissed by Stalin; 1931, returned to government after withdrawing his opposition to Stalin's policies; 1936, charged with being part of an assassination attempt on Stalin; tried and executed.

EXERCISES

1. a What is the difference between a struggle for power, and a struggle over power?
  b Which is the more appropriate description for the events in Russia between 1924 and 1928?
2. Why did Stalin not face a united opposition?
3. What role was played by socialist/revolutionary ideology in the events of 1924–28?
4. Why was Lenin deified? What was the effect of this deification?
5. Who or what was most responsible for Stalin's victories over his opponents in the Politburo?

DOCUMENT STUDY   (No. 10)

Read the following sources and answer the questions which follow.

A view of Stalin   SOURCE 4.A
from British historian A.J.P. Taylor, *The War Lords*, published in 1978
Most people, I suppose, regard Stalin as a monster. Khrushchev said of him: 'Like Peter the Great, he fought barbarism with barbarism.' Yet, for a tyrant, he was curiously unobtrusive, almost unassertive. During the Bolshevik revolution, though he played a part, it was a modest one. Another participant, looking back, said: 'All I remember of Stalin is that he seemed like a grey blur—somebody you would hardly notice against the landscape.'
Of all the war lords I have talked about, or am going to talk about, Stalin was the only

one who saw high command in the First World War or, rather, in the wars of intervention which followed it. He distinguished himself by his defence of Tsaritsyn, which as a result became known as Stalingrad. He also served in Poland. He was extremely insubordinate, taking little notice of the instructions he received from the commissar for war, Trotsky. He even took little notice of the instructions he received from Lenin, the leader of the revolution. He went his own way and stood up for himself: not conduct he would have tolerated from his own generals in the Second World War.

It was not until 1928, some ten years after the Bolshevik revolution, that Stalin manoeuvred himself into supreme power. His title remained general secretary of the Communist Party and, officially, he had no governmental position; but there can be no doubt that from 1928 he was dictator of the Soviet Union.

SOURCE 4.B

A view of Trotsky

from British historian A.J.P. Taylor, *Europe: Grandeur and Decline*, published in 1967

... he was the only Marxist who has possessed literary genius. Time and again the force of this genius posed problems that were still unperceived by others and even pointed to solutions that were unwelcome to Trotsky himself. Immediately after the revolution of 1905, when he was still in prison, he discovered the central dilemma which a victorious Russian revolution would face and which indeed the Soviet Union still faces. How was revolutionary Russia to maintain itself in a hostile world? Backwardness made revolution easy, but survival difficult. Trotsky gave already the answer to which he adhered all his life: permanent revolution. The Russian revolution must touch off revolutions elsewhere. 'The working class of Russia will become the initiator of the liquidation of capitalism on a global scale.' It was in this belief that Trotsky led the revolution of 1917, defied the German empire at Brest-Litovsk, and composed the most ringing phrases in the foundation manifesto of the Communist International. But what if the more advanced proletariat failed to respond? It was useless to maintain for long Trotsky's earliest answer: 'Luckily for mankind, this is impossible.' ... the spirit of man was irrepressible in him. Colonel Robins, The American Red Cross representative at Petrograd, pronounced history's verdict: 'A four-kind son-of-a-bitch, but the greatest Jew since Jesus Christ.'

SOURCE 4.C

Extract from Leon Trotsky, *On the Suppressed Testament of Lenin*, published in 1932
In the eyes of Lenin, Stalin's value was wholly in the sphere of Party administration and machine manoeuvring. But even here Lenin had substantial reservations ... Stalin meanwhile was more and more broadly and indiscriminately using the possibilities of the revolutionary dictatorship for the recruiting of people personally obligated and devoted to him. In his position as General Secretary he became the dispenser of favour and fortune ...

Photograph of Stalin and Lenin in 1922. For many years thought to be a fake, but proved to be genuine by the finding of the original negative   **SOURCE 4.D**

Questions

a **i)** According to Source 4.A, in what way was Stalin a 'grey blur'?
   ii) According to Source 4.B, what was the central dilemma faced by the Russian Revolution?
   iii) According to Source 4.C, what position held by Stalin gave him such great influence over the Party?

b Using Source 4.C and your own knowledge, outline the positions held by Stalin which gave him the advantage in the struggle over power.

c Examine Source 4.A, Source 4.C and Source 4.D. How useful would each of these sources be to an historian attempting to understand the relationships between individuals in the Politburo in the years to 1928? (In your answer you must consider the nature, motive, origin and audience of each source as well as its content.)

d Using all four sources and your own knowledge, how did the attitudes and actions of other people contribute to Stalin's rise to power? In your answer you should consider the role of people other than Stalin.

EXTRA WRITING

Structured Essay

a What were the beliefs of the various factions that made up the Politburo at the time of Lenin's death?

b How did Stalin manipulate developments in the Politburo between 1924 and 1928?

c Why was Stalin successful in achieving the leadership of the Soviet Union by 1928?

Essay

Why was there a power struggle following the death of Lenin in 1924?

EXTRA READING

David Christian, *Power and Privilege*
J.N. Westwood, *Endurance and Endeavour*
G. Gill, *Stalinism*
Alan Wood, *Stalin and Stalinism*
I. Deutscher, *Stalin: A Political Biography*
I. Deutscher, *Trotsky*
T.A. Morris, *European History, 1848–1945*
P. Baker and J. Bassett, *Stalin's Revolution*
L. Kochan and A. Abraham, *The Making of Modern Russia*
Martin McCauley, *Stalin and Stalinism*

THE PROBLEMS AND ISSUES

Consider the Problems and Issues:

Ideology in Theory and Practice
The Role of the Party and the State

in relation to the period 1924 to 1928:

Ideology saw the emergence of the notion of 'socialism in one country' as opposed to the Marxist **theory** of world-wide revolution—there is the debate between Bukharin and the rightists (who are devotees of Marx and argue that moderation and time are necessary and the kulaks/bourgeois are part of the process) against Trotsky and the left who argue for rapid change. Notice the political manipulation by Stalin of one side against the other.

Be aware of the ways in which the **state** becomes increasingly subservient to the **Party** and the Party is being increasingly dominated by Stalin at the policy-making level—take into consideration the arguments of historians such as Gill who point out that at grass-roots/regional level the local loyalties dominate and central control is lessened.

Essay:
Why did Stalin win the struggle over power in the period 1924–28?

When answering this question you should consider the following factors:

FACTORS WHICH WERE CONTROLLED BY STALIN
The positions Stalin held in the Party hierarchy
Stalin's manipulation of Party membership
Stalin's deification of Lenin and his presentation of himself as Lenin's disciple
Stalin's political skills
Stalin's ruthless and tireless pursuit of power

FACTORS WHICH PLAYED INTO STALIN'S HANDS
The embargo placed on Lenin's Testament
The attitude to Trotsky
The lack of cooperation between Stalin's potential opponents
The role played by Zinoviev, Kamenev, Rykov, Tomsky, Bukharin
The nature of the Communist Party—the rules governing Party unity and controlling debate

Consider carefully the actions of the following people in the period 1924–28:
Trotsky, Stalin, Zinoviev, Kamenev, Rykov, Tomsky, Bukharin, and Lenin (through his Testament)

Finally consider the following historical sources:

From L. Kochan and A. Abraham, *The Making of Modern Russia*, pp. 348–50   SOURCE 4.E
Stalin employed the time-honoured methods of 'divide and rule' against his rivals. The question is: why did these methods succeed? . . . it is Trotsky who suggests the answer: 'Stalin's first qualification was a contemptuous attitude towards ideas'. . . they [the Party leaders] all expected Lenin's successor to be a theoretician—the Revolution demanded it—and in this respect Stalin was clearly not a threat . . . [but] the negative side of Marxist thinking is the insistence that since all thought is a manifestation of the class struggle opposing opinions must represent hostile class struggles. This completely blinded the oligarchs to the fact that their differences were minimal in comparison with their common interests . . . To the 'right' Trotsky . . . must represent the reaction of the bourgeois intelligentsia. To the 'left' . . . Bukharin . . . represented the reaction of the peasant bourgeoisie. It was not, therefore that Stalin had too little respect for ideas; his opponents just had too much.
Stalin had his own use for ideas—as weapons. He was adept at picking up other people's ideas and using them as labels. Zinoviev also made a fetish of Leninism, but it was Stalin who profited from it; his own differences with Lenin were minor compared with the fact that Trotsky had not joined the party until 1917, while Zinoviev and Kamenev had denounced the October revolution . . . On more than one occasion, his opponents suggested diluting his control over the Secretariat, but backed off when he offered to resign. He was a master of flattery and arcane manoeuvre . . . By abusing his authority as Gensek, and by sheer force of personality, he early acquired the assistance of the security apparatus . . . It was only in defeat that Stalin's rivals began to understand the significance of 'the personality factor' in Soviet politics. On his defeat in 1928, Bukharin confided to Kamenev his fears about 'this Genghis Khan who is going to kill us all . . .'

From Alan Wood, *Stalin and Stalinism*, pp. 28–9   SOURCE 4.F
Although intellectually Trotsky's inferior, Stalin was by far the cleverer politician. He had

outmanoeuvred his arch-rival on every possible front, not least through his skilful manipulation of the 'cult' of Leninism which was established immediately after the Bolshevik leader's death and in which Stalin, the ex-seminarist, appeared in the role of high priest. In death Lenin was immortalised, almost deified, and a whole idolatrous cult built around his name, with all the ritual trappings, ceremonial, sacred texts and symbols, mythology and hagiography of a major religion. Lenin the atheist, humanist, and materialist would have turned in his grave, if he had been granted the dignity of having one. Instead his body was artificially preserved and placed on public display . . . Like any self-respecting religion, the cult of Leninism also had its early heretics and apostates. Having successfully excommunicated them, Stalin now proceeded to lead the Soviet people into the promised land of Socialism in One Country. The methods he employed were to turn that country into a purgatory of human suffering and grief.

SOURCE 4.G

From Alan Bullock, *Hitler and Stalin: Parallel Lives*, p.200

In the years following Lenin's death, Stalin played a waiting game, leaving it to the other side to move first, and then exploiting its mistakes. Even when the split between them was open, and despite many early threats and warnings, it was not until the end of 1927 that he moved to expel Trotsky and Zinoviev from the party. In the final phase, when he had destroyed the left Opposition and turned against Bukharin and the right, he took great care to keep the quarrel confined within the inner circle until he was sure, after more than a year, that he had isolated Bukharin and only then moved against him in public. Stalin's persistence was phenomenal; so, in this period, was his patience and caution.

Stalin's
Revolution

At the end of this topic you should attempt to answer the following question:
What evidence would you use to provide a balanced view of Stalinism?

THE PROBLEMS AND ISSUES

In this topic the relevant Problems and Issues for analysis in the HSC are:
Revolution and Counter-Revolution
Ideology in Theory and Practice
The Role of the Party and the State
Changes in Society
Collectivisation
Stalinism and Totalitarianism

Revolution may be seen as the way in which Stalin's regime alters the political, social and economic system in a more radical way than Lenin. **Counter-revolution** may be seen in the forces (both within and outside of the Party) that are opposed to Stalin.

The **ideology** may be seen as Marxism, and how this is altered by Stalin.

The **Party** is the Communist Party, while the **state** is the system of government and the institutional structures which allow that government to function.

The **changes in society** involve the alteration of the living and working patterns of the people who live within the Soviet Union.

Collectivisation involves the agricultural changes introduced by Stalin.

Totalitarianism involves examining the nature/extent of Stalinist control over the population of the Soviet Union and the effects of this control.

TIME LINE

1926   Stalin gains control of the Politburo with the defeat of the 'Left Opposition'

1928   Forcible grain requisitioning begun—the Urals-Siberian method
        Shakhty show trial of industrial 'saboteurs'
        The decision is taken to collectivise agriculture
        The First Five-Year Plan begins

1929
  June/July End of the New Economic Policy—rationing of all foodstuffs
        Organisation of the first Motor Tractor Station
        Collectivisation of agriculture begins
        Central Committee decides that 'One-man management' in industry be established, and that the 'enterprise' be established as the basic industrial unit of production

1930		
	February	'Dizzy with success' speech by Stalin
	April	Party begins using 'shock workers' to increase production levels
	July	'Dekulakisation' begins
1930/31		Trials of 'industrial spies' begin
1931		Stalin speaks out against 'egalitarianism' of wages
1932		Second Five-Year Plan begins
	January	The powers of Vesenkha divided up between other government organisations
	April	Death penalty decree passed for stealing from collectives
	May	Decree allowing peasants on collectives to sell surplus food on the market
		78 per cent of all machine tools installed are imported
1933		State grain procurements from peasants increase from 18.5 million tonnes to 22.6 million tonnes
		Famine devastates the USSR
		Defence spending 3.4 per cent of total budget expenditure
1934		Death of Kirov
		Beginning of the great purges
1935		Alexei Stakhanov, a miner, produces 14 times more than the average level for one worker
		83 per cent of peasants in collectives and 94 per cent of total crop area collectivised
		Food rationing abolished
		Kolkhoz declared a voluntary organisation by the Central Committee
	December	Central Committee urges planners and managers to revise technical and output levels upwards
1936		Stalin's Constitution promulgated
		Zinoviev and Kamenev brought to trial
		Defence spending 16.1 per cent of total budget expenditure
1937		Reduction in investment and consequent decline in industrial production
		Less than 10 per cent of all machine tools installed are imported
		Beginning of the Third Five-Year Plan
1938		Maternity leave lowered from 112 to 70 days per annum
		Labour Books introduced to control movement of labour
		Trial of Rykov and Bukharin
1939		Outbreak of Second World War
1940		Expenditure on defence 32.6 per cent of total budgetary expenditure
		Fees for secondary and tertiary studies introduced
		Decrees on labour use, conscription and absenteeism
1941		Outbreak of war with Germany

Industrialisation

FOCUS QUESTIONS Despite the enormous problems facing the Soviet Union in 1929 it was industrialised by 1941. How had this industrialisation taken place?
What were the consequences of this industrialisation?
To what extent was Russia industrialised by 1941?

BACKGROUND 1917–28

RUSSIAN POLITICS in the 1920s was dominated by a struggle over power within the Communist Party. Central to this debate was the question of economic growth. From its earliest days the dilemma was how best to juggle the pressure for industrial growth against the demands of the peasantry, most of whom sought only the freedom to produce their crops and tend their animals. Lenin generally favoured maintaining good relations with the peasants. This point of view was further promoted by Bukharin in the Politburo after Lenin's death.

From the days of the October/November Revolution the Communist control at the grass-roots level was never fully secure. By 1924 the Party had consolidated its rule, but to the majority of the people it was far away in Moscow. Certain elements of the population came to grudgingly accept the Communist government during the difficult days of the Civil War, but it could be said that the great majority remained neutral towards their new masters. The Communists might have controlled the railways, the large industrial enterprises and the armed forces, but not the hearts and minds of the people.

There were also differences within the ranks of the Communist Party. Discipline during the Civil War and the emergence of Stalin as leader had undermined the autonomy of the local soviets and focused increasing power and control in the hands of the Party functionaries. The Party apparatus grew increasingly hierarchic and bureaucratic.

The chief goal of the government was ostensibly the creation of socialism. The old order had been overthrown and the Bolshevik leadership believed that this would foster a revolution abroad, with this international proletarian revolution coming to the economic assistance of Russia. This proved to be a false hope.

Ravaged by a combination of civil war and an economic policy based on coercion, by 1921 Russia was devastated: famine and deprivation were rife and revolt was common in both city and countryside. The palliative of the New Economic Policy saw an immediate improvement in production levels, but members of the Communist leadership recognised that these short run gains were insufficient to fuel a long-term modernisation program based on industrialisation. Some even feared that the 'proletariat' was being eliminated and that the economy was becoming too dependent upon the cooperation of unskilled landless labourers and bourgeois capitalists. In these circumstances how was the Soviet state to be modernised? How were the new socialist rulers going to create the climate for sustained economic growth? How was the finance to be raised? Who was going to pay?

BUKHARIN'S MODERATE POLICIES

Nikolai Bukharin argued that this would be achieved only by encouraging peasant prosperity: allowing them to produce what they desired, taxing them lightly and assisting them to sell their grain to the government, who would then exchange it for foreign currency. In such a way, peasant incomes would increase, the government would gain the capital to invest in industry and there would be a growth in the production of capital goods. It was a policy which involved moderate development, little social dislocation and a continuation of the New Economic Policy.

Opposed to Bukharin were those who argued that while this policy might return Russia to its pre-war production levels, it would provide little industrial capital for future growth. Trotsky and Preobrazhensky denounced Bukharin's scheme, claiming that it would place Russia at the mercy of the capitalist nations and put the economy in the hands of the anti-proletarian forces led by the kulaks and the Nepmen. They believed that for the Soviet state to realise its economic potential a thorough overhaul and modernisation program would have to take place. This would involve the abandonment of the New Economic Policy, higher taxation of the rural classes and rapid industrialisation.

STALIN ABANDONS BUKHARIN

The turning point in the economic history of the Soviet Union came with the continuing poor harvests of the late 1920s. How would the gov-

Workers at a power station in the Dnieper Valley

ernment react? Would it tax the peasants more harshly and thus create even more conflict with the peasantry? Would the peasants respond by producing less, as they had in the past, and thus further reduce possible revenue for industrial growth?

Stalin, now leader of the Party, and outwardly firmly in control, decided to abandon his previous support for Bukharin's moderate agricultural policy of pacifying the peasants. He now argued that the Soviet Union would only prosper economically by confronting, and if necessary eliminating, the peasantry. In late 1927 poor harvests and the continuing kulak determination to keep grain supplies low in order to force up prices combined to anger Stalin. He thus resolved to make industrialisation the country's first priority.

This was the policy of the left wing of the Party, one that had been espoused by Trotsky and Zinoviev before him, and one which Stalin had earlier denounced. It involved forcing the peasants into providing grain for the urban areas so that the number of workers in industry could be increased. The use of the 'Urals-Siberian' method of grain requisitioning in which agricultural produce was forcibly taken from the peasants was reminiscent of the darkest days of War Communism. However, while it helped to relieve the grain crisis temporarily, it also again turned the peasantry against the government.

Within the party there were many who disagreed with Stalin's methods, but this only made him more determined to succeed. He blamed sabotage for poor yields in industry and warned his supporters that unless the Soviet Union moved to industrialise immediately it would

Workers admiring new machinery on a Machine Tractor Station

remain at the mercy of the Western capitalist nations. Bukharin was removed from the Politburo for criticising Stalin, and at the same time many technicians were purged from the economic hierarchy for 'going slow' on the industrialisation programme. Stalin used this occasion for a public trial of technicians arrested for 'sabotage' at the Shakhty mines to show the country how some people were deliberately attempting to destroy the industrial effort.

GOSPLAN AND THE FIVE-YEAR PLANS

In 1927 the government began the industrial projects (dams, iron and steel, automobiles, tractors, railroads and armaments) which became the basis of future growth and expansion. Officially launched in 1928, the industrialisation of the Soviet Union was run by the State Planning Authority through the Gosplan. The state decided what industries were important, what they were to produce and how much was to be produced. All industrial achievement was measured against predetermined targets which formed the basis of a 'Five-Year Plan'. The First-Five Year Plan had unrealistic goals (for example, industrial production to rise by 180 per cent), and it concentrated on heavy industry (iron and steel, coal, tractors, electricity), all of which would be controlled from the centre.

The close relationship between industry and agriculture was continually stressed. Private trade and the employment of labour for private profit were made illegal in 1930. To convince the workers to give of their 'socialist best', various incentive and/or proscriptive schemes were introduced to achieve the set targets. These measures built upon earlier restrictions which the Communists had placed on the activities of the Nepmen. Extra taxation on private freight on the railways, fines and punishments for private speculation and hoarding, and other revenue-raising measures were all designed to stifle, if not kill off, the operation of the moneyed classes.

This discipline and state control at industry level were not new in Stalin's plans: they built upon the earlier programmes of the Bolsheviks during the years of consolidation from 1918 to 1924. Vesenkha, the Supreme Council of National Economy, had already been established during the Civil War to coordinate the economy. As David Christian points out, the Communists held the advantage of having had experience of using centralised planning to overcome a crisis. At the end of the 1920s, Stalin believed that Russia faced such a crisis.

For Stalin, the only way to create 'communism within one country' and be secure from the West was for Russia to be industrialised. His determination to push through with industrialisation and his ruthless obsession with success created a paranoia which was to shape all of his later actions.

The militant revolutionary zeal which had marked War Communism returned to the Party leadership. The results? Many Western analysts have doubted the validity of claimed Soviet achievements during this period. However, the fact remains that industrial expansion by the Soviets was outstanding. The figures that follow tell only part of the story:

Achievements of the Five-Year Plans

(1926–27 as base year of 100)	First Five-Year 1928–32	Second Five-Year 1933–37
National Income		
Official Soviet estimate (1926–27 prices)	91.5	96.1
Western estimates	70.2	66.5
Industrial Production		
Official Soviet estimate (1926–27 prices)	100.7	103.0
Western estimates	64.9	83.3
Official Soviet estimate, producer goods (1926–27 prices)	127.6	121.3
Official Soviet estimate, consumer goods (1926–27 prices)	80.5	85.4
Agricultural Production		
Official Soviet estimates (1926–27 prices)	57.8	62.6–76.9
Western estimates	50.9	70.9
Wages		
Average money wage	143.9	173.6
Average real wage, official Soviet estimate	31.9	102.6
Average real wage, Western estimate	26	65.8
Labour Productivity, Industry		
Official Soviet estimate	65.1	-
Western estimate	39	-

The First Five-Year Plan was launched in 1928. Stalin declared it completed in 1932, stating that it had already achieved its goals. The Plan provided for a doubling of industrial production, especially in the capital goods industries: electricity, metals, fuel, timber, cement. Grain production was increased in

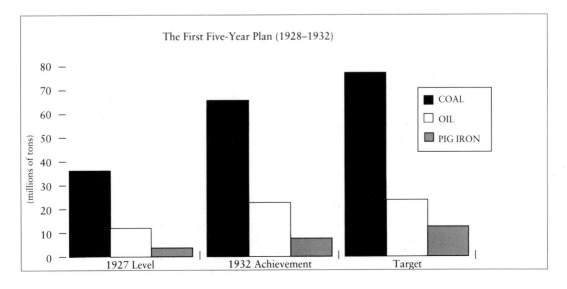

The First Five-Year Plan (1928–1932)

order to pay for imported technical machinery.

The Second Plan (1932–37) consolidated the gains of the First by emphasising the importance of efficiency and industrial techniques, while also promoting the rise of living standards. The Third Plan (1938–43) envisaged that production would again double and the production of consumer goods would increase. It had difficulty achieving its goals because of the purges and the outbreak of the Second World War. Labour shortages and the fuel crisis meant that its targets were not realised. The figures in the graphs on page 141 and below give an indication of what happened.

URBANISATION

One of the most significant effects of the period of rapid industrialisation was growing urbanisation. Some people were drawn to the cities to escape the collective farms which became the basis of Soviet agricultural policy, others moved in search of the incentives offered by the government in return for efficiency and determination. Collectivisation may have pushed many workers off the land, but they proved to be an unskilled, untrained and undisciplined work force.

The emphasis upon heavy industry led to the expansion and renewal of existing industrial centres, while new industrial areas, such as Magnito-gorsk, appeared out of nowhere. In some production areas targets were not reached, but the increases were substantial. In some areas, such as housing, production decreased.

THE HUMAN COST

The change in direction from a 'mixed economy' under the NEP to a 'command economy' under Gosplan meant the removal of much of the 'human element' from the Soviet economic system. The industrial emphasis of the plans caused Russia to fall behind in consumer goods production and in the introduction of new technology. With the emphasis on fulfilling targets, efficiency and the quality of the finished product became a secondary concern to planners and workers alike.

Some people embraced this single-minded pursuit of industrial

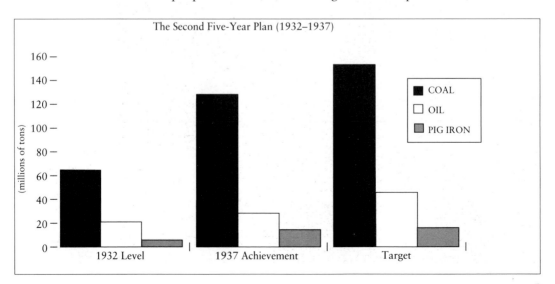

expansion with enthusiasm. Many worked overtime; role models such as the 'super human' miner worker, Alexei Stakhanov, were used to great effect. Also, Soviet economic expansion was occurring while the Western world was in the midst of economic depression—the rightness of the Stalinist method could have no clearer proof and the Seventeenth Party Congress in 1934 was marked by a wave of self-congratulatory militant enthusiasm.

However, these achievements were made at a terrible cost: millions lost their lives, victims of a system in which the use of force and the insistence upon discipline were paramount. To make the best use of workers, incentive schemes were introduced—rewards, social service benefits, higher wages for the skilled workers, fewer hours for 'exceptional people'. When these did not succeed force and coercion were used in their stead. Absenteeism became a capital offence, and job-changing could only occur with permission. Legislation was passed to control every activity of the urban worker, from hours of work to time of

Blast furnaces at Magnitogorsk, one of the many new industrial centres which developed under the Five-Year Plans

leisure. For the majority, living and working conditions were appalling: price increases, overcrowding, lack of skilled labour, and bribery were the norm in many areas. For those who tried to escape or speak out against the system, there were two solutions: the camps in Siberia (the gulags) or death.

To all intents and purposes, the Soviet Union had industrialised by the beginning of the Second World War and its international position was changed as a result. By 1941 the Soviet Union was second only to the USA in economic performance and output. It was far superior to its Western European neighbours. Stalinism brought industrial growth, but it did so by bullying, browbeating and belligerence. There was no room in the Stalinist system for those who would not conform or contribute.

SUMMARY

- Debate over economic policy was divided between the Bukharinites who sought moderate development based upon the peasantry, and the Trotskyites who argued for rapid industrialisation based upon attacks on the peasantry.
- Stalin initially supported Bukharin, but by 1927 he had decided to confront the rural classes and force industrialisation upon the country.
- Significant gains were made, despite the appalling living and working conditions.
- Industrialisation marked a return to the militant revolutionary enthusiasm of War Communism.
- Stalin saw industrial development as a fundamental element in the establishment of a secure socialist state.
- The emphasis of industrialisation was upon material production levels—the human element was seen primarily as the means by which industrialisation could be achieved.
- The human cost of industrialisation was extraordinarily high.

KEY PERSONALITIES, GROUPS, TERMS

Alexei Stakhanov: Soviet miner; exceeded the daily work output by 14 times—became the model Soviet worker; toured the country exhorting his fellow workers to do the same, and was elected to the Supreme Soviet.

Gosplan: State Planning Commission; formed in 1921 as part of Vesenkha; main task was to prioritise the economic plans for the Soviet Union by setting guidelines and production targets.

Shock Brigades: Groups of young workers used by the state to move into factories and industries to set an example of 'correct' work habits; competed with other groups to improve output and were never absent from work; their example was used to put pressure upon fellow workers.

The Shakhty Affair: 1928, a group of mining engineers was charged by the state with sabotage and collaboration with foreign powers to overthrow the government; guilty verdict established the notion that there could be no 'fence sitters' in the class struggle which was being waged by the Communists—people were either for it or against it.

EXERCISES

1. Describe the nature of Soviet industrialisation before the introduction of the Five-Year Plans.
2. Why did Stalin promote industrialisation as a major priority in Soviet economic policy?
3. **a** Which group(s) within the Soviet Union would have been most opposed to industrialisation? Why?
   b Which group(s) within the Soviet Union would have been most in favour of industrialisation? Why?
4. To what extent were the Five-Year Plans successful in creating industrial development in the Soviet Union?

DOCUMENT STUDY No. 11

Read the following sources and answer the questions which follow.

Stalin justifies the pace of industrial development
SOURCE 5.A
from an article written by Stalin in 1931

It is sometimes asked whether it is not possible to slow down the tempo a bit, to put a check on the movement. No, comrades, it is not possible! The tempo must not be reduced! On the contrary, we must increase it as much as is within our powers and possibilities. This is dictated to us by our obligations to the workers and peasants of the USSR. This is dictated to us by our obligations to the working class of the whole world. To slacken the tempo would mean falling behind. And those who fall behind get beaten. But we do not want to be beaten. No, we refuse to be beaten! One feature of the history of old Russia was the continual beatings she suffered for falling behind, for her backwardness . . . for military backwardness, for cultural backwardness, for political backwardness, for industrial backwardness, for agricultural backwardness. She was beaten because to do so was profitable and could be done with impunity . . . It is the jungle law of capitalism. You are backward, you are weak therefore you are wrong; hence, you can be beaten and enslaved. You are mighty—therefore you are right; hence, we must be wary of you. That is why we must no longer lag behind . . . Do you want our socialist fatherland to be beaten and to lose its independence? If you do not want this you must put an end to its backwardness in the shortest possible time and develop a genuine Bolshevik tempo in building up its socialist system of economy. There is no other way. That is why Lenin said during the October Revolution: 'Either perish, or overtake and outstrip the advanced capitalist countries.' We are 50 or 100 years behind the advanced countries. We must make good this distance in ten years. Either we do it, or they crush us.

SOURCE 5.B

Statistical evidence
from David Christian, *Power and Privilege*, 1989, pp. 212–13

Index numbers of Soviet economic development, 1928–40

Year	Iron	Steel	Coal	Oil	Electricity	Motor vehicles
1928	1.00	1.00	1.00	1.00	1.00	1.00
1932	1.88	1.37	1.81	1.84	2.70	29.88
1937	4.39	4.12	3.61	2.46	7.24	249.88
1940	4.52	4.26	4.67	2.68	9.66	181.25

SOURCE 5.C

Extract from British historian Alec Nove, *An Economic History of the USSR*, 1969

The proper assessment of living standards at this time is rendered almost impossible not only by the existence of rationing, price differences, and shortages, but also of queues, decline in quality, neglect of consumer requirements ... Therefore any figures comparing wages and prices are bound greatly to understate the decline in living standards ...

In order to facilitate the mobilisation of the working class for the 'great tasks of building socialism', and so as to avoid any organised protest against living standards or working conditions, the trade unions ... were instructed to act primarily as organisers and mobilisers in the interests of plan fulfilment ... The protective role of the unions was greatly reduced ... The inclusion in the picture of the peasants would certainly make it worse, in particular in the period 1928–34 ... 1933 was the culmination of the most precipitous peacetime decline in living standards known in recorded history.

SOURCE 5.D

Photograph of members of the Young Pioneers organisation—young boys whose task was to monitor work habits and production levels in factories and farms

Questions

a i) According to Source 5.A, why was it necessary for the Soviet Union to industrialise?

ii) From Source 5.B, which two areas had the greatest relative increase between 1928 and 1940?

iii) Explain the differences in the figures in Source 5.B.

b Using Source 5.A and your own knowledge, describe the process of industrialisation which took place in the Soviet Union between 1928 and 1941.

c Examine Source 5.B and Source 5.C. In what ways would sources such as these be useful but possibly unreliable for an historian attempting to understand developments in the Soviet Union under Stalin? (In your answer you must consider the nature, origin, motive and audience of each source, as well as its content.)

d Using all four sources and your own knowledge, explain the impact of industrialisation on the people of the Soviet Union between 1928 and 1941.

Collectivisation

FOCUS QUESTIONS What was the purpose of collectivisation? How did the peasants react to this process?

FROM THE EARLIEST DAYS of the revolution relations between the peasants and the central government had been strained. There were many in the Party who disliked the emergence of the richer peasants (the kulaks), but with the introduction of the New Economic Policy, the Party accepted Lenin's smychka for the sake of the revolution. The relationship was not harmonious.

RELATIONS WITH THE PEASANTS

The poor harvests of the late 1920s prompted many party officials to again seek an alternative to the inefficient agricultural production and distribution systems. Grain collection for 1927 was well below forecast totals. The government once again resorted to forced requisitioning. This quickly destroyed any remaining notion of cooperation with the peasantry. In 1928 the harvest was again down—this time to the point that bread rationing had to be introduced. Farmers reacted by slaughtering animals, destroying or hiding grain and neglecting the fields. All classes of peasant were angry at the government for its actions.

The combination of poor harvests, peasant discontent and concern for the future among the inner-Party circle led Stalin to move in late 1929 to the rapid collectivisation of agriculture. He argued that such a measure was necessary in order to make use of more modern agricultural methods and that the collectivisation of large scale-farms would create a surplus of labour who would then be gainfully employed in the factories. He also believed that the peasants would be easier to control once on the collectives. If Soviet agri-

THE DECISION TO COLLECTIVISE

culture was to be of any benefit to industry it could not remain backward.

In simple terms, collectivisation meant the establishment of large-scale farming. The collectives (which would be either state-run or cooperatively supervised) would take over from individual kulak holdings the role of producing food for the towns. The initial plan was for the peasants to hand over their land voluntarily, but their resistance, and Stalin's desire to match the progress being made in industry, led to a quickening of the pace. Collectivisation techniques were compulsory, forced and brutal. The full weight of Stalin's authority came to be felt at the lowest levels of society. The peasants' hatred of the central government's interference in their affairs increased as a result. Historians such as Graeme Gill suggest that this was indicative of the gulf that existed between the central decision makers in Moscow and the ordinary people in the provinces. For example, even the Commission on Collectivisation, established by the Politburo in 1929 to monitor the rate of collectivisation, warned against the 'ecstacy of dictation' which was taking place.

The major feature of Stalin's programme of collectivisation was the war against the richer peasants, or kulaks. 'Kulak' had traditionally been a derogatory term in Russia and was associated with ideas of exploitation and misery. Now, any peasant who was against the forced requisitioning and collectivisation was branded as a kulak. 'Kulaks' were either deprived of their land, sent to Siberia, or shot. The war against the kulaks was to serve as a warning to all other peasants of the consequences of dissent.

Tractors at the entrance to a model collective farm

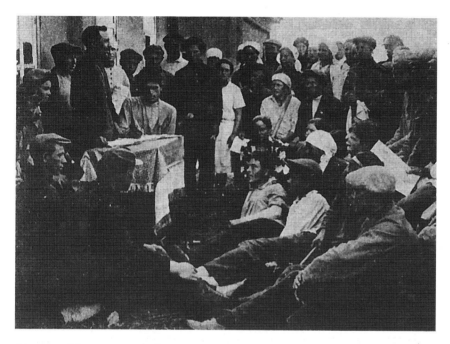

Meeting of farmers on a collective farm

Workers on a collective farm being taught to read

Stalin claimed that his actions were necessary if everyone was to be equal. This was social equality in its most brutal form.

Many attempted to resist Stalin's directives by burning their crops, killing their animals and by hiding anyone sought by the officials. The resistance only increased Stalin's resolve to push ahead with the programme, and to increase its pace. The dissent, however, proved too great and in 1930 Stalin was forced to call a temporary halt to collectivisation. He justified this stay in proceedings by stating that the lower echelons of the Party had become 'dizzy with success' and had become over-enthusiastic in their treatment of the peasants. It was time to pause and consolidate before moving on to greater gains.

Stalin's belief that this truce would mollify the peasants was mistaken. Many took the opportunity to leave the collectives and by the middle of 1930 only 25 per cent of the peasants remained on the collective farms. Stalin was not to be intimidated. He resumed collectivisation immediately—he needed grain for export to pay for the large amounts of imported industrial machinery. The end result was twofold: by 1941 over 90 per cent of Soviet agriculture had been collectivised; the cost was millions of lives lost as a result of famine, eviction or imprisonment. Grain production levels and animal numbers decreased and the 'party experts' who were sent to the countryside proved of little value to the farmer. By 1941 the desired smychka between agriculture and industry had still not been reached.

SUMMARY

- Collectivisation of agriculture was undertaken in order to provide a revenue source for industrialisation and a more reliable food supply for the urban areas.
- Opponents of collectivisation were labelled as 'kulaks' and dealt with brutally.
- Collectivisation actually led to a fall in the agricultural production of the Soviet Union.

Machine Tractor Stations: Supplied the collective and state farms with tractors when required; tractors were leased to the farms; they were, despite initial peasant distrust, important agents for successful collectivisation.

Kolkhoz: Collective farms; peasants worked the soil as a group and also had the luxury of small private plots to farm for their own use; obligation was to provide the state with a fixed quota of produce each year; peasants retained any surplus produced; the type of farm most commonly used to organise the peasants.

Sovkhoz: State farms; peasants worked as hired labourers of the state; received wages whatever the result of the harvest; all produce went to the state; workers used wages to buy food and other necessities.

EXERCISES

1. a What were the advantages of collectivisation to the Soviet government?
   b What were the advantages of collectivisation to agricultural workers?
2. a What were the disadvantages of collectivisation to the Soviet government?
   b What were the disadvantages of collectivisation to the agricultural workers?
3. Why was the link between agriculture and industry so important to Stalin?
4. Describe Stalin's attitude towards the peasants from 1917 to 1940. How do you explain any changes which took place?
5. a Why were the kulaks specifically targeted for extermination?
   b How valid do you find the reasons put forward by Stalin for these actions?
6. a How did the kulaks respond to collectivisation?
   b What were the long-term consequences of their reactions?

DOCUMENT STUDY   No. 12

Read the following sources and answer the questions which follow.

The reasons for collectivisation   SOURCE 5.E
from M. Lewin, *The Immediate Background of Soviet Collectivisation*, 1965
. . . the decision to undertake overall collectivisation had its roots in the grain crisis at the beginning of 1928. Stalin's ideas on policy germinated during the testing time of this crisis, though only in essentials, for at that stage he was concerned only with a short-term policy of moderate aims, but by reason of the growing crisis he was constantly obliged to extend the objectives with which he had set out at the beginning of the year . . .
During his visit to Siberia, where he had gone to urge and compel the party officials to take the grain ruthlessly . . . he became aware of the urgent necessity for establishing strong points in the countryside, similar to those the regime had built up in the towns . . . It is at this point also that he expressed the thought that the Soviet regime was 'walking on two unequal legs'—the socialist sector in the towns and the private sector in the villages—and that this could not go on indefinitely. It can be deduced from this . . . that he no longer believed in NEP as a viable policy. . . As he saw it, matters must be so arranged that the state would be absolutely sure of having at its disposal some 250 million poods of grain (in other words, about a third of the quantity required by the end of the Five-Year Plans) . . .
Stalin knew, and told the Central Committee in a speech which was secret at the time, that the peasants would have to pay a tribute for the requirements of industrialisation.

Extract from an article by Stalin in *Pravda*, 2 March 1930   SOURCE 5.F
. . . by 20 February 1930, we had over-fulfilled the Five-Year Plan of collectivisation by more than 100 percent . . .
But successes have their seamy side . . . People not infrequently become intoxicated by such successes; they become dizzy with success, lose all sense of proportion and the

capacity to understand realities . . . Collective farms must not be established by force. That would be foolish and reactionary. The collective-farm movement must rest on the active support of the main mass of the peasantry . . .

We know that in a number of areas of Turkestan there have already been attempts to 'overtake and outstrip' the advanced areas of the USSR by threatening to use armed force, by threatening that peasants who are not ready to join the collective farms will be deprived of irrigation water and manufactured goods . . .

How could there have arisen in our midst such block-headed exercises in 'socialisation', such ludicrous attempts to overleap oneself?

SOURCE 5.G

The peasants give their views on collectivisation
from letters quoted in V. Serge, *From Lenin to Stalin*, 1937

The members of the kolkhoz have for two months received no pay for their labour, which consists of transporting wood and feed. Of the revenue, 50 percent goes to the kolkhoz treasury, 50 percent for taxes and rent. What remains for the workers? No one knows . . . All this lends credence to the kulaks' assertion that a 'new serfdom' is being instituted . . . The kolkhozes are emptying. Eighty peasants in this hole-in-the-ground came to the public prosecutor to complain that they have been forced by violence to join the kolkhoz . . . The peasants have replied to the forced collectivisation by selling their possessions, sabotaging the work and revolting . . . The peasants' assemblies are being purged. A nearby soviet has just announced the expulsion of 20 poor peasants, some of whom are sincerely devoted to the regime. All are condemned as 'agents of the kulaks'. Their crime is that they have not always kept silent, that they have said their condition has grown worse, and asked if there could be another Five-Year Plan.

SOURCE 5.H

Statistics on collectivisation from a Soviet source

	1928	1929	1930	1931	1932	1933	1934	1935
Grain harvest (million tons)	73.3	71.7	83.5	69.5	69.6	68.4	67.6	75
Cattle (million head)	70.5	67.1	52.5	47.9	40.7	38.4	42.4	49.3
Pigs (million head)	26	20.4	13.6	14.4	11.6	12.1	17.4	22.6
Sheep/goats (million head)	146.7	147	108.8	77.7	52.1	50.2	51.9	61.1

Questions

a From Source 5.H, describe the impact of collectivisation upon agricultural production levels between 1928 and 1935.

b Using Source 5.G and your own knowledge, describe how the rural population responded to collectivisation.

c How useful would an historian find each of these four sources when attempting to understand the nature and impact of collectivisation on the lives of the Soviet people? (In your answer you must consider the nature, origin, motive and audience of each source as well as its content.)

d Using all four sources and your own knowledge, explain how and why the lives of the rural population changed as a result of Stalin's policies.

Social and Cultural Change under Stalin

FOCUS QUESTIONS In what ways did Stalinism involve a 'social revolution'?
What were the main cultural features of Stalinism?

SOCIAL AND CULTURAL CHANGES were part of a wider revolution instituted by Stalin from the late 1920s. The entire nature of the Soviet state was altered so that no one could claim to have escaped the touch of 'Stalinism'. (It should be noted that Stalin never permitted the use of this term—it was always 'Marxist-Leninism'.)

STALIN'S INFLUENCE OVER THE PARTY

Stalin became supreme master of the Party by closely aligning himself with the career and ideas of Lenin. In many ways Stalin would prove to be Lenin's best and brightest pupil, putting into operation the policies and practices of Lenin in a way which could not have been achieved by any of the other original Bolshevik leaders. At heart Stalin was the consummate political pragmatist. He had a particular vision of the revolution (albeit an increasingly distorted and paranoid one) and he was prepared to pursue that vision ruthlessly to its realisation. His willingness to take on the kulaks won Stalin increased prestige within the Party. The peasants and their backward methods of agriculture were seen by many as the major stumbling block to Soviet economic development; Stalin's marshalling of labour against their will, and for the greater benefit of the entire country, increased his standing in the hearts and minds of the Party. The rank-and-file membership, the great majority of whom owed Stalin their positions, delighted in their hero's actions.

'Deviations' against the Party line became a major crime in Stalinist Russia. Anyone who did not work as hard as the best in the group was immediately under suspicion for attempting to sabotage the revolution.

THE NOTION OF THE 'COMMON GOOD'

Stalin attacked the problems of agriculture and industry in a similarly militaristic/mechanical manner. He believed that when all sections of society worked in harmony, the country would advance. When it did not, the machine would break down and someone had to be blamed for the stoppage. Discipline and conformity were the catchcries of the period. Workers were encouraged to produce more through the promise of decorations, better housing, holidays and higher wages. The Stakhanovites, the model workers who exceeded their quotas, were one expression of this new 'socialist spirit'. Women were urged to have more children. It was all part of the notion that the individual was to be completely subsumed by service to the state. Free will and personal expression gave way to collective action for the 'common good'.

When problems occurred, it was the lower Party officials who were at fault.

Stalin was blameless. It was a recurrence of the Tsarist technique of explaining difficulties away by blaming an incompetent bureaucracy. In the same way the Party suffered widespread condemnation for the rapid rush to industrialise. Instead of cowing him into making concessions, it simply stiffened Stalin's resolve. Saboteurs and Trotskyites were to blame; Party members were accused of being soft and lacking commitment to the cause; Party members lost their positions and privileges. By the mid-1930s over half of the membership of the Communist Party was new to its ranks.

Churches and organised religions were condemned. The League of Militant Atheists was established in 1924 and had a membership of over five million in the 1930s. There could be no commitment to any other 'god'. Children were taught to think of the 'common good' and not for their own benefit. The revolution was glorified and its targets became doctrine. The future, rather than the present, was the key.

The 1935 Education Law made classrooms and the curriculum more disciplined. The progressive moral standards promoted by Alexandra Kollontai in the 1920s were replaced by traditional and rigid versions of family life and the role of women. The shock brigades, industrial spies and Stakhanovites ensured that the work ethos became the dominant social philosophy, while a new class emerged in Soviet society: the slave labourer. Many classes, such as the kulaks and the bourgeois technicians, lost

*Red Army
soldiers looting
a church*

An example of 'Socialist Realism' – note that the emphasis is upon Stalin and the bureaucrats

status. Others, both inside and outside the Party, disappeared during the purges. In the 1920s the major victims of repression and elimination had been ex-Tsarists and the middle class. In the 1930s the Stalinist system turned increasingly in on itself and targeted its own membership.

THE SOCIAL REVOLUTION

However, this downward movement was counterbalanced by the opportunities for the upward mobility of members of the peasantry and proletariat. The introduction of collectivisation and industrialisation created new positions in administration and in factories. Regardless of the deteriorating urban working conditions, people moved to the cities in large numbers. They continued to believe that such a move would lead to an improvement in their standing in society. This upward mobility was not only associated with a rapid expansion in technical education, but was also linked to the coming of the purges in the mid-1930s. The disappearance of large numbers of former officials or supervisors created advancement opportunities for the new Soviet elite. As Gill mentions, by 1939 the revolution of 1917 had all but achieved its aim of creating a working-class/peasant governing elite. The point was that it was a governing elite completely dominated by the new bureaucracy—the so-called 'apparatchiks' who were under the sway of Stalin.

SOCIALIST REALISM

Changes on the cultural front took place in two phases: from the late 1920s to the early 1930s; and during the rest of the 1930s. The first phase was marked by an emphasis upon the proletarian on the shop-floor and at the coal-face. The virtues of the ordinary worker were stressed; the focus was upon the class struggle. Working-class values were emphasised; the 'bourgeois experts' of the Tsarist period and the 1920s were denounced. This phase was then replaced by the period of 'Socialist Realism'. Stalin reshaped Soviet culture in order to promote and reinforce the Soviet advance. Culture and entertainment had to be happy, productive and utilitarian. Composers such as Shostakovich and Prokofiev were instructed to write music which was 'directly accessible to the masses'. Visual artworks were dominated by images of workers and planners and the benevolent visage of Stalin. The true 'Soviet expert' or apparatchik/bureaucrat played an increasing role in the iconography of the nation. With the Communist Party becoming more hierarchic, authoritarian and inequitable, the role of the 'worker' gave way to the 'cult of the big man'. Associated with this change in cultural values came other changes in public life: privilege and inequality, increasing wage differentials and material incentives became the rule rather than the exception.

THE CULT OF STALIN

Most typical of this manipulation of popular culture was the development of 'the cult of Stalin'. The deification of Stalin as leader—with the use of terms such as 'Granite Bolshevik', 'Shining Sun of Humanity', 'Universal Genius', 'Iron Soldier', as well as 'Man of Steel'—emphasised and reinforced his domination of the country. He had gained this position through his control of the Party and its membership and his leading role in the collectivisation and industrialisation of Russia. He was now universally praised for his achievements and sacrifices for the good of the Russian people. All of his actions and words were honoured. Plays, novels and poems were written about his life. The Soviet people were left in no doubt as to whom they should thank for the emerging greatness of the nation. Stalin became the keystone of the entire social, political and economic revolution. Without him the changes would never have taken place. The irony, as Deutscher points out, was that the whole Stalinist revolution was based upon 'terror and illusion'.

SUMMARY

- The Stalinist revolution was a social revolution.
- The social revolution was initially marked by social mobility for the working and peasant classes and the elimination of the bourgeoisie.
- The social revolution was later marked by the rise of the apparatchik and a return to a society based upon rank, status and privilege.
- Culturally all sections of society were brought to serve the political aims of the leadership.

- The state deliberately manipulated cultural values through the development of the 'cult of the big man' and the 'cult of Stalin'.
- These changes were initially revolutionary, but by the mid-1930s conservatism was again the dominant social force.

KEY PERSONALITIES, GROUPS, TERMS

Apparatchik: Soviet bureaucrat; term used to describe the new kind of civil servant who emerged during the 1920s and 1930s; derived from the notion of complete loyalty to the state apparatus; many owed their positions and influence to Stalin; developed into a class of people known as the *dvoriane* who, like the nobles who had given unquestioning service to the Tsarist regime, owed their power and position to their willingness to do whatever the state required of them.

Socialist Realism: Artistic movement of the late 1920s, 1930s; major elements were the depiction of the working people involved in the progress of communism; strength, joy and a sense of common purpose were important characteristics.

EXERCISES

1. Make a list of the major social and cultural changes introduced into the Soviet Union in the 1930s.
2. a What aspects of these social changes can be regarded as 'progressive'?
  b What aspects of these social changes can be regarded as 'regressive'?
3. In what ways did the changes brought by Stalin to Russia in the 1930s amount to a cultural revolution?

DOCUMENT STUDY No. 13

Read the sources and answer the questions which follow:

Extract from a speech presented at the 1935 Congress of Soviets   SOURCE 5.I
All thanks to thee, O great educator, Stalin. I love a young woman with a renewed love and shall perpetuate myself in my children—all thanks to thee, great educator, Stalin. I shall be eternally happy and joyous, all thanks to thee, O great educator, Stalin. Everything belongs to thee, chief of our great country. And when the woman I love presents me with a child the first word it shall utter will be: Stalin.

Rule One of the twenty rules of behaviour which had to be learnt by Soviet school children   SOURCE 5.J
It is the duty of each school child to acquire knowledge persistently so as to become an educated and cultured citizen and to be of the greatest possible service to his country.

SOURCE 5.K

Painting from 1924 entitled *Friendship of the People*

SOURCE 5.L

Extract from Paul Baker and Judith Bassett, *Stalin's Revolution: The USSR 1924–57*, published in 1988

Artists and writers joined the struggle for Russia's industrial revolution. Artists painted Stakhanovites exceeding their production norms and happy collective farmers at harvest festivals. They drew posters which urged workers to ever greater productive efforts. For a time it was fashionable to paint 'Fighting Art', that is art which helped to fight the class war.

Writers were expected to produce work which would help the industrial effort. They wrote simple stories explaining Stalin's economic policies or novels about model workers. One slogan said 'For Coal! For Iron! For Machines! Each Literary Group Should Work for These!' Some writers worked in factories for a while to learn more about workers.

Fantasy and emotional writing such as poetry was disapproved of. It was considered escapist and self-indulgent. The style required was called 'socialist realism'— writing about real things and ordinary people in an encouraging way. But writing about real problems and difficulties was not allowed. A poet who wrote a poem called 'Get Off the Stove' urging workers to stop being lazy was first praised for encouraging production; then Stalin said the poem unfairly criticised Soviet workers, and it was banned. 'Socialist realism' was not an easy style to master.

Questions

a i) According to Source 5.I, to whom were all things due?
ii) From Source 5.J, list two benefits from the acquisition of knowledge.
b Using Source 5.L and your own knowledge, describe the major cultural changes which took place in the Soviet Union during the 1930s
c How useful and reliable would each of these sources be to an historian attempting to understand the attitudes held by the Soviet people during the 1930s? (In your answer you must refer to the nature, origin, motive and audience of each source, as well as its content.)
d Using all four sources and your own knowledge, to what extent did Stalinism represent a social and cultural change for the people of the Soviet Union?

The Purges and the Great Terror

FOCUS QUESTIONS What role did the purges play in the Stalinist Revolution? Were they successful?

THE USE OF PURGES was not new to the Communist Party of the 1930s. In the early 1920s Lenin had held 'show trials' of the Socialist Revolutionaries and launched an all-out assault on the power and influence of the church. Ever since the turn of the century this device had also been used to rid the Party of its undesirable elements. When Stalin gained ascendancy within the Party in the late 1920s he purged sections of it to rid himself of potential rivals. Some suggest that at least one-tenth of the Party was eliminated at this time. This search for enemies within the Party became acute during the New Economic Policy and collectivisation programmes. Even people who were considered experts in their field and those who showed too much enthusiasm fell victim to the ruthless denunciations of the regime. In 1928 mining engineers at Shakhty were publicly tried, then executed, for allegedly undermining the industrialisation movement.

THE EARLY PURGES

The purges of the 1930s followed the 1934 death of Sergei Kirov, the Leningrad Party boss and member of the Politburo. Stalin used this murder, which many believe he masterminded, to push through legislation which effectively meant that 'Party membership' was no longer a protection against denunciation or punishment. He staged three show trials to

THE SHOW TRIALS

Stalin, as chief mourner, at the funeral of slain Party member Sergei Kirov, 1934

rid himself of potential rivals from within the old Bolshevik elite. Many of the original Bolshevik leaders were tried and shot, most of them confessing to crimes they had not committed: Zinoviev, Kamenev, Bukharin and Rykov were all tried and executed. Those who were not killed were sent to the labour camps in Siberia, the 'gulags'. The rounding up of all suspects was carried out by the secret police, now known as the NKVD (The People's Commissariat for Internal Affairs). It has been suggested that the NKVD carried out many of these arrests and executions in an attempt to protect itself against its enemies within the Party and state. While this may have some validity, the role of Stalin in these purges remains paramount.

THE EZHOVSCHINA

Out of these state-driven purges grew a period in Soviet history known as the *Ezhovschina,* or 'Great Terror'. From 1937 onwards the process of denunciation, punishment and persecution took on a life of its own as thousands of people became caught up in the wave of fear and suspicion which swept the countryside and cities. Of course, many people benefited from this feeling. The elimination of state officials created great opportunities for social mobility! Unfortunately, institutionalised terror became part of the social and political framework of the Soviet state and left a legacy of fear which lasted for many decades. The purges also eliminated large numbers of people with 'talent' from the institutions of the Soviet state. Thus the bureaucracy and the armed forces came to be dominated by the 'mediocre', those who were seen as no threat to the leadership. Again, this was to have long-term consequences for the development of the Soviet state.

Victims of the Purges, 1928–1946

Year	Type of Victim	Alleged Crime	Sentence
1928	Shakhy Mines engineers	Sabotage	Show trial – 15 executed, 49 imprisoned
1929–39	Up to 24 million	Being kulaks, criminals, wreckers, or failing to inform	Labour camps – 13 million died
1930–31	Industrialists	Sabotage	Show trial – imprisonment
	Mensheviks	Political crimes	Show trial – imprisonment
	Scientist	Sabotage of economy and spying	Secret trials – execution
1933	Sovkhoz officials	Sabotage and creating food shortages	Secret trials – 70 executed
1934	Kirov	Favoured to replace Stalin	Murdered
1935	1 million people in Moscow/Leningrad	Links with Kirov murder	Arrested and executed
1937	Pyatakov and Serebryakov	Spying for Germany	Show trial – executed
	Sokolnikov and Radek	Spying for Germany	Show trial – executed
1937	Yagoda (Head of NKVD)	Treason, murder, corruption	Show trial – executed
1937	3/5 Marshals in Red Army	Treason	Executed
	14/16 Army Commanders	Treason	Executed
	60/67 Corps Commanders	Treason	Executed
	136/199 Divisional Commanders	Treason	Executed
	221/397 Brigade Commanders	Treason	Executed
	11/11 Deputy Commissars for Defence	Treason	Executed
	78/80 members of Supreme Military Council	Treason	Executed
	17 500/35 000 Officers	Treason	Executed or imprisoned
	Foreign trade officials	Treason	Executed or labour camps
	Intelligence agents	Treason	Executed or imprisoned
1938	Bukharin, Rykov	Treason	Show trial – executed
	All Party and state leaders in the Soviet republics	Treason, or 'Bourgeois Nationalism'	Executed

Year	Type of Victim	Alleged Crime	Sentence
1939	Yezhov (Head of NKVD)	Spying for Britain	Show trial – executed
1940	2 million people in Baltic States	Being an 'enemy'	Deported to gulags
1941	3 million people from Germany, Chechnya and Crimea	Disloyalty to USSR	Deported to gulags
1944–46	10 million returned prisoners of war	Political contamination by foreigners	Deported to gulags

As part of this process of terror, Stalin deliberately set out to break down the old loyalties people had to their families, their church and to their friends. At the same time Stalin's power increased, and his image as the great leader grew. A personality cult developed round Stalin, aided by his control over every aspect of the Party apparatus and his patronage in every corner of the Soviet Union. The successes of the Soviet Union in the 1930s were because of Stalin; all the hardships of the times were blamed upon lower Party subordinates. Stalin fostered this leadership cult, and his place in the history of the Soviet Union from 1917 was played up at the expense of the other revolutionary leaders. Stalin became Lenin's co-worker in the fight to achieve the socialist utopia.

How did Stalin see the purges of the 1930s? Possibly he viewed them as necessary to purge all bad elements from the Party, but it has also been suggested that Stalin had very little feeling for the problems and hardships of the people and that he was only interested in the future of the Soviet Union. Either way it seems that he cared little for his people.

SUMMARY

- The Soviet was a highly centralised, directed system.
- Under Stalin the Soviet Union developed into a dictatorship which was based upon the use of terror.
- Institutionalised terror found expression in the purges and show trials of the 1930s.
- The terror came to take on a life of its own in the Ezhovschina.
- The purges and the terror brought all aspects of Soviet life under the influence of the state and its leadership.

KEY PERSONALITIES, GROUPS, TERMS

Sergei Kirov: Communist Party official and member of the Politburo; born 1886, died 1934; leader of the Leningrad Party machine in 1925 when Zinoviev was defeated by Stalin and others over the role of the Party and its right to enforce the majority decision; popular and charismatic; murdered in

Forced labourers working on the construction of the Belomor Canal—a massive project, and ultimately pointless effort which resulted in the deaths of hundreds of thousands

A watchtower at a Siberian labour camp—symbol of the gulags

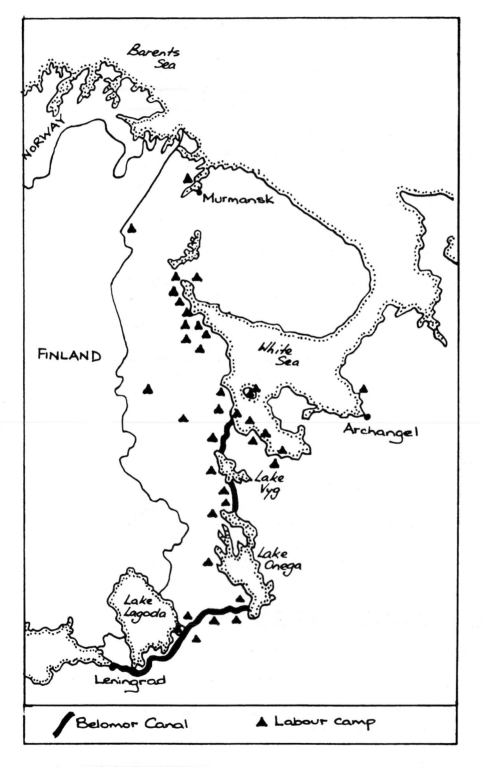

Map showing the location of the major labour camps in North West Russia, 1917–1936

1934, supposedly on Stalin's orders because he was a threat to the latter's power within the Party.

Gulags: Series of detention camps scattered about the eastern Siberian regions of the Soviet Union; used by Stalin to exile/punish anyone accused of working against the revolution; the camps differed in severity; many had been used by the Tsars from the beginning of the nineteenth century .

NKVD: The Peoples' Commissariat for Internal Affairs; replaced OGPU (Unified State Political Administration)—which had replaced the GPU in 1924 following the creation of the Soviet Union—as the internal security force; used by Stalin to remove enemies from within the Party, the armed forces, the state bureaucracy and the general community; under the leadership of Lavrenti Beria it became a dominant part of the Soviet power system.

Ezhovschina: The so-called 'Great Terror'; the climate of fear, suspicion and denunciation which gripped the Soviet Union from 1938; tens of thousands of people fell victim, including many for simply refusing to denounce others; named after Yezhov, Head of the NKVD, who was also one of its victims.

Show trials: Public trials of prominent 'enemies' of the Soviet state from within the Party membership; used by Stalin to eliminate possible opponents and further entrench his position as leader; most important of these took place in 1936, 1937 and 1938, when virtually all of the remaining Bolshevik leadership from 1917 confessed to treasonous actions against the socialist cause and were executed.

EXERCISES

1. Why did Stalin embark on the purges of the 1930s?
2. **a** Why was Kirov murdered?
   b What techniques were used to extract confessions during the show trials?
3. What evidence is there to suggest that the Ezhovschina developed a life of its own?
4. What were the functions of the labour camps?
5. To what extent can Stalin be referred to as the 'Red Tsar'? Give evidence to support your opinion.

STUDYING AN HISTORICAL SOURCE   No. 4

Read the historical sources and answer the questions which follow.

Extracts from Alexander Solzhenitsyn, *One Day in the Life of Ivan Denisovich*, 1962.   SOURCE 5.M
Shukov decided to report sick.
At that very moment his blanket and jacket were imperiously jerked off him. He flung his coat away from his face and sat up. Looking up at him, his head level with the top bunk, was the lean figure of The Tartar.

So the fellow was on duty out of turn and had stolen up.

'S 854,' The Tartar read from the white strip that had been stitched to the back of his black jacket, 'Three days' penalty with work'.

The moment they heard that peculiar choking voice of his, everyone who wasn't up yet in the whole dimly-lit hut, where two hundred men slept in bug-ridden bunks, stirred to life and began hurriedly dressing.

'What for, citizen chief?' asked Shukhov with more chagrin than he felt in his voice.

With work—that wasn't half so bad. They gave you hot food and you had no time to start thinking. Real lock-up was when you were kept back from work.

'Failing to get up at reveille. Follow me to the camp commandant's office', said The Tartar lazily.

His crumpled, hairless face was imperturbable. He turned, looking for another victim but now everybody, in dim corners and under the lights, in upper bunks and lower, had thrust their legs into their black wadded trousers, or, already dressed, had wrapped their coats round them and hurried to the door to out of the way until The Tartar had left. (pp. 10–11)

No sense in getting your boots wet in the morning. Even if Shukhov had dashed back to his hut he wouldn't have found another pair to change into. During eight years' imprisonment he had known various systems for allocating footwear: there'd been times when he'd gone through the winter without valenki at all, or leather boots either, and had had to make shift with best sandals or a sort of galoshes made of scraps of motor tyres—'Chetezes' they called them, after the Cheliabinsk tractor works. Now the footwear situation seemed better; in October Shukhov had received (thanks to Pavlo, whom he trailed to the store) a pair of ordinary, hard-wearing leather boots, big enough for a double thickness of footcloth. For a week he went about as though he'd been given a birthday present, kicking his new heels. Then in December the valenki arrived, and, oh, wasn't life wonderful?

But some devil in the bookkeeper's office had whispered in the commandant's ear that valenki should be issued only to those who surrendered their boots. It was against the rules for a prisoner to possess two pairs of footwear at the same time. So Shukhov had to choose. Either he'd have to wear leather throughout the winter, or surrender the boots and wear valenki even in the thaw. He'd taken such good care of his new boots, softening the leather with grease! Ah, nothing had been so hard to part with in all his eight years in camp as that pair of boots! They were tossed into a common heap. Not a hope of finding your own pair in the spring. (pp. 14–15)

He still had to fit in a visit to the sick-bay. He was again all aches and pains. And there was that guard outside the mess-hall to be dodged: the camp commandant had issued strict orders that prisoners on their own were to be picked up and thrown into the lock-up.

That morning—a stroke of luck—there was no crowd, no queues, outside the mess. Walk in.

The air was as thick as in a bath house. An icy wave blew in through the door and met the steam rising from the skilly. The teams sat at tables or crowded the aisles in between, waiting for places to be freed. Shouting at each other through the crush, two or three men from each team carried bowls of skilly and porridge on wooden trays and tried to find room for them on the tables. Look at that bloody stiff-backed fool. He doesn't hear. He's jolted the tray. Splash, splash! You've a hand free, swipe him on the back of the neck. That's the way. Don't stand there blocking the aisle, looking for something to filch!

There at a table, before dipping a spoon in, a young man crossed himself. A west Ukrainian, that meant, and a new arrival too.

As for the Russians, they'd forgotten which hand to cross themselves with.

They sat in the cold mess-hall, most of them eating with their hats on, eating slowly, picking out putrid little fish from under the leaves of boiled cabbage and spitting the bones out on the table. When the bones formed a heap and it was the turn of another team, someone would sweep them off and they'd be trodden into a mush on the floor. But it was considered bad manners to spit the fishbones straight out on the floor. (pp. 16–17)

It was still dark, though in the east the sky was beginning to glow with a greenish tint. A light but piercing breeze came to meet them from the rising sun.

There is nothing as bitter as this moment when you go out to the morning muster—in the dark, in the cold, with a hungry belly to face a whole day of work. You lose your tongue. You lose all desire to speak to anyone. (p. 26)

Extract from Alexander Solzhenitsyn, *The Gulag Archipelago*, 1974.   SOURCE 5.N

Scattered from the Bering Strait almost to the Bosporus are thousands of islands of the spellbound Archipelago. They are invisible, but they exist. And the invisible slaves of the Archipelago, who have substance, weight, and volume, have to be transported from island to island just as invisibly and interruptedly.

And by what means are they to be transported? On what?

Great ports exist for this purpose—transit prisons: and smaller ports—camp transit points. Sealed steel ships also exist: railroad cars especially christened zak cars (prisoners cars). And out at the anchorages, they are met by similarly sealed, versatile Black Marias rather than by sloops and cutters. The zak cars move along on regular schedules. And, whenever necessary, whole caravans—trains of red cattle cars—are sent from port to port along the routes of the Archipelago.

All this is a thoroughly developed system! It was created over dozens of years—not hastily. Well-fed, uniformed, unhurried people created it . . .

All this is happening right next to you, you can almost touch it, but it's invisible (and you can shut your eyes to it too). At the big stations the loading and unloading of the dirty faces takes place far, far from the passenger platform and is seen only by switchmen and roadbed inspectors. (pp. 489–90)

Extract from Boris Pasternak, *Doctor Zhivago*, 1957.   SOURCE 5.O

. . . We were told: 'Here you are. This is your camp'—An open field with a post in the middle and a notice on it saying: 'Gulag 92 Y.N. 90'—that's all there was . . . First we broke saplings with our bare hands in the frost, to get wood to build our huts with. And in the end, believe it or not, we built our own camp. We put up our prison and our stockade and our punishment cells and our watch towers, all with our own hands. And then we began our work as lumberjacks. We felled trees. We harnessed ourselves, eight to a sledge, and we hauled timber and sank into the snow up to our necks.

Questions

a **i)** From Extract 5.M, what sort of life was experienced by the political prisoners?

ii) Write a report on the prisoners' life in one of these camps. Consider the accommodation, food, diseases, working conditions, temperature, guards, hygiene.

iii) Compare this lifestyle with that of the political prisoners sent to the camps under the Tsars. What major differences can be identified? How do you account for the changes/differences?

b **i)** Explain the meaning of the term 'Gulag Archipelago'.

ii) What does Extract 5.N tell us about the Archipelago?

c What evidence of conditions in the labour camps is provided by Source 5.O?

d How useful are historical novels to someone seeking to understand the lifestyle and attitudes of people in the past? Give examples from Sources 5.M, 5.N and 5.O to support your ideas.

The Stalinist Constitution

FOCUS QUESTION   What were the major features of the 1936 Constitution?

AIMS

ONE AIM of the Stalinist revolution was to portray to the outside world the victory of socialism. This found its expression in the 1936 Constitution, and was based on the assumption that the defeat of the kulaks meant that the internal class struggle was over and the true socialist order could now be constructed.

DETAILS

The 1936 Constitution greatly extended the power of the central federal government. Moscow took on administration of defence, foreign affairs and the budget. The old representative body, the All-Union of Congress of Soviets, was replaced as the chief legislative body by the Supreme Soviet. This was a two-chamber assembly made up of the Soviet of the Union and the Soviet of the Nationalities. The Soviet of the Union was based on electorates of approximately 300 000 citizens. Thus the more populated areas of European Russia had greater representation and authority. To balance this, the Soviet of Nationalities had an equal number of deputies from each of the republics. Other innovations included the direct election of soviets every four years by all citizens over the age of eighteen using secret ballot; former 'class enemies' such as clergy, ex-Tsarist officials and kulaks were granted full civil rights so long as they exercised them in accordance with 'the interest of the working class'. The Constitution also legitimised the notion of the one-party state by pointing out that political parties were produced by classes, and since the class war was now over there was no need for any political party other than the Communists.

However, the power of the Supreme Soviet was very limited. It met for only a few days of the year, and when it did it merely 'rubber-stamped' decisions already made by the higher organs of the state. It was elected every four years, and the people standing had to be Communist Party members, and had to be approved by the Party. Control was maintained through Party members throughout the country and through the fact that all decisions came from the central organisation. Power remained in the hands of the members of the Politburo.

SUMMARY

- The 1936 Constitution was used to legitimise the position of the Communist Party.
- While the Constitution appeared democratic, power remained firmly in the hands of the leaders of the Communist Party.

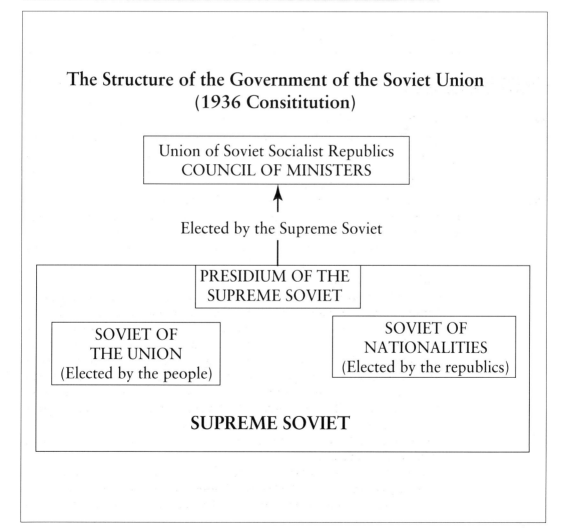

The Structure of the Government of the Soviet Union
(1936 Consititution)

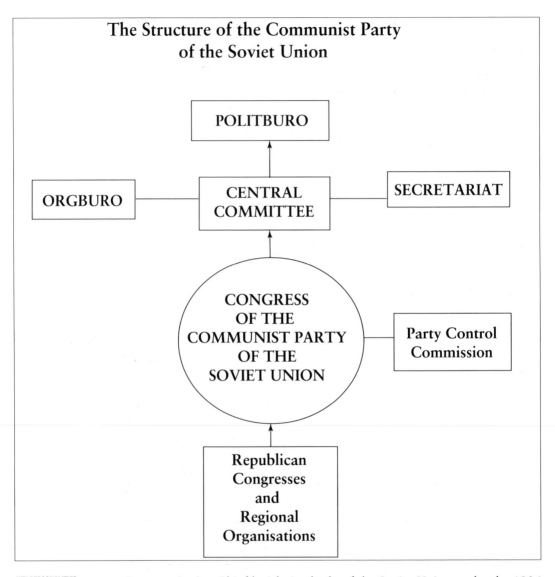

The Structure of the Communist Party
of the Soviet Union

POLITBURO

ORGBURO — CENTRAL COMMITTEE — SECRETARIAT

CONGRESS
OF THE
COMMUNIST PARTY
OF THE
SOVIET UNION

Party Control
Commission

Republican
Congresses
and
Regional
Organisations

KEY PERSONALITIES, GROUPS, TERMS

Supreme Soviet: Chief legislative body of the Soviet Union under the 1936 Constitution; divided into two houses—the Soviet of the Union and the Soviet of the Nationalities; power was actually limited with most legislation being generated by the Politburo.

Presidium: The executive body of the Supreme Soviet.

EXERCISES

1. Consider the following two views of the 1936 Constitution.
   - J.N. Westwood: 'It bore much of the outward form of the U.S. Constitution but in fact most of its provisions were either meaningless or misleading.'

- L. Schapiro: '[The Constitution was] worthless as a guarantee of individual rights.'
Are these two views accurate? Support your opinion with evidence.
2. A. Ulam has argued that the 1936 Constitution was a significant document for the following reasons:
   - it sought to protect the continuity of the Soviet state
   - it sought to impress foreign opinion (which was at the time under threat from fascism)
   - it showed that the Soviet Union had emerged from the period of revolutionary buffetings and mumbo jumbo, and was once again a stable and progressive state.
   To what extent can this view be justified?

Stalinism—an Assessment

FOCUS QUESTION What was Stalinism?

THE SYSTEM OF GOVERNMENT under Stalin in the years 1928 to 1945 rested upon the twin pillars of centralised direction and the use of force. What were its roots and how can it be viewed in retrospect?

HISTORICAL BACKGROUND

After seven years of war and the total collapse of the Tsarist system the new Communist government in 1921 was increasingly isolated from its original support base. The urban working classes had either been removed by death or deprivation, or had moved to the countryside in search of a more secure living. The political history of the Soviet Union in the 1920s did little to consolidate the regime's power. The introduction of the NEP, the intra-Party faction struggles and the continuing hostility of foreign powers maintained and broadened the Party's insecurity. Ever since 1917 the Communists had treated both their supporters and their enemies harshly. Not only were its political rivals eliminated in 1917–18, but frequent purges rid the Party of some of its more valuable supporters.

Throughout these years Stalin manipulated the organisation to achieve power for himself. As a member of the Orgburo, Politburo and Secretariat he had established by the late 1920s an unassailable power base from which to institute 'his' revolution. His defeat of Zinoviev in 1926 as a result of his organisational links within the Party is an example. While the coercive power of the regime at the peripheries of society was marginal and loose, Stalin's control at the centre was absolute. This was the essence of Stalinism.

The Stalinist revolution of the late 1920s and 1930s sought to achieve socialism in a backward country. The decisions Stalin took in 1928 and 1929

LINKS WITH THE PAST

were not a break with the past but had definite links with the original purpose of the 1917 Revolution. The absence of a middle class, the lack of true proletarian organisations and a disciplined Party organisation allowed Stalin to institute his revolution from above.

The Stalinist revolution emerged in a series of phases. The revolutionary economic, cultural and social changes began in the late 1920s and early 1930s; the political changes came with the purges and the terror of the mid-1930s.

STALIN'S LEGACY

Stalin was not 'simply another bureaucrat', as suggested by Trotsky. His role was much more significant. It was Stalin who collectivised agriculture and instituted and maintained rapid industrialisation. Of course there were members of the regime who assisted in the completion of these tasks and believed that centralised direction was necessary. However, there was never any doubt as to the origins of these directions: it was Stalin who managed the economy, controlled Party membership, began the purges, and maintained the system.

For Lenin, the notion of 'party' had never been important. His emphasis, along with Trotsky, had been upon governing Russia and securing power. With Lenin's death and the ostracism of Trotsky, a major sea-change took place: the 'Party', headed by General Secretary Stalin took on an increasing role in the life of the Soviet state and came to subsume the bureaucratic structures which maintained the day-to-day functioning of the nation. Lenin's 1919 Constitution made no mention of the Bolshevik/Communist Party; Stalin's 1936 Constitution stressed the Party's primacy.

It should be noted, however, that a further change came in the 1930s. The purges, show trials and personal paranoia of Stalin led the Party to come under attack as the self-seeking, Stalin-serving apparatchik came to the fore. Between 1934 and 1953 there were only two Party Congresses held. When war came in 1941 the Communist Party was, to all intents and purposes, actually in decline. It would be left to Stalin's successors to reassert its authority.

SUMMARY

- Stalin was the essential figure in the development of the Soviet Union between 1928 and 1945.
- The Stalinist revolution had firm links with the Bolshevik past.
- By the end of the 1930s, the Stalinist 'revolution' had given way to a conservative and reactionary desire to maintain the new institutions and power structures which had been established.
- Stalinism involved revolutionary social and economic change as well as massive repression and terror.

DOCUMENT STUDY No. 14

Examine the sources and answer the questions which follow.

Cartoon, published by Soviet exiles in Paris in the 1930s
depicting a meeting of the Supreme Soviet

SOURCE 5P

Statistics from Alec Nove, *An Economic History of the USSR*, published in 1969.

SOURCE 5.Q

Industrial Production (millions of tons)

	1927/28	1937
Coal	35	128
Oil	12	28.5
Pig iron	3	14.5
Steel	4	18

Agricultural Production (millions of tons)

	1928	1933
Grain harvests	73	68

Livestock (millions of head)

Cattle	70.5	38
Pigs	26	12
Sheep and goats	147	50

SOURCE 5.R

Extract from an account of the 1930s written by Nadezhda Mandelstam, whose husband died in a labour camp

Nobody trusted anyone else, and every acquaintance was a suspected police informer ... Every family was always going over its circle of acquaintances, trying to pick out the provocateurs, the informers and the traitors. After 1937, people stopped meeting each other altogether, and the secret police were thus well on the way to achieving their ultimate objective ... they had isolated people from each other.

SOURCE 5.S

Extract from a speech by Stalin, February 1931

It is sometimes asked whether it is not possible to slow down the tempo some-what, to put a check on the movement. No, comrades, it is not possible! The tempo must not be reduced! On the contrary, we must increase it as much as is within our powers and possibilities. This is dictated to us by our obligations to the workers and peasants of the USSR. This is dictated to us by our obligations to the working class of the whole world.

Question

a **i)** Explain the point being made by the cartoon in Source 5.P.
  ii) According to Source 5.S, what pressures were dictating the course of developments in the Soviet Union?
  iii) From Source 5.Q, which areas of output saw the largest increase and decrease?

b Using Source 5.S and your own knowledge, explain how Stalin attempted to put his doctrine of 'socialism in one country' into operation in the Soviet Union between 1928 and 1941.

c Explain how an historian would find each of these sources useful in attempting to understand the effects of Stalinism on the Soviet Union. (In your answer you must refer to the nature, audience and motive of each source as well as its content.)

d Using all four sources and your own knowledge, explain the importance of Stalin in the functioning of the Soviet Union between 1928 and 1941.

EXTRA WRITING

Essays

Stalin established a dictatorship which was a betrayal of both Marxism and Leninism. To what extent do you agree with this statement?

Josef Stalin was another Tsar, only in different clothes. To what extent is this an appropriate description of Stalin and Stalinism?

EXTRA READING

Alec Nove, *An Economic History of the USSR*
David Christian, *Power and Privilege*
J.N. Westwood, *Endurance and Endeavour*
G. Gill, *Stalinism*
Alan Wood, *Stalin and Stalinism*
I. Deutscher, *Stalin: A Political Biography*
I. Deutscher, *Trotsky*
T.A. Morris, *European History, 1848–1945*
P. Baker and J. Bassett, *Stalin's Revolution*
L. Kochan and A. Abraham, *A History of Modern Russia*
Boris Pasternak, *Doctor Zhivago*
Alexander Solzhenitsyn, *The Gulag Archipelago*
Alexander Solzhenitsyn, *One Day in the Life of Ivan Denisovich*

THE PROBLEMS AND ISSUES

Consider the Problems and Issues:

Ideology in Theory and Practice
The Role of the Party and the State
Collectivisation
Changes in Society
Stalinism and Totalitarianism

in relation to the period 1928 to 1941.

Notice the way in which **ideology** has shifted to 'socialism in one country' with the desire to secure the revolution and the achievements of the Party leadership against all enemies (both internal and external)—**collectivisation**, industrialisation and foreign policy are all used for these ends—the social revolution creates a new leadership class in the Soviet Union—the purges, terror, OGPU/NKVD are used to eliminate the real and imagined enemies—centralisation of all economic, social and political life—the emphasis upon planning, the cult of the leader and the subjugation of the individual.

Notice the way in which the **Party** has become the **state**—this is enshrined through the 1936 Constitution—remember the distinction between central directives and the compliance of the regions and the rise of the bureaucracy—were the purges a mechanism for Party purification and control?

All of this is associated with the desire for national security and rapid industrial progress in the wake of perceived external threats—what was the human cost? what was the Party cost?

When considering **totalitarianism** and **Stalinism**, keep in mind the 'totalitarian model' proposed by American political scientist Carl Freidrich in the 1950s—it is based on the control of each of the following factors—does Stalinism conform in each?

• control of economy:	centralisation of control
	collectivisation
	industrialisation
• control of the armed forces:	monopoly of control
	purges
• control of the Party:	single-party government
	one leader
	interconnectedness of Party and state
• control of ideology:	direction given to all aspects of Soviet life
• control of the media:	the cult of Stalin
	control and elimination of enemies
	propaganda
	education
• use of terror:	dekulakisation
	the purges
	elimination of enemies (real and imagined)

WRITING THE ESSAY

Essay:
What evidence would you use to provide a balanced view of Stalinism?

In answering this question you should consider the following:

THE POSITIVE ASPECTS OF STALINISM
Its links with the Bolshevik past
The desire to create a 'classless society'
The industrial success of the Five-Year Plans

Improvements in education
Improvements in the status of women

Versus

THE NEGATIVE ASPECTS OF STALINISM
The growth of the one-party state
The use of institutionalised terror
The purges, show trials and absence of opposition
Massive dislocation of the population
The effects of collectivisation
The social effects of industrialisation
The loss of individuality and the legacy of fear and suspicion

Consider the actions of the following people:
Stalin, Trotsky, Beria, Kirov, Rykov, Tomsky, Yagoda, Yezhov, Zhdanov, Zinoviev,
Kamenev, the kulaks, the Stakhanovites.

Consider the following events:
Collectivisation, industrialisation, the purges and show trials, the Ezhovschina,
the 1936 Constitution, the social and cultural changes.

Finally, consider the following summary of Stalinist historiography:

SOURCE 5.T

From T.A. Morris, *European History, 1848–1945*, pp. 206–7

In forming so much of the modern structure of the Soviet Union, Stalin and his government engineered one of the most monumental achievements of the twentieth
century. The human cost of that achievement was so high that not even Stalin's successors in power could openly accept it. As a result of this unique combination of
factors, historical judgements on Stalin have varied more widely than those on
any other modern political figure. Nowhere has this been more evident than in the
U.S.S.R. itself. During his tenure of office he was of course praised as the all-wise
leader, the natural continuor of the ideology of Marx and Lenin, guiding his
country through the various perils of the epoch. Much of the history of the revolution was rewritten to support this view, as in Stalin's own work, *Short History of the
Communist Party of the Soviet Union* (1938). Much was swallowed wholesale by
sympathetic foreign writers such as Stalin's French biographer H. Barbusse
(Stalin: A New World Seen Through One Man, 1936). Between 1956–1961,
however, official historiography in the Soviet Union sought to reverse the process
entirely. Stalin, it was now declared, had perverted the course of the revolution by
allowing the 'cult of the personality' to develop in the 1930s and by taking
savage and unwarranted action against other sound communists in the purges.
His body was removed from Lenin's mausoleum in Red Square. It was, however,
reburied in a place of honour alongside the Kremlin wall. In reality, the approved
view of Stalin in the Soviet Union today is probably close to that stated by N.S.
Khrushchev in a speech in 1957. 'It is, of course, a bad thing that Stalin launched into
deviations and mistakes which harmed our cause. But even when he committed mistakes and allowed the laws to be broken, he did that with the full conviction that he
was defending the gains of the Revolution, the cause of socialism. That was
Stalin's tragedy.'
The most violent opposition to Stalin in his lifetime and since his death has come, not
from the west, but from the followers of L.D. Trotsky. Trotsky's own works, such as
The Revolution Betrayed (1937), will admit no compromise with Stalinism.
Instead, they portray Stalin's whole career in power, the building of the Party

bureaucracy, the development of personal leadership, the whole concept of 'Socialism in One Country', as a betrayal of the principles of Marx and Lenin. The man responsible for this perversion of the revolution was thus, in Trotsky's famous phrase, the 'gravedigger of the revolution'.

Western commentaries upon Stalin's life and policies have generally been characterised by a mixture of awe and disapproval. They seem to be roughly divided into two 'schools'. The first is that which views the personality and psychology of Stalin as vital formative factors in the events of the 1930s. This school might be represented by the work of R.C. Tucker (*Stalin as Revolutionary*, 1973). He argues in 'psychohistorical' terms that Stalin's inflated self-image of himself as Lenin's natural successor was a crucial factor in Soviet developments in the 1920s and 30s, which might otherwise have followed a rather different path. More writers have preferred to view Stalin as the agent of other impersonal forces released, but not mastered in the earlier stages of the revolution. For A. Ulam (*Stalin: The Man and His Era*, 1974), he represents a remarkable continuity with earlier Bolshevism. He was forced to deal with problems created by Lenin's opportunism, and solve them by methods quite consistent with earlier Bolshevik practice. He, rather than Lenin, is the greatest and most successful of the Bolsheviks. For I. Deutscher (*Stalin: A Political Biography*, 1949), it was less the impetus of Bolshevism than that of centuries of Russian history to which Stalin was the heir. His comparison is less with Lenin than with Ivan the Terrible and Peter the Great who similarly forced the inert mass of Russian society and tradition into new paths by extreme and inhuman methods. Deutscher is also one of the many writers who have stressed the absence in Russia after the revolution and civil war of the proper economic and social conditions for the development of the free revolutionary society originally envisaged by the Bolsheviks. Similar lines of argument have been followed by A. Nove (*An Economic History of the U.S.S.R.*, 1969) and by R. Pethybridge (*The Social Prelude to Stalinism*, 1974). They lay their stresses respectively upon the economic and social backwardness of post-revolutionary Russia, which faced Stalin with the alternatives of drastic action or ultimate political failure. By avoiding the latter fate, by whatever means, Stalin stands as a dominant figure in the formation of the modern world.

6

The Soviet Union at War

At the end of this topic you should attempt to answer the following question:
Why did the Soviet Union defeat Germany in the Great Patriotic War?

THE PROBLEMS AND ISSUES

In this topic the relevant Problems and Issues for analysis in the HSC are:
Changes in Society
Stalinism and Totalitarianism
Communism and the Great Patriotic War

Changes in society involves the industrial, agricultural and lifestyle changes introduced by Stalin and the role of these in the defence of the Soviet Union against the German invasion.

Stalinism as a **totalitarian** phenomenon must again be considered—in relation to both the coming of the war (and Soviet foreign policy in the 1920s and 1930s) and in the waging of the war after 1941.

Communism's role in the victory must also be taken into account. How important was centralised control? Balance this against the part played by the patriotism of the Soviet peoples as they fought to defend the 'motherland' rather than communist principles.

Soviet Foreign Policy

FOCUS QUESTIONS

What were the major directions of Soviet foreign policy under Lenin?

What were the major directions of Soviet foreign policy under Stalin?

In what ways did Stalin's notion of 'socialism in one country' influence Soviet foreign policy to 1941?

How did the Western nations respond to the actions and/or reactions of the Soviet Union between 1917 and 1941?

What role did the Soviet Union play in the outbreak of war in 1939?

TIME LINE

1918		Georgy Chicherin appointed Commissar for Foreign Affairs
	March	Germany and Russia sign the Treaty of Brest-Litovsk
		British forces land at Murmansk
	April	Japanese forces land at Vladivostok
	November	French forces land at Odessa
		Armistice ends the fighting between Germany and the Allies
1919		
	January	Paris Peace Conference convenes
		Civil war in Russia between Red and White forces
	March	Meeting of the Third International—Comintern
	June	Treaty of Versailles signed between Germany and Allies
	September	Treaty of St Germain signed between Austria and Allies
		White forces attack Moscow
	November	Treaty of Neuilly between Bulgaria and Allies
1920		
	January	Moscow announces the Twenty-One Demands of the Third International
	March	US Congress rejects the Paris Peace Settlement
	April	War begins between Russia and Poland
	June	Treaty of Trianon between Hungary and Allies
	August	Polish forces defeat six Red armies in the Battle for Moscow
	October	Russo-Polish War ends
	November	Allies withdraw from Russian Civil War
1921		
	March	Treaty of Riga sets Russian and Polish borders
	April	Widespread famine in Russia
1922		
	April	Treaty of Rapallo between Russia and Germany
	December	Formation of the Union of Soviet Socialist Republics
1924		
	February	Formal British recognition of Soviet Union—other countries follow
	October	France recognises Soviet Union
1926		
	April	Treaty of Berlin between Germany and Soviet Union extends Rapallo agreement
1927		
	May	Britain breaks diplomatic relations with Soviet Union
1929		
	October	Britain resumes relations with Soviet Union
	1930	Maxim Litvinov becomes Soviet Commissar for Foreign Affairs: within three years he organises non-aggression pacts between the Soviet Union and Finland, Estonia, Latvia, Poland
1932		
	November	Non-aggression pact signed between France and Soviet Union

1933		
	January	Hitler becomes Chancellor of Germany
	February	Soviet Foreign Minister Litvinov supports call for French security
	June	Secret military training agreement between Germany and Soviet Union ends
1934		
	April	Renewal of non-aggression pact between Soviet Union and Poland
	August	Hitler assumes the title 'Fuhrer'
	September	Soviet Union admitted to the League of Nations
1935		
	May	Franco–Soviet Mutual Assistance Pact
		Czech–Soviet Mutual Assistance Pact
	June	French Premier Laval makes overtures to Soviets with regard to forming an alliance
	July	Comintern Conference in Moscow establishes a 'Popular Front' against fascism
1936		
	November	Germany and Japan form Anti-Comintern Pact
1937		
	August	Chinese–Soviet Non-Aggression Pact
	November	Italy joins Anti-Comintern Pact
1939		
	March	Spain joins Anti-Comintern Pact
		Stalin condemns the policy of appeasement adopted by Britain and France
	April	Litvinov proposes alliance between Soviet Union, Britain and France
	May	Vyacheslav Molotov replaces Litvinov as Commissar for Foreign Affairs
		Soviet forces defeat Kwantang Army on Siberia–Manchuria border
	August	Soviet–Anglo–French talks in Moscow
		Nazi–Soviet Non-Aggression Pact
	November	Soviet troops invade Finland
	December	Soviet Union expelled from League of Nations
1940		
	March	Soviet Union and Finland sign peace treaty
	June	Soviet Union occupies the Baltic states
1941		
	April	Soviet–Japanese Neutrality Pact signed
	June	Germany invades the Soviet Union

GUIDING PRINCIPLES

THROUGHOUT the inter-war period the guiding principle in all Soviet foreign policy decisions was the survival of the revolution. Initially this was founded upon the notion of a permanent world revolution which was espoused at the time of the Bolshevik seizure of power. As time passed, however, and it became obvious that such a revolution was unlikely to take place, the focus became the survival of the Soviet Union itself. The Soviet leadership (both Lenin and Stalin alike) were prepared to put aside strict ideological considerations in order to avoid war at all costs until the Soviet Union was strong and stable enough to defend itself. As Richard Overy points out:

> During the inter-war years Soviet foreign policy was dominated by the desire to stand aside from the conflicts of the capitalist world, to become, in Lenin's memorably mixed metaphor, an 'oasis of Soviet power in the middle of the raging imperialist sea'.
>
> (Richard Overy and Andrew Wheatcroft, *The Road to War*, 1989 p. 184)

It is for this reason that the events of August 1920 take on great importance. The failure of the six Red armies led by Mikhail Tukhachevsky to defeat the Polish legionnaires in the battle for Warsaw during the Russo-Polish War marked the end of the hopes held by Lenin and the Bolsheviks to extend their revolution across Western Europe. A central plank in the Bolshevik ideology had been the belief that their revolution would unleash a social revolution which would sweep across all of Europe. Lenin even believed that communism would not survive in Russia without the support of the rest of the world's proletariat. By 1920, though, all other potential revolutions had disappeared and the Bolsheviks themselves had been brought to the brink of defeat in the Civil War in Russia. An ideological about-face consequently took place in relation to Bolshevik foreign policy: from being based upon expansion and advancement, it became based upon internal consolidation and defence against outside threats: 'world revolution' became replaced by 'world isolation'. It was from this that Stalin's guiding belief of 'socialism in one country' emerged. As with all foreign policy matters, however, the course of events would not be determined solely by the actions or efforts of the Soviet Union itself. The preparedness of the outside world to tolerate the continued existence of the Soviet Union (and/or go so far as to cooperate with it) would also influence the course of international events.

THE BATTLE FOR WARSAW, 1920

With the end of the Civil War and the withdrawal of foreign troops, Lenin believed that the Communists had achieved a 'breathing space'. The problem was that there was no indication of how long it would last. He therefore turned to a policy of 'revolutionary pragmatism': the Soviet Union publicly declared that it stood for peaceful coexistence and economic cooperation with the capitalist powers, while at the same time exploiting situations to gain whatever it could whenever it could. Again as Richard Overy points out:

REVOLUTIONARY PRAGMATISM

> Where possible Lenin hoped the Soviet Union could play off one imperialist power against another; when necessary the Soviet Union would even co-operate with imperialist powers if there was something it needed badly enough. Anything, Stalin later wrote, 'which is a necessity from the standpoint of Soviet Russia, is also

a necessity from the standpoint of the world revolution'. Tactical flexibility was possible because Russia had everything to gain and little to lose.
(Richard Overy and Andrew Wheatcroft, *The Road to War*, p. 187)

GEORGY CHICHERIN

One of the earliest examples of this 'tactical flexibility' was in Lenin's choice as the first Soviet Commissar for Foreign Affairs: Georgy Chicherin. Chicherin embodied everything the Communists supposedly opposed: he was an aristocrat from the Tsar's Foreign Office, and he had been a Menshevik. However, he was a skilled diplomat with a mastery of many foreign languages, and he was a revisionist opposed to the Treaty of Versailles and the League of Nations (which he saw as an instrument for capitalist aggression and expansion). Chicherin was typical of many of the officials recruited to head government departments in the early years of the Communist regime. He was a 'bourgeois specialist'. His skills were exploited by the Communists, but he was never admitted to the Party's inner circle.

Along with many of the leading Communists, Chicherin believed that the major early threat to the Soviet Union was Great Britain. Britain was seen as the major promoter of the Allied intervention in the Civil War and British imperial power was viewed as the greatest threat to a possible world revolution.

Out of this suspicion of Britain grew Chicherin's determination to forge friendships or alliances or understandings wherever he could. The Soviet Union initially formed an agreement with Germany, their recent enemy, and now fellow world outcast. The Treaty of Rapallo (1922) and the Treaty of Berlin (1926) saw Germany and the Soviet Union agree to work together in a number of areas: economic cooperation and the renunciation of all reparations demands from the First World War; benevolent neutrality in the event of invasion from another power—that is, neither side would directly intervene in support of the other, but would give moral and material assistance if necessary; the Soviet Union gained advanced industrial equipment and technology; and the German armed forces gained the training facilities forbidden them by the Treaty of Versailles, such as tank units in Kazan and the use of the Lipetsk airfield as a testing and training ground for the latest aircraft. This relationship with Germany was typical of Soviet international moves in the inter-war period. By forging such an alliance with a possible aggressor, the Soviet Union kept its potential enemies from forming their own agreements. It was all about ensuring that the Soviet Union, regardless of the ideological or physical cost, survived.

A good example of this pragmatism was the attitude of the Soviet Union to the United States of America during the 1920s. Ideologically, the Communists should have viewed this bastion of capitalism with suspicion and loathing, yet economic relations were established between the two countries very early in the decade. The Soviets drew heavily upon American technological and industrial expertise and much was made of the achievements of men such as Henry Ford. The justification was, as usual, that:

Soviet industry needed the collaboration and technical equipment of the industrialised West, but only in order to strengthen communism. The same was true of Germany, where Soviet officials collaborated not with the large and powerful German labour movement, but with the most reactionary sections of the German armed forces and big business. They fully recognised the political limits of co-operation. The survival of communism and the safety of Russia produced strange bedfellows, but hostility was never far beneath the surface. (Richard Overy and Andrew Wheatcroft, *The Road to War*, p.189)

This hostility found expression in a number of instances: the Red Scare and so-called Palmer Raids in the USA, the Zinoviev Letter which brought down the British Labour government, the Soviet perception that the main purpose of the Locarno Treaty was to lay the basis for a war against them, and the 'war scare' in the Soviet Union in 1927 following attacks on communists in Britain and China. Stalin was successfully able to use the catch-cry that 'the revolution was in danger' to further institute the notion of 'communism in one country'—from 1927 the remaining internationalists were removed from influence within the Party and the programs of industrialisation and collectivisation were commenced.

Added to this was the existence of the Communist International (Comintern). While this body (whose avowed aim was the organisation, coordination and promotion of the communist parties of the world) was supposed to be completely independent of the Soviet government, this was not the way it was perceived in the West—nor was it actually the case. Comintern itself shifted focus, and turned from promoting 'communism' to promoting the interests and survival of the Soviet Union. This change of emphasis eventually trapped Comintern in what was to prove to be a self-destructive paradox: in order to survive the Soviet Union needed Lenin's 'breathing space'; this breathing space depended upon the capitalist nations being economically and socially stable; communist parties, however, were supposed to be working to create economic and social instability. By linking Comintern to the needs of Moscow rather than to the needs of the working class in general, the Soviet Union negated any possibility of cooperation between all sections of the political left wing. Therefore when fascist organisations emerged in the West they were not faced with a united political and/or philosophical opposition.

THE COMMUNIST INTERNATIONAL

One significant development in the inter-war period did, for a time, work in the Soviet Union's favour. This was the onset of the Great Depression in 1929. The capitalist world was plunged into economic crisis just at the time Stalin embarked upon his own massive economic expansion. The Soviet Union's industrialisation therefore became a readily accepted market for Western resources. Germany and Britain became major trading partners with the Soviets as they put issues of immediate economic need to the fore of foreign policy decisions.

THE GREAT DEPRESSION

However, the Depression also created uncertainties for the Soviet Union. While the economic crisis created increased support for communism abroad, it also led the Western nations to abandon collective action through organisations such as the League of Nations and seek national security through rearmament. Stalin was convinced that the target of these capitalist weapons would be the Soviet state. This attitude was strengthened by the Japanese occupation of Manchuria in 1931 and then completely entrenched with Adolf Hitler's assumption of power in 1933. But even at this stage the Soviets were prepared to compromise, albeit for only a short time:

> In 1933 Hitler, the most vocal and uncompromising of the new generation of anti-Bolsheviks, assumed power in Berlin. For some months the Soviet Union made desperate attempts to maintain the connection with Germany which had been at the centre of her strategy since 1922. German machine tools were vital for Soviet industrial expansion; in 1931 there were over 5,000 German engineers working in Soviet industry. Soviet officials and commissars went out of their way to assure the Nazi regime that the change of government made no difference to the Soviet friendship. The Soviet Union stood back while the largest communist party in Europe was broken up and terrorised by the Nazi SA. Only by the end of 1933 did relations perceptibly cool with the German refusal to tone down press attacks on the Soviet Union. Co-operation with German armed forces came to an end in October 1933. But even in 1934 Molotov, Chairman of the Council of Commissars, could publicly announce that the Soviet Union had no other wish 'than to continue further good relations with Germany . . . one of the great nations of the modern epoch'. Only the Nazi-Polish pact, signed in 1934, brought the relationship to an end. Not even the Soviet Union could swallow German concessions to the state in Europe it hated most. (Overy and Wheatcroft, *The Road to War*, p. 197)

MAXIM LITVINOV

The emergence of Japan and Germany as potential threats to Soviet security caused a change of emphasis in Soviet foreign policy. From the start of the 1930s it was decided that 'communism in one country' would be maintained by the Soviet Union's giving its support to the Western notion of collective security and active participation in the League of Nations. Maxim Litvinov (the Commissar of Foreign Affairs following Chicherin's retirement in 1930) pointed out:

> What other guarantee of security is there? Military alliance and the policy of balance of power? Pre-war history has shown that this policy not only does not get rid of war, but on the contrary unleashes it. (A. Ulam, *Expansion and Co-existence: A History of Soviet Foreign Policy 1917–1967*, pp. 218–19)

Litvinov was the best man to achieve this aim: he was outgoing, pro-European, popular in Western diplomatic circles, and he recognised that the best way to contain the perceived fascist threat was for the Soviet Union to work closely with Britain and France.

During this period of goodwill between the Soviet Union and the West, Litvinov signed non-aggression pacts with Finland, Latvia, Estonia, Poland and France. He established formal diplomatic relations with the United States of America, and in 1934 secured the Soviet Union's membership of the League of Nations. The Comintern also conformed to this new image and adopted the strategy of cooperating with democratic and republican parties in the conflict against the fascist enemy. This was the 'Popular Front'. It was not that the Comintern (or even the Soviet government) had changed or abandoned its ultimate goal of world revolution and the destruction of capitalism. It was a case of making it appear otherwise in order to ensure Soviet survival.

The problem for the Soviets was that the major Western nations never completely fell for the ruse. In 1935 France signed a mutual assistance treaty with the Soviet Union but never undertook any discussions in relation to military support for this agreement. When Italy attacked Abyssinia in 1935 and Germany reoccupied the Rhineland in 1936 the Soviet Union argued for the strict imposition of collective action and international law against the fascist expansionists. Instead France and Britain compromised. Similarly with the outbreak of the Spanish Civil War in 1936, Britain and France did little to support the Popular Front government:

REACTION FROM THE WEST

> The failure of co-operation over Spain was a painful lesson for Soviet strategy. It served to confirm what Soviet leaders had suspected all along, that Western statesmen were only half-hearted defenders of collective security, more hostile to communism than to fascism. The ideological divide was as great as ever, but it was self-interest as much as ideology that seemed to govern Western attitudes. Stalin had never shed his dislike of the British Empire, and he interpreted British inaction over Spain as a calculated attempt to drive the Soviet Union into a war with Germany from which the imperial powers alone would profit. This attitude was to colour Soviet attitudes to the West profoundly throughout the period leading to German invasion in 1941. (Overy and Wheatcroft, *The Road to War*, p. 200)

The Soviet Union once again came to see itself as isolated, and the threat of Japan and Germany was reinforced in Soviet eyes by the formation of the Anti-Comintern Pact between Japan, Germany and Italy in 1936–37. To make matters worse, in 1937 the Ezhovschina was unleashed within the Soviet Union as the Party and provinces were purged of enemies (some real, most imagined). While Litvinov survived, his two deputies, his personal secretaries and many ambassadors did not. More than half the officer corps were purged from the armed forces, as were all the major strategists and technicians from the air force. The victims included 90 per cent of all generals and 80 per cent of all colonels, with virtually the entire Soviet General Staff being tried and executed as German spies.

The international ramifications of the purges were disastrous. France became even more reluctant to cooperate with the Soviets, fearing that its own secrets would be passed straight on to the Germans. The elimination of so many of its major military figures meant, from the British and French standpoint, that the Soviet Union was no longer a viable counterweight to Japanese and German expansion. The Soviet Union consequently found itself more isolated than it had been before. The Soviet perception of these events was of course slightly different: as far as Stalin was concerned the British and French were once again embarking on a policy of strengthening Germany in order to unleash it in a war to destroy Russia.

THE EFFECTS OF THE PURGES

The real test of the relationship came over Czechoslovakia in 1938. Like France, the Soviet Union had a mutual assistance treaty with Czecho-

THE CZECH CRISIS, 1938

slovakia, but with the important proviso that Soviet action would occur only if France honoured its pact. Throughout the Czech crisis, the Soviet Union insisted it would stand by its commitment to Prague. However, for France to do the same it would have had to convince Poland and Rumania to permit Soviet troops to move across their territory—something neither country was willing to allow. Stalin was determined that the Soviet Union would not face Germany alone while Britain and France sat back and watched. Yet British Prime Minister Neville Chamberlain was hardly likely to call upon Stalin for support when the Soviet Union was again speaking of moving against Poland and at the same time killing off its military commanders. Czechoslovakia's fate was sealed, and the possibility of cooperation between the Soviets and the West again disappeared. The exclusion of the Soviets from the Munich negotiations simply reinforced Stalin's view that the capitalist states were acting in cooperation against the Soviet Union.

However, the Soviet Union found itself no longer isolated from Europe following the Nazi occupation of the rest of Czechoslovakia in 1939 and Britain's guarantee of support to Poland. Moscow's support was being sought not only by London and Paris, but also by Berlin. Britain and France began overtures to the Soviets in an attempt to reconstruct the pre-1914 encirclement of Germany. At the same time Hitler attempted to neutralise this threat by driving a wedge between the potential allies. Without doing anything the Soviet Union had become the key to war or peace, and Stalin was determined to adopt the course which would do the Soviet state the least possible damage.

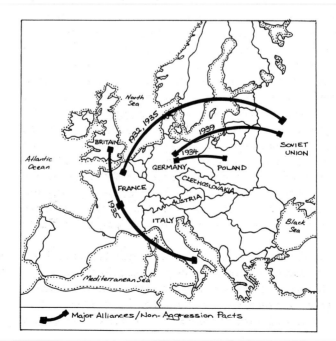

European Diplomacy in the 1930s

Initially Stalin felt that this lay in an alliance with Britain and France: he saw their combined might as exceeding that of Germany. The Soviets, though, put a price upon this support: guarantees from Britain and France of the territorial integrity of each of the remaining states of Eastern Europe, and the promise of mutual assistance in the event of a German attack. The French, and particularly the British, dithered and delayed. Britain had given Poland a guarantee but it was not prepared to fight to support Latvia or Estonia.

The problem was that by the time Chamberlain agreed to begin negotiations (May 1939) the situation had again changed. Western delays had reinforced Stalin's distrust of their resolve. He therefore became more sympathetic to the pro-Soviet noises emanating from Berlin. In May 1939 Litvinov was sacked and replaced as Commissar of Foreign Affairs by Vyacheslav Molotov who favoured a pro-German foreign policy. The Soviet Union, while still publicly courting the favour of Britain and France, then embarked upon secret negotiations with the Germans.

VYACHESLAV MOLOTOV

The one development which could have destroyed Stalin's careful juggling act was a separate agreement between Germany and the West. To negate this possibility the Soviets invited representatives from Britain and France to Moscow to begin military negotiations. However, the Western representatives who attended were neither senior officials nor did they possess the authority to sign binding agreements. This was again interpreted as evidence that the West did not trust Moscow. The negotiation of a political and economic agreement with Germany was therefore completed, and was followed immediately by the Nazi–Soviet Non-Aggression Pact of 24 August 1939. In return for Soviet neutrality, Germany promised the return of the Polish lands lost in 1917, the creation of a Soviet sphere of influence in Finland and the Baltic, as well as access to German industrial and military equipment.

THE NAZI–SOVIET PACT, 1939

The announcement of this agreement was viewed with dismay in Britain and France, yet it should not have been unexpected—there had been overt cooperation between Germany and the Soviet Union for twelve of the preceding seventeen years. Also, the Germans were promising the return of the territory which the Communists had been seeking since the revolution: Poland. The fundamental flaw in the Western strategy throughout the negotiations was that they had expected the Soviet Union to defend and support the existence of the one state in Europe which it would never accept as legitimate. When this was added to the continuing Soviet suspicion of the motives of the West and a belief that Britain was militarily too weak ever to be a useful ally to the Russians, Stalin simply seized the opportunity which gave the Soviet Union its long-sought-for neutrality and protection.

This breathing space did not last for long. As the German tanks rolled into Poland on 3 September 1939, the Japanese engaged Soviet forces in a large-scale battle on the Manchurian border. The Germans then swept across Poland with such rapidity that there was a real fear that they would be able to occupy the whole country, reach a truce with the West, and leave Russia under

THE GERMAN INVASION OF POLAND

threat on its own border. The Soviet Union therefore quickly reached its own truce with Japan and on 17 September entered Poland from the east, justifying its actions by saying that the war between Germany and Poland had clearly shown the internal problems of the Polish state and that these problems were in fact a threat to the Soviet state.

Both the Soviets and the Germans argued that any continuation of the war from this point would be the responsibility of the British and French. Some Communists even argued that Poland, like Belgium in 1914, was being used as a pawn of British imperialism. Now that the 'breathing space' had finally been achieved the Soviet Union turned its attention to the development of its armed forces in preparation for the inevitable war against capitalism which was to come. By 1941 the Soviet army had grown by 150 per cent and the air force was larger than those of Britain, France and Germany combined. The Five-Year Plans had worked; the Soviet Union was the second largest industrial nation in the world.

THE WINTER WAR

Inevitably this industrial and military muscle was flexed. The first victim was Finland. In October 1939 the Finns refused to heed a Soviet demand for a strip of territory to the north of Leningrad. The 'Winter War' between the two countries resulted in a Soviet victory in March 1940, but at great cost. In the first months of the war, the Finnish troops, led by Marshal Mannerheim, imposed defeat after defeat upon the Soviet forces, but were eventually overwhelmed by weight of numbers. The war cost the Soviet Union 200000 men, 700 planes and 1600 tanks; the Finns lost 25000 men. But there was also more than just a material cost: the Soviet Union was expelled from the League of Nations for its actions; and the weakness of the Soviet army against the Finns gave Hitler confidence that his own army could easily overwhelm the Soviet Union.

With Hitler preoccupied with his war in the west, Stalin took the opportunity to expand the Soviet Union's territory in Eastern Europe: north Bukovina, Bessarabia, Lithuania, Latvia and Estonia were all incorporated into the Soviet Union in 1940. This had not been within the terms of the Nazi–Soviet Pact and Stalin's actions annoyed Hitler. Relations between the two men cooled, and in July 1940 Hitler ordered the German economy to build the resources for an army bigger than all of the enemy armies combined. The Tripartite Pact was signed between Germany, Italy and Japan in September 1940 and Hitler ordered that plans be put together, under the greatest secrecy, for 'Operation Barbarossa'. In April 1941, Stalin secured his eastern border with the signing of a Neutrality Pact with Japan. On 22 June German forces invaded the Soviet Union.

SUMMARY

- Soviet foreign policy from 1918 to 1941 was determined by the desire to protect the revolution against external enemies.
- During the 1920s, Germany was the Soviet Union's major

ally—based on the fact that both countries had been ostracised by the Western world.
- After being opposed initially to the League of Nations and the notion of collective security, the Soviet Union in the 1930s became the strongest supporter of the League and its philosophy.
- The Communists were prepared to adopt a pragmatic attitude towards foreign affairs in order to protect and preserve their own interests.
- The existence of Comintern worked against the possibility of cooperation between the Soviet Union and the West.

Georgy Vasilyevich Chicherin: Soviet diplomat; born 1872, died 1936; served in the Russian foreign office under Tsar Nicholas II, but resigned to join the Social Democrats; from 1904 he lived abroad as a Menshevik; 1917, arrested in London, then returned to Russia in exchange for the return of the British ambassador; 1918, became Commissar for Foreign Affairs and signed the Treaty of Brest-Litovsk; 1922, negotiated the Rapallo Treaty which aligned Germany and the Soviet Union; retired in 1930; died 1936.

Maxim Maximovich Litvinov: Soviet diplomat; born 1876, died 1951; real name Maxim Maximovich Vallakh; Bolshevik and friend of Lenin; worked in London and married an Englishwoman; from 1917 he was Russia's diplomatic agent in Britain; 1930, appointed Commissar of Foreign Affairs; attempted to make the Soviet Union more internationally accepted; publicly supported collective security; created a number of treaties of non-aggression and/or mutual assistance with other European powers; 1934, secured the admission of the Soviet Union into the League of Nations; replaced in 1939; died 1951.

Vyacheslav Mikhailovich Molotov: Soviet politician; born 1890, died 1986; real name Vyacheslav Scriabin; joined the Bolsheviks in 1906; changed his name to Molotov, meaning 'hammer'; an ardent supporter of Stalin; 1925, became a full member of the Politburo; Premier of the Soviet Union 1930–41; replaced Litvinov as Commissar for Foreign Affairs in 1939; negotiated the Nazi–Soviet Non-Aggression Pact (sometimes referred to as the Molotov–Ribbentrop Pact); Deputy Premier 1941–57; again Foreign Commissar 1953–57; formed triumvirate with Beria and Malenkov to rule following Stalin's death but lost power struggle against Khrushchev; 1957–60, Ambassador to Mongolia; 1960–62, Ambassador to the International Atomic Energy Agency; 1964, expelled from Communist Party; died 1986.

Comintern: Abbreviation of Communist International—formed in Moscow in 1919, its purpose was to link and coordinate the efforts of all Communist parties throughout the world in the effort to spread the revolution.

1. What was Lenin's foreign policy?
2. What foreign policy directions were favoured by Trotsky and Bukharin in the early 1920s?
3. What was meant by Stalin in the doctrine 'communism in one country'?
4. In what ways were the foreign policy ideas of Stalin, Trotsky and Bukharin linked to their ideological beliefs about the Soviet state?
5. Why were the Western nations so suspicious of the Soviet Union and reluctant to cooperate with it throughout the inter-war period?
6. **a** What was Comintern?
   b What were the Twenty-One Conditions issued by Comintern in 1920?
   c Make a list of the ways in which the existence of this organisation came to work against the interests of the Soviet Union.
7. **a** What was the 'Popular Front'?
   b Why was it unsuccessful?
8. **a** In what ways did the Soviet Union contribute to the adoption of the policy of appeasement?
   b How important was the role of the Soviet Union in bringing about the war between Germany and Britain and France over Poland in 1939?
9. **a** What was the Ezhovschina?
   b Why did this occur?
   c Who were its victims?
   d What were the consequences?
10. How important was ideology in determining the course of the Soviet foreign policy in the inter-war period?
11. In what ways was Soviet foreign policy linked with internal social, political and economic developments?
12. Rather than being positive and active, Soviet foreign policy in this period can be viewed as negative and reactive. In other words, it was the actions and attitudes of other countries which determined the direction of Soviet diplomacy.
    What evidence is there to support or refute this interpretation?
13. **a** What different attitudes to diplomacy and international relations were held by Chicherin, Litvinov and Molotov?
    b How influential was each of these men in determining the course of the Soviet Union's dealings with other nations in the inter-war years?

DOCUMENT STUDY **No. 15**

Read the historical sources and answer the questions which follow.

SOURCE 6.A

The effect of the Comintern on Soviet foreign policy
from J.N. Westwood, *Endurance and Endeavour*, p. 268

The Comintern did little good for the Red cause. It failed to make revolutions, and its machinations gained support for right-wing governments and fascist movements abroad. In Italy, Bulgaria, and Germany its directives to local communists to struggle against the other socialists, sometimes in alliance with fascism, was a crucial factor enabling the extreme right to defeat the left in those countries. It embarrassed the commissariat of foreign affairs because foreigners could not accept that it had no connection with Soviet foreign policy; in the thirties the distrust which it had sown was one of the factors discouraging a common front of the west and Russia against fascism. And it discouraged the initiatives of foreign communist parties, while making them vulnerable to accusation of putting the interests of Moscow before those of their own peoples.

The effect of the Comintern on Soviet foreign policy
from P.M.H. Bell, *The Origins of the Second World War in Europe*, pp. 118–19

SOURCE 6.B

In every country there was an organised body on which the Soviet government could rely to promote its interests, as they were interpreted in Moscow at any given time. Equally, every other government in Europe knew that an organised group of its own citizens owed its primary allegiance to a foreign state, and was working openly or in secret for the overthrow of the existing social order. It was impossible to treat the Soviet Union simply as another state, even though for practical purposes it was necessary to have dealings with it, and on calculations of power politics it might be desirable to form alliances with it. Both practical dealings and diplomatic negotiations were made difficult by the nature of the Soviet state, and by the fact that relations with the Soviet Union were always a contentious issue in domestic politics. Above all, the existence of the foreign Communist Parties and the sympathisers focused the attention of all governments on the fact that the USSR was both a state and the centre of an international revolutionary movement. Communism and its homeland were in existence before Italy became fascist, and long before Germany turned to Nazism. It was natural, and in many ways reasonable, that other European states, and especially the great imperial powers, Britain and France, should continue to regard Soviet communism as a dangerous enemy. From this it was a short step for some to the assumption that the enemies of communism were your friends; and that fascist Italy and Nazi Germany were sturdy bulwarks against communism. Once this notion had taken root, it was hard to believe that the Nazi regime was itself a threat, nearer and more powerful than the Soviet Union. Even if Nazism was perceived as a threat, the background of hostility, rooted in ideological antagonism and fostered by Comintern activity, could not be instantly dispelled or ignored, but remained to clog and hamper all dealings with the Soviet government—as was shown in the British and French negotiations for a Soviet alliance in the summer of 1939.

Winston Churchill on Communism, 1919

SOURCE 6.C

Communism is not a policy, it is a disease. Communism means war of the most ruthless character, the slaughter of men, women, and children, the burning of homes, and the inviting of tyranny, disease, and famine

Lenin on the League of Nations

SOURCE 6.D

The League is a robbers' den to safeguard the unjust spoils of Versailles.

The Soviet view of the League of Nations in the 1920s, from *Izvestiya*

SOURCE 6.E

[The League of Nations is] a wasps' nest of international intrigue where political sharpers [cheats] and thieving diplomatists cheat with marked cards, strangle weak nations, and organise war against the USSR.

Stalin's address to the Eighteenth Congress of the Communist Party of the Soviet Union, 10 March 1939

SOURCE 6.F

Pacifism and disarmament schemes are dead and buried. Feverish arming has taken their place. Everybody is arming, small states and big states, including primarily those which practise the policy of non-intervention. Nobody believes any longer in the unctuous speeches which claim that the Munich concessions to the aggressors and the Munich agreement opened a new era of 'appeasement' . . . Naturally the USSR could not ignore these ominous events . . . At the end of 1934 our country joined the League of Nations, considering that despite its weakness the League might nevertheless serve as a place where aggressors can be exposed, and as a certain instrument of peace however feeble, that might hinder the outbreak of war. The Soviet Union considers that in alarming times like these even so weak an international organisation as the League of Nations should not be ignored. In May 1935 a treaty of mutual assistance against possible attack by aggressors was signed between France and the Soviet Union.

A similar treaty was simultaneously concluded with Czechoslovakia. In March 1936 the Soviet Union concluded a treaty of mutual assistance with the Mongolian Peoples' Republic. In August 1937 the Soviet Union concluded a pact of non-aggression with the Chinese Republic.

It was in such difficult international conditions that the Soviet Union pursued its foreign policy of upholding the cause of peace.

The foreign policy of the Soviet Union is clear and explicit.

1. We stand for peace and the strengthening of business relations with all countries. That is our position; and we shall adhere to this position, so long as these countries maintain like relations with the Soviet Union, and so long as they make no attempt to trespass on the interests of our country.

2. We stand for peaceful, close and friendly relations with all the neighbouring countries which have common frontiers with the USSR. That is our position; and we shall adhere to this position so long as these countries maintain like relations with the Soviet Union, and so long as they make no attempt to trespass directly or indirectly on the integrity and inviolability of the frontiers of the Soviet state.

3. We stand for the support of nations which are the victims of aggression and are fighting for the independence of their country.

4. We are not afraid of the threats of aggressors, and are ready to deal two blows for every blow delivered by instigators of war who attempt to violate the Soviet borders.

SOURCE 6.G

Transcript of the meeting between the delegates of France, Britain, and the Soviet Union, 14 August 1939

Marshal Voroshilov [Soviet Commissar for Defence]: I want a clear answer to my very clear question concerning the joint action of the Armed Forces of Britain, France and the Soviet Union against the common enemy—the bloc of aggressors, or the main aggressor—should he attack . . .

Do the French and British General Staff think that the Soviet land forces will be admitted to Polish territory in order to make direct contact with the enemy in case Poland is attacked? And further:

Do you think that our Armed Forces will be allowed passage across Polish territory, across Galicia, to make contact with the enemy and to fight him in the south of Poland? Yet one more thing:

Is it proposed to allow Soviet troops across Rumanian territory if the aggressor attacks Rumania?

These are the three questions which interest us most.

[Admiral Drax confers at length with General Doumenc.]

General Doumenc [Head of the French delegation]: I agree with the Marshal that the concentration of Soviet troops must take place principally in the areas indicated by the Marshal, and the distribution of these troops will be made at your discretion. I think that the weak points of the Polish–Rumanian front are their flanks and point of junction. We shall speak of the left flank when we deal with the question of communications.

Marshal Voroshilov: I want you to reply to my direct question. I said nothing about Soviet troop concentrations. I asked whether the British and French General Staffs envisage passage of our troops towards East Prussia or other points to fight the common enemy.

General Doumenc: I think that Poland and Rumania will implore you, Marshal, to come to their assistance.

Marshal Voroshilov: And perhaps they will not. It is not evident so far. We have a Non-Aggression Pact with the Poles, while France and Poland have a Treaty of Mutual Assistance. This is the reason why the question I raised is not an idle one as far as we are concerned, since we are discussing the plan of joint action against the aggressor. To my mind, France and Britain should have a clear idea about the way we can extend real help or about our participation in the war.

[There is a lengthy exchange of opinion between Admiral Drax and General Heywood.]

Admiral Drax [Head of the British delegation]: If Poland and Rumania do not ask for Soviet help they will soon become German provinces, and then the USSR will decide how to act. If, on the other hand, the USSR, France and Britain are in alliance, then the question of whether or not Rumania and Poland ask for help becomes quite clear.

Marshal Voroshilov: I repeat, gentlemen, that this question is a cardinal question for the Soviet Union.

Admiral Drax: I repeat my reply once again. If the USSR, France and Britain are allies, then in my personal opinion there can be little doubt that Poland and Rumania will ask for help. But that is my personal opinion, and to obtain a precise and satisfactory answer, it is necessary to approach Poland.

Marshal Voroshilov: I regret that the Military Mission of Great Britain and France have not considered their question and have not brought an exact answer.

SOURCE 6.H

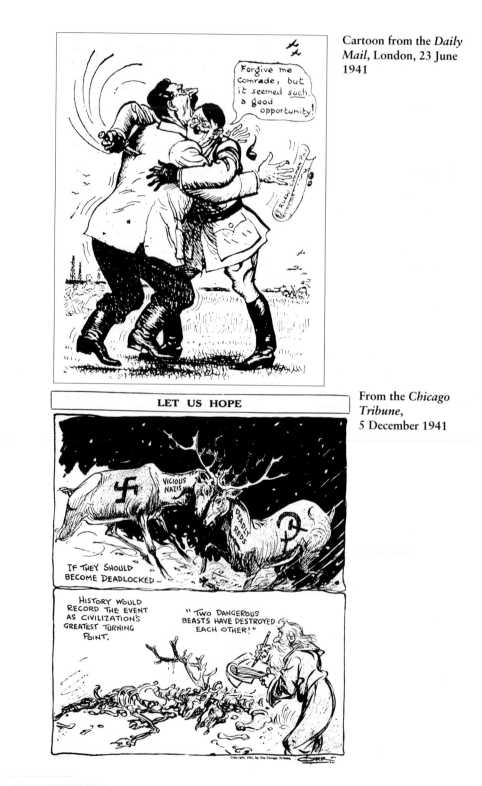

Cartoon from the *Daily Mail*, London, 23 June 1941

SOURCE 6.I

From the *Chicago Tribune*, 5 December 1941

Questions

a What evidence is provided by Sources 6.A–6.E for an historian attempting to work out why there was so much mutual mistrust between the Soviet Union and the Western nations in the 1920s and 1930s?

b **i)** Make a list of the Soviet foreign policy aims, as expressed by Stalin in Source 6.F.

ii) According to Source 6.F, why did the Soviet Union join the League of Nations?

iii) Given the nature of Source 6.F, how reliable do you regard it as a source of information about Soviet foreign policy aims?

c **i)** What is the tone of statements made by Marshal Voroshilov in Source 6.G?

ii) In what way does Source 6.G explain why the Soviet Union signed a non-aggression pact with Germany in 1939 rather than reaching agreement with Britain and France?

d Explain in your own words the messages being presented in Sources 6.H and 6.I.

e The *Chicago Tribune* was perhaps the most stridently anti-communist newspaper in the United States during the 1930s.

i) How is this attitude reflected in Source 6.I?

ii) How can Source 6.I be used by an historian to explain Soviet foreign policy decisions throughout the inter-war years?

The Great Patriotic War

FOCUS QUESTIONS
What were the major factors contributing to the victory of the Soviet Union in the war against Germany?
How important were the roles of individuals in bringing about the Soviet victory?
What was the impact of the Second World War upon the Soviet home front?
What role was played by ideology in the Great Patriotic War?

TIME LINE

1941

June	22	Operation Barbarossa—Germany invades the Soviet Union
	24	German forces capture Brest-Litovsk
July	3	Stalin orders 'Scorched Earth' Policy
	9	German forces take 300 000 prisoners near Minsk
	25	German forces reach Smolensk
	27	Tallinin, capital of Estonia, captured
August	5	Russian resistance at Smolensk ends
	12	German forces advance on Leningrad
September	15	German forces encircle Leningrad
	19	Fall of Kiev
October	6	Germans launch offensive towards Moscow
	19	Stalin announces state of siege in Moscow

	24	Fall of Kharkov
	27	German forces defeat Soviet armies in the Crimea, though Sebastopol does not fall
November	20	Fall of Rostov
	29	Russians recapture Rostov
December	5	Hitler abandons Moscow offensive for the winter
	6	Soviet forces under Zhukov begin counter-offensive outside Moscow
	14	German forces retreat from Moscow
	19	German Army Commander-in-Chief, Brauchitsch, relieved of his command—Hitler takes personal command of the German army

1942

January	18	Soviets launch counter-attack in the Ukraine
May	8	Germans launch spring offensive
	12	Soviets begin Kharkov offensive
	18	Germans counter-attack at Kharkov
	28	Soviets defeated at Battle of Kharkov
June	28	Germans launch summer offensive in Caucasus
July	2	Fall of Sebastopol
	6	Fall of Voronezh
	23	Fall of Rostov
August	12	First Moscow Conference begins
	24	German attack on Stalingrad begins
September	10	German forces enter Stalingrad
November	19	Soviets begin counter-offensive at Stalingrad
	23	Soviets encircle Stalingrad
December	12	Germans attempt to relieve forces trapped in Stalingrad

1943

January	3	Germans retreat from Caucasus
	14	Soviets break the encirclement of Leningrad
February	2	German forces surrender at Stalingrad
	8	Soviets retake Kursk
	14	Soviets retake Rostov
July	4	Battle of Kursk begins
	12	Soviets launch counter-offensive extending from Smolensk to Black Sea
August	5	Soviets recapture Kharkov
September	25	Soviets recapture Smolensk
November	6	Soviets liberate Kiev
	28	Teheran Conference begins

1944

January	19	Soviets recapture Novgorod
	26	Liberation of Leningrad
April	2	Soviets enter Rumania
May	12	Soviets recapture Sebastopol
June	22	Operation Bagration—Soviets open massive counter-offensive on central front
July	4	Soviets recapture Minsk
	28	Soviets recapture Brest-Litovsk

September	5	Soviets declare war on Bulgaria
	19	Armistice signed between Soviet Union and Finland
October	20	Soviet and Yugoslav forces recapture Belgrade
	23	Soviet forces enter East Prussia
December	24	Soviets surround Budapest

1945

January	12	Soviets open winter offensive
	17	Warsaw falls
February	4	Yalta Conference begins
	13	Soviets capture Budapest
March	30	Soviets capture Danzig
April	13	Soviets capture Vienna
	16	Soviets begin assault on Berlin
	25	Soviet and US forces meet near Torgau, joining the fronts in north-west Europe
May	2	Fall of Berlin
	7	Formal surrender of German forces
	13	Soviets overcome remaining resistance in Czechoslovakia

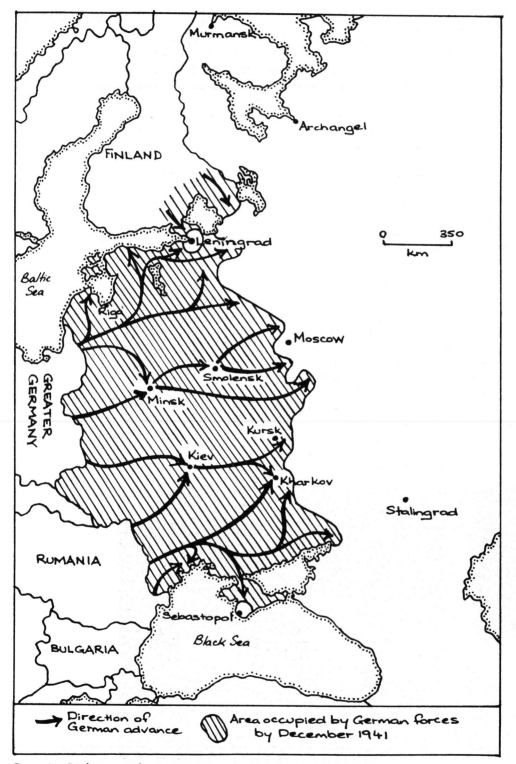

Operation Barbarossa—the German invasion of the Soviet Union, 1941

O N 22 June 1941 Foreign Commissar Molotov informed the Soviet people that the Germans had embarked on 'a perfidious act, unparalleled in the history of civilised nations'. It was Molotov who referred to the conflict as a 'patriotic war' and promised eventual victory. Stalin, the all-knowing, all-powerful 'Granite Bolshevik' seemed to have disappeared. In Moscow the general atmosphere was one of depression rather than excitement. It was ten days after the invasion before Stalin addressed the nation and from his first words it was clear that a major change had occurred:

> Comrades, citizens, brothers and sisters, men of our Army and Navy! It is to you I am speaking, dear friends!
>
> The treacherous military attack launched by Hitlerite Germany on our motherland on 22 June is continuing. In spite of the heroic resistance of the Red Army, and although the enemy's best divisions and best air force units have already been destroyed and have found their graves on the field of battle, the enemy continues to advance, throwing fresh troops to the front. Hitler's troops have succeeded in capturing Lithuania, most of Latvia, the western part of Belorussia and part of the western Ukraine. Fascist aircraft are extending the range of their operations . . . Grave danger threatens our country.
>
> How has it come about that our glorious Red Army surrendered a number of our cities and districts to the Fascist armies? Is it really true that the Fascist German troops are unbeatable, as the boastful Fascist propagandists are endlessly claiming? Of course not! History proves that there are no unbeatable armies and there never have been unbeatable armies.
>
> It may be asked, how could the Soviet government have agreed to sign a Non-Aggression Pact with such treacherous people, such monsters, as Hitler and Ribbentrop? Was this not a mistake by the Soviet government? Of course not! I think that no peace-loving state would decline a peace agreement with a neighbouring state, even though the latter was headed by such monsters and cannibals as Hitler and Ribbentrop . . .

Munitions workers

The enemy is cruel and implacable. He is out to seize our lands watered by the sweat of our brows, to seize our grain and oil secured by the labour of our hands. He is out to restore the rule of the landlords, to restore tsarism, to destroy the national culture and the national existence as states of the Russians, Ukrainians, Moldavians, Georgians, Armenians, Azerbaijanians and the other free peoples of the Soviet Union, to Germanise them, to turn them into the slaves of German princes and barons. Thus the issue is one of life and death for the Soviet State, of life and death for the peoples of the USSR; the issue is whether the peoples of the Soviet Union shall be free or fall into slavery. The Soviet people must realise this and abandon all complacency; they must mobilise themselves and reorganise all their work on a new wartime footing, where there can be no mercy for the enemy.

Further, there must be no room in our ranks for whimperers and cowards, for panic-mongers and deserters; our people must know no fear in the fight and must selflessly join our patriotic war of liberation against the fascist enslavers . . .

The enemy must not be left a single engine, a single railway truck, not a single pound of grain or gallon of fuel . . . in occupied areas partisan units must be

Soviet propaganda posters from the Second World War: the one on the left calls on women to increase their commitment to the war effort; the one on the right calls for an increase in industrial production.

formed, sabotage groups must be formed . . . to blow up bridges and roads, damage telephone and telegraph wires, set fire to forests, stores and transport . . . conditions must be made intolerable for the enemy and all his accomplices.

Stalin was attempting to distance himself from the Party and all it stood for. Instead, the appeal was to the patriotism of the people. It was Stalin, for the first time, acting as the 'leader' of the people rather than as the bureaucratic dictator.

To many this speech was reassuring. Others, however, were not so convinced. For example, people in the Ukraine and Belorussia viewed the advancing Germans as a force liberating them from the Communist tyranny. The Communist Party and the police were able to maintain a tighter control in the cities, and here the citizens were quickly marshalled to dig defensive works such as anti-tank ditches, while in many factories the workers undertook basic military training. Different cities and regions presented different reactions, but in general there was a patriotic uplift as people volunteered for work and service rather than wait for coercion.

Adding to this spirit of the 'Great Patriotic War' was the return of organised religion as a legitimate part of Soviet life. Russian Orthodox priests were brought to the fore of pro-war rallies. The Communists' campaign against organised religion was halted and the Orthodox Church, the spiritual foundation of 'Mother Russia', was presented as under threat from the Teutons. By 1942, Soviet and church leaders were exchanging messages of support and cooperation in the press:

THE RETURN OF THE CHURCH

> I cordially and devoutly greet you in your person the God-chosen leader of our military and cultural forces . . . (Patriarch of the Orthodox Church to Stalin)
> May Allah help you to bring to a victorious end your work of freeing the oppressed peoples. Amen. (The Mufti of the Muslims to Stalin)
> . . . the Almighty has prepared for the fascist horde the inglorious and shameful destruction suffered by all the Pharoahs, Amelekites and Ammonites . . . (President of the Moscow Jewish community to Stalin)

Part of this domestic response to the war was the movement of factories and businesses to the east of the Urals, beyond the range of the Luftwaffe. The industrial centres of Minsk and Riga had been captured by the Germans early in the war and their factories were lost. From July 1941 factories in other towns began to close down and their equipment was loaded onto freight trains as the great evacuation began. For example, in the first week of July twenty-six munitions works were moved from the Moscow and Leningrad area along with an armour-plate works from the Black Sea.

THE MOVEMENT OF INDUSTRIES

Once the decision to evacuate was issued, the dismantling of a factory went ahead twenty-four hours a day. For large works, like a steel mill, 6000 to 10 000 railway freight cars would be employed. Then, depending upon the supply of raw materials, components and workers, the factory would resume production about three months after leaving its original site.

At the height of this evacuation—from July to November 1941—

about 1500 different factories were dispatched, some 300 going south to central Asian regions. Despite the hardships inflicted on the workers and the regular chaos involved in the movement, this industrial evacuation was an unprecedented achievement which, by 1942, enabled the Soviet Union to keep its forces supplied despite the German occupation of its traditional industrial areas.

Life was equally hard for the rest of the Soviet population. Rationing was introduced, with the food allocation being determined by the nature of employment. For example, the workers in heavy industry received double the amount of non-working dependents. Holidays were abolished as all possible labour, regardless of age and sex, was mobilised. J.N. Westwood estimates that the combination of overwork, malnutrition, cold and enemy action resulted in fifteen million civilians giving their lives to the Soviet war effort. Combine this with the seven to ten million military personnel who did not return home, and it can be seen that one in ten of the entire population died during the war with Germany.

ANTI-SOVIET FORCES

It should be remembered also that there was not a total commitment to the war effort. Anti-Soviet partisan movements developed in the Ukraine and the Baltic states. Many prisoners of war formed an anti-Soviet army which sided with the Germans. This army, led by Lieutenant General Andrei Vlassov, actually proved so successful against its former Red Army comrades that some experts believe it could have changed the course of the war in Eastern Europe. This was not to be, because Hitler, with his entrenched ideas of racial superiority, could not harbour the notion that the 'slavs' of the anti-Soviet army could succeed where the mighty Wehrmacht had failed. Vlassov's units were therefore primarily deployed in non-combat roles. Vlassov was handed over to the Soviets at the end of the war and publicly hanged in Red Square.

All this of course must be understood within the context of the major battles and the nature of the fighting which took place during the four years of the war. The fighting between the Germans and Russians possessed an underlying savagery which was absent in the clinical and precise encounters in the West. The reason for this difference was race. Hitler's intentions for the West were cooperation (at best) and domination (at worst); his overt intentions for Eastern Europe were enslavement and elimination.

THE BATTLE OF MOSCOW

Operation Barbarossa, the invasion of Russia, had been launched on 22 June 1941 and the Germans made rapid inroads against disorganised Soviet resistance. The key battle of the first phase of the German invasion of the Soviet Union was the Battle of Moscow, 1941. The German assault on Moscow began on 2 October 1941 following Germany's annihilation of the Soviet armies in the Ukraine. The German Army Group Centre struck eastwards in three waves of advance capturing more than 650000 prisoners. With no air cover and the Soviet battalions reduced to improvisation, a state of siege was declared in Moscow on 19 October by its recently appointed commander General Zhukov. However, the German advance slowed as the two main roads to Moscow became congested, and then turned to bogs, while the dense forests to the north of the city slowed and divided the German panzer divisions.

Russia's time-honoured saviour, 'General Winter', then intervened. The sudden onset of the cold froze German engine oil, packing grease and firing mechanisms. Lacking winter uniforms, the German soldiers began to fall victim to frostbite and morale sank quickly as the German offensive stalled. On 15 November, Army Group Centre launched a final lunging attack at Moscow which broke through to within 30 kilometres of the Kremlin.

On 6 December, having persuaded Stavka (Soviet High Command) to withdraw Russia's remaining eight tank brigades and huge Siberian infantry reserves from the Far East, Zhukov launched a massive counter-offensive which the Germans were unable to withstand. Literally freezing in their tracks and unable to reinforce their armies or their positions, the German lines fell away. Despite Hitler's furious orders to stand and resist (following his own assumption of the position of Commander-in-Chief) the German offensive was reversed. To all intents and purposes, Operation Barbarossa had been negated.

Soviet soldiers raise their flag above the Reichstag building in Berlin

The decisive battle of the war on the Eastern Front, and the first indication to the Allies that the German forces could be defeated, was the Battle of Stalingrad, 1942–43. Having failed to win a decisive victory against the Soviets in 1941, Hitler returned to the offensive in 1942. The order was given to Sixth Army commander, General Paulus, to attack Stalingrad, a key point on the Volga controlling the rail and waterway communications of southern Russia.

The attack began on 19 August 1942 with a pincer assault by the Sixth Army from the north-west and the Fourth Panzer Army attacking the south-west. Although mobile German units reached the Volga above Stalingrad, breaking into the northern suburbs in a few days, the Russian 66th Army under General Chuikov kept the two arms of the German forces apart.

In a bitter war of attrition, concentrated German attack was countered by equally concentrated Soviet defence. As German troops entered the suburbs, the Luftwaffe inflicted a massive aerial bombardment. Paradoxically, this devastation only made the city easier to defend. The Germans had to work through the rubble, building by building, room by room, to remove each Soviet soldier.

The Soviet launched its counter-offensive on 19 November and within days Paulus found his forces trapped within the city with no possibility of withdrawal. The Germans' 'Operation Winter Storm' in December was a failed attempt to break the encirclement. Hitler continually denied Paulus' requests to surrender the German forces and so supplies became the key to their survival. Hermann Goering initially promised that the Luftwaffe would deliver 700 tons of supplies per day. He then reduced this promise to 300. Even this lesser figure could not be met. Again the Russian winter set in and the transport wing of the Luftwaffe found itself decimated by the rapidly rebuilding Red Air Force.

In January 1943 the Soviets offered the Germans in Stalingrad surrender terms. Hitler ordered Paulus to fight on. The Soviets then launched another counter-offensive which brought about the German surrender. Paulus' Sixth Army had originally numbered close to 300 000 men; at the time of surrender only 94 000 remained. Although the Fourth Panzer Army had escaped before the full Soviet counter-offensive came into operation, the scale of the German defeat at Stalingrad could not be redressed.

The German armies in the Soviet Union were forced into retreat, a retreat which was intensified following the Battle of Kursk, 1943. Often described as the largest tank battle in history, this battle began on 5 July 1943. Bolstered by intelligence information supplied by the so-called 'Lucy Ring' which had infiltrated German High Command, the Soviets were able to counter a German offensive and force the Germans to retreat to the Dnieper River. From this battle onwards, the Soviets were on the offensive along the whole Eastern Front. The Communist state had survived its greatest test.

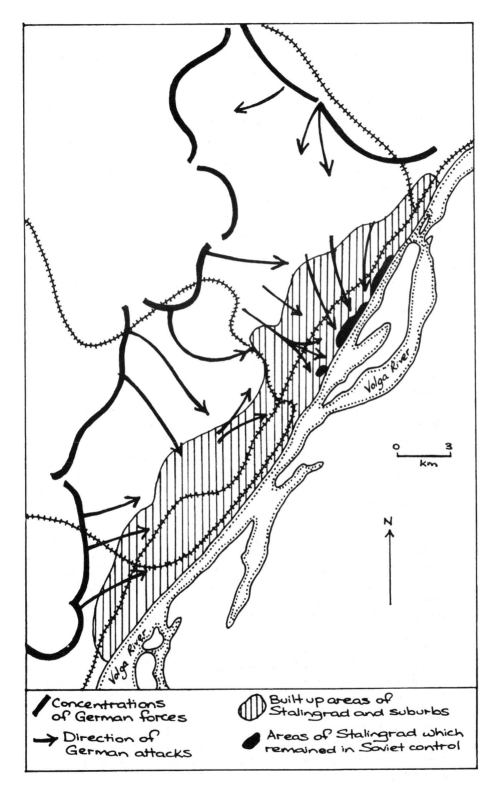

Concentrations of German forces

Direction of German attacks

Built up areas of Stalingrad and suburbs

Areas of Stalingrad which remained in Soviet control

The Siege of Stalingrad 1942–1943 — the decisive battle of the Eastern European war

SUMMARY

- The Soviet Union was successful because of a combination of Soviet tactics and Nazi mistakes.
- Geography and climate, along with the actions of individuals, played a major part in the Soviet success.
- Stalin was instrumental in the Soviet victory.

STAVKA: The Soviet High Command; established 23 June 1941; initially headed by General Timoshenko; within days Stalin altered its powers with the establishment of a five-man State Defence Committee (GKO) made up of himself, Molotov, Malenkov, Voroshilov and Beria; its purpose was changed to the directing of military operations with Stalin as its Chairman; 8 August 1941, Stalin named himself Supreme Commander-in-Chief of the Soviet Armed Forces in place of Timoshenko; early tactical deployments, disastrous battles in the initial stages of the German advance, chaos created by the lack of a defensive plan, and rapid destruction of the Red Air Force were symptomatic of this organisational monomania.

Marshal Georgi Konstantinovich Zhukov: Soviet General; born 1896, died 1974; Commander-in-Chief of the Red Army from October 1941; distinguished himself against the Japanese in Mongolia; appointed Chief of Staff in the final stages of the Russo-Finnish War; replaced Voroshilov in command of defence of Leningrad; recalled to Moscow; most famous achievement was the 1941 defence of Moscow; went on to oversee successful counter-offensives at Stalingrad (November 1942), Kursk (July 1943) and in the Ukraine; primary tactic was to deliver a series of continuous blows along the vast stretch of the Soviet front, supported by huge concentrations of armour, and without any consideration of the cost of human

Production of the T-34 tank—one of the most effective Soviet weapons of the war

lives; headed the First Ukrainian Front in March 1944; transferred to the First Belorussian Front in the early summer; directed the advance on Warsaw; April 1945, ordered the launch of the final offensive against Berlin that resulted in the German surrender, 2 May 1945.

Marshal Kliment Efremovich Voroshilov: Soviet General; born 1881, died 1969; 1934–39, Commissar for Defence; became Deputy Premier in the reshuffle of positions which followed the Russo-Finnish War; July 1941, became Deputy Chairman of the State Defence Committee and the STAVKA representative on the north-west front at Leningrad; lacked knowledge of modern military tactics and failed to halt German advance; recalled to Moscow; attended the Teheran Conference and took part in various talks between the Soviet Union, and the Allies; President of the Soviet Union, 1953–60.

Marshal Simeon Konstantinovich Timoshenko: Soviet General; born 1895, died 1970; personal friend of Stalin, he was appointed Commissar of Defence following the Russo-Finnish War; given the responsibility for reorganising and training the Red Army; hampered by the lack of modern equipment, so introduced harsh discipline and training techniques; accelerated the program of replacing the traditional horse-mounted cavalry with light tanks; 1941, appointed to STAVKA; his forces suffered major defeats along a 500-kilometre front; transferred to the South-west Front in September 1941, but was unable to salvage the disastrous defeats suffered here by his predecessor, Marshal Budënny; May 1942, planned an offensive against Kharkov, unaware of the build-up of German troops in the area; the Soviet defeat gave Stalin an excuse to demote him; he became the scapegoat for the Soviet Union's lack of military preparedness at the start of the war.

Lavrenti Pavlovich Beria: Soviet bureaucrat; born 1899, died 1953; 1938–53, Chief of the NKVD; member of the five-man State Defence Committee; provided Stalin with intelligence information; under his leadership, the NKVD gained a reputation for unsurpassed brutality with its main tasks being the large-scale purges in occupied territories, the deportation of minority nationalities, control of Soviet partisans and POW camps, and counter-intelligence; determined to make his security organisation the ultimate power in the Soviet Union; after Stalin's death he assumed power in a triumvirate with Molotov and Malenkov; denounced as a traitor and executed.

Vyacheslav Mikhailovich Molotov: Soviet diplomat; born 1890, died 1986; 1939–52, Commissar for Foreign Affairs; announced the German invasion to the Soviet people; served on the State Defence Committee throughout the war, and formalised Allied assistance to the Soviet Union with the signing of the Mutual Assistance Pact with Britain in July 1941, and the Lend-Lease Agreement with Britain and the USA; negotiated 20-year Anglo-Soviet Treaty in May 1942; his chairmanship of the Moscow Foreign Ministers' Conference in 1943 laid the groundwork for the Teheran Conference, at which a European invasion date was finally agreed; 1945, accompanied Stalin to the major Allied conferences at Yalta and

Potsdam which established the post-war political structure of the world; lost favour following the death of Stalin; 1964, expelled from the Communist Party; rehabilitated only in 1984; died 1986.

Josef Vissarionovich Stalin: Soviet leader; assumed Chairmanship of the Council of Peoples' Commissars for the first time in June 1941; took command of the Soviet Armed Forces; seems to have been totally surprised by the timing of Germany's attack; first reaction was the historic appeal to the Soviet people to leave the invader nothing but scorched earth; scale of the early defeats of the Soviet armies created a perception of panic in the Kremlin, and it was not until the Soviet defence of Moscow began that he clearly reasserted his authority; from the Zhukov counter-attack which drove the Germans from Moscow in December 1941 to the final assault on Berlin in May 1945, he was served by an increasing number of generals who were distinguished in their own right; initial lack of readiness of the Soviet armed forces was in large part due to the Stalin purges; came to appreciate the art of generalship as the war progressed; viewed by the Nazis as an implacable enemy; often an argumentative and demanding ally to the British and Americans with his continuing demands for the opening of a second front; attended the Allied Conferences at Teheran, Yalta and Potsdam; emerged from the Second World War as a major figure in world politics.

Marshal Ivan Stepanovich Konev: Soviet General; born 1897, died 1973: one of the outstanding Soviet field commanders of the war; began career as a private in the Tsar's army in 1912; 1941, in charge of the Kalinin Front Army Group, which played a vital role in holding the northern flank during the German assault on Moscow; forced German armies back 150 kilometres in subsequent counter-offensive; greatest successes came as commander of the Soviet counter-offensives of 1943–45; directed the northern assault to link up with Zhukov's First Ukrainian Front to complete the encirclement of German forces south of Kiev; drove westward into Poland and though suffering heavy casualties, his forces devastated the German armies in their path; led the First Ukrainian Front in the Battle of Berlin which brought the European war to an end.

Marshal Konstantin Konstantinovich Rokossovsky: Soviet General; born 1896, died 1968; highly regarded front commander; had been conscripted into the Tsarist army and imprisoned during the purges of the 1930s; reinstated as a corps commander in the Kiev Military District; commanded the 16th Red Army with distinction in the Battle for Moscow; transferred to Stalingrad, and directed the decisive breakthrough which led to the encirclement and surrender of the German forces; commanded the Central Front during the Battle of Kursk; pushed westward into Poland but failed to assist the people of Warsaw in attempted insurrection against the Germans; 1945, led the northern Soviet armies which entered East Prussia and into Germany.

Siege of Leningrad: German forces advanced mid-August 1941 and were on the outskirts of the city by the start of September; Germans attempted to cut off major supply lines and starve the civilian population into surrender; Zhukov was placed in charge of defences, resistance stiffened and both sides dug in; siege lasted for 890 days; constant aerial bombardment added to food supply problems; strict enforcement of rationing, with violators shot or sent to the front; small amount of supplies maintained via a Red Navy ferry flotilla across Lake Lagoda; 1943, bigger supply route opened; liberated by Soviet troops 19 January 1944; civilian death toll was enormous—over 600 000 from starvation and 200 000 from the bombing.

T-34 Tank: Soviet tank—probably the most important tank of the war; distinguished by its shaped armour, which greatly improved its resistance to shellfire; easy to mass-produce and maintain; all-round performance was superb and its heavy main armament was a formidable innovation in a medium battle tank; its existence had remained a well-kept secret from the Germans, who were unpleasantly surprised by its apparent invincibility.

Katyusha: Soviet multiple-rocket launcher—first of its kind to reach active service; used this weapon against the Germans from July 1941; equipped with sixteen 132mm free-flight rockets, and with a range of 9.6 km; easily mass-produced and placed on the back of lorries; its multiple barrage capacity could wipe out a column of troops or tanks in minutes; the piercing scream of the rockets was equally damaging to German morale.

EXERCISES

1. Fill in the missing spaces in the table below.

The Reasons for the Soviet Victory

Reason	Contribution to the Soviet victory
German tactical mistakes	
The geography and climate of the Soviet Union	
The size of the Soviet armed forces	
The tactics adopted by the Soviet commanders	
Stalin's leadership and centralisation of control of the war effort	
Allied military and economic assistance	

2. Read the sources and answer the questions which follow.

Extract from Alan Bullock, *Hitler and Stalin: Parallel Lives*, pp. 850–2   **SOURCE 6J**
The eventual Soviet victory can be attributed to two things. The first was the fact that the Red Army survived the disasters of the first six months of the war as

an organised fighting force. The second, hardly less important, was the removal of industry from the threatened western areas and the expansion of production in the east which enabled the Soviet Union to survive as an industrial power. The movement of between ten and twelve million workers to the east was an incredible achievement by itself in the confusion of wartime, and on inadequate railways already over-burdened by the movement of men and supplies and men to the west . . . When Leningrad was cut off, the Soviet Union lost the production from one of its most important industrial centres; but, before the siege was complete, no less than two-thirds of the city's capital equipment, buildings excepted, had been moved away . . .

Control over all resources was highly centralised. Gosplan, under the leadership of Voznesensky, produced an emergency war plan for 1941–42, and thereafter annual military-economic plans. Decisions were centralised in the small but all-powerful State Defence Committee (GKO), which met almost daily under Stalin's chairmanship . . . Plenty of mistakes were made, as they were in the wartime expansion of all the belligerents' industries, but the achievement of the Russian people on the economic front under the Soviet system and Stalin's leadership was remarkable and in the end more than offset Stalin's dismal record in the same period on the military front.

SOURCE 6.K

Extract from Alan Wood, *Stalin and Stalinism*, pp. 48–9

From Russia's point of view, the war was probably the greatest Pyrrhic victory in history. Twenty million of the Soviet population—one in ten—were killed, around half of them civilians and the majority of them males of the virile age-group. The resulting sexual imbalance and demographic consequences were to last for many years to come. Of those that survived, hundreds of thousands were left crippled, maimed, and unfit for work. Apart from the physical mutilations, whole cohorts of Soviet citizens were left psychologically scarred for life. Indeed, the shocking slaughter left a deep and ineradicable trauma in the mind and soul of the Soviet people which has only quite recently begun to heal, though the visible and invisible scars still remain. The sheer scale of the human suffering and material destruction is unimaginable. Complete cities, towns, villages, and settlements were obliterated, leaving about twenty-five million homeless. In Stalingrad, 90 per cent of the city was flattered. In Leningrad, more people died through shelling, cold or starvation than were killed by the American atomic bombs dropped on Hiroshima and Nagasaki.

SOURCE 6.L

A.J.P. Taylor on Stalin's role in the war
from *The War Lords*, pp. 100–26

Every line of policy ran, had to run, through Stalin's study. Stalin alone made every great decision throughout the war and many of the small ones, too . . .

Stalin continued for most of 1941 to be obsessed with his belief that to be on the offensive was the only answer. It brought upon the Soviet armies greater catastrophes than any other armies have ever known. Between June 1941 and the tailing-off of the German offensive, which came in October, the Russians lost something like four million dead, and at least two million Russians were made German prisoners-of-war, many of them later being murdered. It was the inexhaustible human resources of Soviet Russia which kept her going . . .

Sometimes, in the early days of the war, he was savage. He would ring up perhaps half-a-dozen generals whose armies had retreated during the day, and tell them to come to Moscow at once. Immediately on arrival in Moscow, they were brought before a court martial and then, in the evening, shot. Stalin was the only war lord of the Second World War who shot his generals for failure in the field. Hitler, of course, shot some generals who conspired against him, but that was something very different.

No wonder, then, that Stalin's generals were all his absolute subordinates. There was never an instance of one directly defying him. There were some generals who argued, some who evaded, but the combination of terror and loyalty maintained Stalin's supremacy. After all, he was the boss, the centre of everything.

. . . there was never a moment from the time when the Russian fronts became something like stabilised that Stalin was not in complete personal control.

People often talk about Stalin's political designs during the Second World War: they seem to think that communists never stop thinking about political conquests. In my opinion, Stalin could have said what Churchill said: 'I have only one aim in life— that is to beat Hitler. This makes everything simple for me.'

a   According to Alan Bullock (Source 6.J), why did the Soviet Union emerge victorious from the war against Germany?

b   Why do you believe Bullock places so much emphasis upon the relocation of Soviet industry in his assessment of the Soviet victory? Do you agree with his interpretation? Why or why not?

c   Alan Wood (Source 6.K) describes the Soviet Union's success as a 'Pyrrhic victory'. What does he mean by this description?

d   From your own knowledge, how accurate is Wood's analysis of the effects of the war on the Soviet Union?

e   According to A.J.P. Taylor, how important was Stalin in the ultimate success of the Soviet Union in the war against Germany?

f   What evidence can you produce either to support or refute each of the assertions A.J.P. Taylor makes in Source 6.L?

DOCUMENT STUDY (No. 16)

Read the historical sources and answer the questions which follow.

SOURCE 6.M

British cartoon published in 1939

WONDER HOW LONG THE HONEYMOON WILL LAST?

SOURCE 6.N

Extract from Alan Bullock, *Hitler and Stalin: Parallel Lives*, published 1992
The explanation [for the Ezhovschina against the army] can only be that Stalin was prepared to run the risk of drastically weakening the Soviet Union's capacity to defend itself in order to make sure that there should be no command group which, in the event of war and serious initial reverses, might seize the opportunity to carry out a coup against them. It was not the actions of the Soviet generals that aroused his suspicion, but that same attitude of mind which led him to judge them capable of acting independently, and therefore politically unreliable.

Photo of Stalingrad, 1942–43

A joke current in the USSR during the late 1930s, reprinted in an article
on Soviet anecdotal humour in 1957

A flock of sheep were stopped by frontier guards at the Russo-Finnish border.
'Why do you wish to leave Russia?' the guards asked them.
'It's the NKVD,' replied the terrified sheep. 'Beria's ordered them to arrest all ele-
phants.'
'But you aren't elephants!' The guards pointed out.
'Try telling that to the NKVD.'

Questions

a i) What event is the subject of the cartoon in Source 6.M?
   ii) What position was held by Beria, mentioned in Source 6.P?
   iii) From Source 6.N, explain in your own words why Stalin purged the armed
        forces.
b From your own knowledge, how important was the doctrine of 'socialism in
   one country' in determining the direction of Soviet foreign policy in the period
   1928–41?

c In what ways can each of these four sources be of use to an historian
   attempting to understand the nature of life in the Soviet Union under Stalin? (In
   your answer you must consider the nature, origin, motive and audience of
   each source as well as its content.)
d Using all four sources and your own knowledge, how essential was Stalin to the
   successful functioning of the Soviet Union in the period 1928–45?

Structured Essay

a What were the main features of Soviet foreign policy in the period 1918–39?
b How did the Soviet leadership attempt to secure the revolution against external
   enemies during this period?
c Why did the Soviet Union sign a non-aggression pact with Germany in 1939?

Essays

The Soviet Union's defeat of Germany in 1945 proved the success of Stalin's policy of 'socialism in one country'. To what extent does this explain the Soviet victory?

How important was Stalin in Russia's victory over Germany, 1941–45?

How significant was the industrialisation of the 1930s in the Soviet defeat of Germany during the Second World War?

In what ways is 'The Great Patriotic War' an appropriate description for the conflict between Germany and the Soviet Union, 1941–45?

EXTRA READING

David Christian, *Power and Privilege*
J.N. Westwood, *Endurance and Endeavour*
G. Gill, *Stalinism*
Alan Wood, *Stalin and Stalinism*
I. Deutscher, *Stalin: A Political Biography*
I. Deutscher, *Trotsky*
T.A. Morris, *European History, 1848–1945*
P. Baker and J. Bassett, *Stalin's Revolution*
L. Kochan and A. Abraham, *A History of Modern Russia*
A. Bullock, *Hitler and Stalin: Parallel Lives*

THE PROBLEMS AND ISSUES

Consider the Problems and Issues:

Stalinism and Totalitarianism
Communism and the Great Patriotic War

in relation to the period 1941–45

Modernisation of the Soviet economy allows production to centre upon war materials—the decline in production of consumer goods, 1941–45; the role of women in the workforce; the movement of the industrial plants beyond the Urals.

The **totalitarian** methods are increased: the special oath of the armed forces; Stalin as Commander-in-Chief; the establishment of the Defence Committee in 1941; the image of 'Marshal Stalin'; the increased control and influence of the army which results from the Soviet victory.

WRITING THE ESSAY

Essay:

Why did the Soviet Union defeat Germany in the Great Patriotic War?

In answering this question you should consider each of the following factors:

German tactical mistakes
The geography and climate of the Soviet Union
The size of the Soviet armed forces
The tactics adopted by the Soviet commanders
Stalin's leadership and centralisation of control of the war effort
Allied military and economic assistance
The movement of key industries beyond the reach of German planes
The patriotism of the people of the Soviet Union
Make a judgement about the way in which some, or all, of these factors are

working in combination in the period 1941–45.

Consider the actions of the following people:
Stalin, Hitler, Zhukov, von Paulus, Molotov, Rokossovsky, Voroshilov, Timoshenko, Beria.

Consider the resources which the Soviet Union had at its command, and the nature of the social, economic and political structures which had been established under the Communists.

Finally, consider the following historical sources:

From Roy Medvedev, quoted in P. Baker and J. Bassett, *Stalin's Revolution*, p. 52   SOURCE 6.Q
... Of course attacking the U.S.S.R. was a risky adventure for Germany, especially since Hitler gambled on victory in a few weeks, in any case before winter. The German war plan did not provide for adequate reserves of manpower or industrial production. The Nazi Army could beat the Red Army in some battles, but Germany could not enslave the whole Soviet people in addition to all the nations of Europe. Considering that the German Army suffered defeat in spite of its unbelievably favourable situation in 1941, it is useful to imagine what would have happened to it if the Soviet government had been properly prepared. Hitler was also a dictator: he too based his actions on imaginary rather than real factors. Intoxicated by the German victories in the West, he overestimated the strength of the German army, and underestimated the strength of the Soviet people and the cohesion of Soviet society. He thought that after early defeats the U.S.S.R. would collapse like a house of cards. Hitler was an adventurist and a reckless maniac, but Stalin perceived him as a rational statesman. Stalin's tendency to mistake illusions for reality prevented him from seeing the same fault in Hitler. That is one of the main reasons why both Hitler and Stalin miscalculated in 1941.

From N. Khrushchev, quoted in Baker and Bassett, *Stalin's Revolution*, p.64   SOURCE 6.R
The Germans reached the Volga and half-encircled us, closing off our railroad contact with the North and stopping all navigation on the river. I got a call from Stalin. He asked me menacingly, 'What's this about you starting to evacuate the city?'
'Comrade Stalin, who said anything about evacuating the city? Who reported this to you? Nothing of the kind is even planned. I don't know how you came by this information, but it's absolutely untrue.'
He hung up. I began wondering, who could have concocted this filthy lie? It was obviously aimed against me personally. I decided to call Malychev, although I didn't think he would stoop that low. I told him about Stalin's call and he said, 'Yes, I just got an indignant call from Stalin myself. He said the very same thing to me that he said to you. I have no idea who could have planted this lie.'
Then I thought maybe it was Chuyanov, but Chuyanov was hardly the sort to stoop that low either. I called him anyway. He said that he'd had a nasty call from Stalin, too.
Stalin never mentioned the evacuation again. Later I realised that the rumour about an evacuation was Stalin's own doing. It was what he would have called a preventive device. For anyone else to have suggested an evacuation would have been to invite some very unpleasant consequences, so Stalin took the initiative of planting the idea himself, just to let us know how he felt about it in case the idea were ever to come up. This was typical of Stalin's conduct of the war. He wanted to regulate everything from Moscow. By carrying centralised control to such an extreme, Stalin hamstrung his commanders and commissars at the front.

Index

Page numbers in *italics* refer to illustrations. Page numbers in **bold** print refer to main entries.